# THE DUTCH PLURAL SOCIETY

The Institute of Race Relations was founded as an independent body in 1958. The main aims are to promote the study of the relations between groups racially defined, to make available information on race to different groups, and to give advice on proposals for improving relations. In its work, the subject of 'race relations' is regarded as primarily referring to the social relationships between groups that are influenced by prejudices and beliefs about race, but 'race' is inevitably related to the many factors affecting group relations including the major problems of political and economic relationships. The Institute has responded to a changing situation by extending its work and services to members of minority groups and by increased study of racist societies. The Institute cannot itself hold a corporate opinion: the opinions expressed in this work are those of the authors.

The research, on which this book is based, was made possible by an anonymous grant given to the Race Relations Committee of the Society of Friends.

# THE DUTCH PLURAL SOCIETY

## A COMPARATIVE STUDY IN RACE RELATIONS

CHRISTOPHER BAGLEY

*Published for*
*the Institute of Race Relations, London*
*by*
OXFORD UNIVERSITY PRESS
LONDON NEW YORK TORONTO
1973

*Oxford University Press, Ely House, London W.1*

GLASGOW NEW YORK TORONTO MELBOURNE WELLINGTON
CAPE TOWN IBADAN NAIROBI DAR ES SALAAM LUSAKA ADDIS ABABA
DELHI BOMBAY CALCUTTA MADRAS KARACHI LAHORE DACCA
KUALA LUMPUR SINGAPORE HONG KONG TOKYO

ISBN 0 19 218405 9

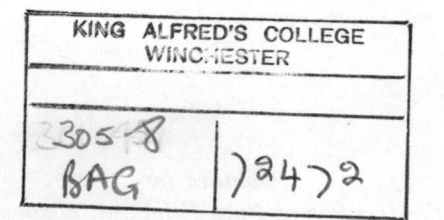

*Printed in Great Britain*
*by Ebenezer Baylis and Son Limited*
*The Trinity Press, Worcester, and London*

*Love alone constructs. Hatred and violence serve to destroy. What remains, therefore, to the underdeveloped country as a democratic and viable means of opening the eyes of the power classes to the necessity of educating the masses, making them aware of their situation, and disposing them to development and to the indispensable reform of mediaeval structures? Personally, I favour a large-scale experiment in non-violent action in the whole of the North-East, along the lines of the great movement for racial integration led by Martin Luther King.*

*When I was very young, I thought Christ was exaggerating when he spoke of the danger of riches. Now I know that it is extraordinarily difficult to combine wealth and human sensitivity. Sooner or later, money covers the eyes with dangerous scales and freezes the lips and the heart of the creature. From this I draw the conviction that it is democratic and christian to assist human weakness by a balanced, firm and just moral pressure based on non-violent action.*

Archbishop Helder Camara *of Recife, Brazil, 1968.*

# PREFACE AND ACKNOWLEDGEMENTS

My first brief in this study was to inquire how immigrants, and especially coloured immigrants, have fared in the Netherlands in comparison with Britain. A number of short articles and newspaper reports have given the impression that in comparison with Britain, race relations in the Netherlands are in a much happier state.[1] The Dutch, to the casual observer at least, seem to have absorbed a large number of coloured immigrants into their society with a minimum of strain, and with maximum effectiveness.

The first task in fieldwork was to inquire in detail how the Dutch had handled the immigration, first of coloured immigrants from the former colonial territory of Indonesia, and then of workers and students from Surinam in South America, and the Antilles in the Caribbean.

As the study proceeded I became aware of the nuances and complexities of the Dutch situation; it seemed important to specify as clearly as possible the nature of the society to which the immigrants had to adapt, and also to consider quite fully the relations of the Netherlands with its East Indies possessions (now Indonesia), and with Surinam and the Antilles. I have tried also to fit the adaptation and integration of immigrants of all kinds in the Netherlands into a theoretical framework, derived largely from Eisenstadt's work on migration.

I have attempted to draw specific parallels with the British situation, suggesting wherever appropriate how the British can learn from the Dutch. Two special inquiries were undertaken to provide objective evidence on the nature of Dutch attitudes to and treatment of coloured minorities—a survey of attitudes using a

[1] See for example, Renee Short's articles in *The Times* (28 and 29 January 1969); the article by Jack Halpern in the *Observer* (25 April 1971); and the short account in Huggett's *The Modern Netherlands* (1971).

questionnaire for which British norms are known; and an inquiry into the degree of discrimination using 'situation tests' to find out how acceptable coloured people are in jobs and housing. Again, evidence is available on the extent of such discrimination in Britain as a result of the tests carried out by Political and Economic Planning in 1967.

Finally, this study has implications for race relations which I had not envisaged when I began fieldwork. The Netherlands, the East Indies, Surinam, and the Antilles were, or still are, *plural societies* in which largely endogamous groups of marked ideological separateness, and sometimes ethnic distinctiveness as well, live side by side and also coexist amicably. This apparent paradox has considerable importance for understanding the sociology of plural societies. Such plural societies are of interest for the student of race relations since the terms 'the problems of plural societies' and 'the problems of race relations' are almost interchangeable. How can groups of people—Jews, Arabs, Chinese, Malays, Ibos, Yorubas, Bantus, Whites, East Indians, Creoles—maintain the distinctive elements of their cultures, and yet share in nation-building with other ethnic groups who maintain a large degree of ideological and cultural separateness?

This is a vitally important question, and the experience of the Netherlands and its former East and West Indian territories is of peculiar importance in considering solutions to the problems of the co-existence of ethnic groups. Such a study provokes interesting questions of comparison—why have there been serious interethnic conflicts in Guyana, and no such conflicts in the contiguous and demographically and economically similar neighbour, Surinam? Answering this question fully would require a separate study, but the information in the present inquiry may provide at least some hypotheses for such a study.

The initiative and the early finance for this study came from the Race Relations Committee of the Society of Friends, and I am grateful to the anonymous donor who made this study possible.

I am deeply indebted to my many Dutch colleagues who provided so much assistance in this study. My academic base in the Netherlands was the Institute of Social Studies, The Hague, and I would like to dedicate this report to the I.S.S. Class of 68–9, students from many parts of the world who provided so much cheerful support for my wife and myself.

Sheila and I arrived in the Netherlands to begin fieldwork on 15 April, 1969. The writing of this report was completed on 2 March 1972.

Christopher Bagley

*Department of Sociology*
*University of Surrey*

# CONTENTS

# LIST OF TABLES

## CHAPTER I

# DUTCH SOCIETY

This rather arbitrary way of imposing order, the satisfaction of our need to round off, straighten, and smooth out the illusion of well-functioning systems, are partly a result of the fact that even after concluding an investigation the anthropologist or sociologist still has a very imperfect knowledge of the society he has studied. Anyone who does not agree would do well to read the reports of foreign observers on his own society. For is not our appreciation of such writing due, in part, to the fact that the author's observations are sometimes not altogether wide of the mark? And due to their amusing conclusions and their rectilinear exposé, based on a minimum of knowledge?

—A Dutch professor on 'anthropologists in the field' (Hollander, 1967).

In the centuries before the Normans invaded England, English influence on the 'Netherlands' was strong. England had command of the Channel, and the Netherlands was virtually an island cut off from the rest of Europe by deep swamps. The language of the two countries was similar. But two things happened which diminished English influence. After 1066 the English no longer had dominance of the sea; and the swamps isolating the Netherlands from the rest of Europe were drained. In consequence, Germanic influences had an important effect on Dutch language and culture. Links between Britain and the Netherlands have remained, however, and were specially strengthened by the acceptance of William of Orange as sovereign of England.

Querido (1968) suggests that: 'Whatever their local conflicts might have been, the inhabitants had to fight their way against their eternal and common enemy: the water. They had to unite for this purpose, and, in order to conduct the struggle, power had to be shared among equals: power to control, to direct, to allocate tasks, to define duties and rights' (p. 8). But despite this sense of common purpose in building and maintaining defences against the sea, Dutch society has been marked by severe conflict between religious groups. It is this conflict and the emergence of a social system with mechanisms to cope with these potentially disruptive forces which has given Dutch society many of its most important characteristics.

Historically, individualism has been a leading feature of Dutch life. This individualism has been of groups rather than of individuals: the individual has afforded deference, often extreme deference, to the elders of his group. But the group to which he belonged was often independent of, and perhaps in conflict with, other groups.

The state, as Goudsblom (1967) says, has always been highly decentralized. According to what is usually regarded as its founding charter, the Union of Utrecht in 1579, the seven provinces remained sovereign 'allies' each of which sent its own delegates to the federal assembly, the States-General in The Hague. Querido's account (1968) of the development of public health legislation illustrates the degree of autonomy which towns and cities had (and still have) in fields such as sanitation and housing.

Netherlands society consists of four blocs, or *verzuiling* (pillars) as the Dutch call them. These pillars of society are separate from one another; yet without any one of them the society which they support would be considerably weakened. The pillars of society are Catholic, Protestant, and secular (or 'Humanist'). The Protestant bloc is divided into Dutch Reformed and Re-Reformed. Both these groups have Calvinist origins, but the Re-Reformed group adhered much more strictly to their Calvinist origins.

The advent of Calvinism in the Netherlands which followed the Reformation, coincided with the rising tide of revolt against Spain. Calvinism became almost synonymous with Dutch patriotism as a result of the war of independence, which was a struggle against both Spanish rule as such and the Spanish attempt to re-impose Roman Catholicism on the Dutch. Calvinism became the dominant force in the Netherlands, and Calvinists continued to enjoy a privileged position until the nineteenth century. The freethinking or secular bloc also had good reasons for national allegiance. Many of them had Calvinist origins and thus inherited patriotic feelings, and they were well represented among the better educated in the ruling elite.

The Catholics—a substantial minority of the Dutch population—were in a difficult position. The war of independence against Catholic Spain caused Roman Catholicism to be regarded as implying disloyalty, and Catholic churches and services were banned in 1573. Catholics were also forbidden to assume public office or establish their own schools. When the two largely Catholic southern provinces had been conquered by the Netherlands they did not become part of the seven United Provinces but were ruled as colonies and exploited economically. As Lijphart observes (1968, p. 80) it is surprising that this history of discrimination and denial of religious freedom and self-government did not turn Catholics against the Dutch nation. Instead, the Catholic minority always fought for emancipation *within* the nation. The main reason for this, Lijphart suggests, was that *some* degree of Catholic aspirations was not entirely precluded. Furthermore, the doctrine of the Catholic Church does not counsel revolution or secession, a factor of particular significance because Catholic political leadership in the nineteenth century was to a greater extent in the hands of priests rather than laymen.

The present pattern of 'accommodation'—in which the separate pillars or blocs of society accord rights and deference to members of the other pillars—crystallized in the period 1878 to 1917, and centred round three issues—the question of church and state, particularly with regard to education; the franchise issue, and the question of collective bargaining and the rights of labour. The schools issue became acute with the extension of public education to the masses; it centred around the demand made by the Roman Catholics and the orthodox or 'Re-Reformed' Calvinists. These two religious groups demanded that the state should support schools of specific religious denominations on an equal basis with non-denominational schools, a demand which placed them in opposition to the more secular-minded Protestant liberals. The issue came to a head in 1878 when a Liberal government introduced an education bill which kept the old rule in force: not one penny of public aid to private schools. Catholics and Calvinists were united —if temporarily—in their opposition to the bill. A large-scale popular protest movement against this bill was organized by the Calvinists. Out of this movement the Anti-Revolutionary political party was born. In 1889 a limited degree of public support for private schools was introduced, and in 1904 and 1908 limited public aid was also extended to private secondary schools and universities; but Catholics and Calvinists demanded more.

Parallel to this struggle over education was that over suffrage. It caused a three-way split in the liberal movement and also the secession of conservative Calvinist elements from the Anti-

Revolutionary party who later founded the Christian Historical Union.

The third dominating issue concerned the question of whether the state should initiate social legislation to protect workers in the rapidly spreading industrial system. The debate on this issue caused considerable tension within the religious or confessional parties, and gave rise also to a large socialist party confronting the liberals in the non-confessional sphere. The present party structure still revolves around the same two axes: confessional versus non-confessional on the one hand, and liberal versus socialist on the other. This means that since both axes contain varieties of the right–left dimension; the actual distinction between right and left may vary depending on the issue at stake.

The following table (Table 1:1) shows the division of parliamentary seats in the two years 1897 and 1963.

*Table 1:1. Division of Parliamentary Seats in 1897 and 1963 (Second Chamber)*

| | *1897* % | *1963* % |
|---|---|---|
| Liberals | 52 | 11 |
| Socialists | 2 | 31 |
| Communists | — | 3 |
| *Total Non-confessional* | *54* | *45* |
| Roman Catholics | 22 | 33 |
| Anti-Revolutionary Party | 17 | 9 |
| Christian Historical Union | 6 | 9 |
| *Total Confessional* | *45* | *51* |
| Others | 1 | 4 |
| Total number of seats | 100 | 150 |

*Source*: Goudsblom (1967) pp. 86–7.

Politically and economically speaking, the liberals in the Netherlands today are a conservative party, and ought not to be equated with the much more radical Liberal party of Britain.

Around 1910 the political situation, according to Lijphart, was very serious. The three major issues had reached a peak of tension, and the lines between the rivals were sharply drawn. Especially the issues of the schools, and the right to vote remained fundamentally unresolved with all of the contending groups hardening in their contention not to yield. An initiative to break the deadlock was taken in 1913 by the Cabinet, and a special commission was formed to attempt a solution to the schools question. All seven political parties were represented, each party sending its leader and its principal education expert. A similar commission to consider the franchise question was set up in the same year.

The schools commission presented its report in 1916: all elementary schools, public and private, were to get the same financial assistance from the Government in proportion to their enrolments. The suffrage commission advocated universal manhood suffrage on the basis of proportional representation. The recommendations of these two commissions were adopted by parliament in 1916 and 1917, with only a handful of dissidents. The fact that this was the time of a world war accentuated the feeling that these issues should not be allowed to divide or to destroy the Dutch nation. During these crucial years the pattern of the 'politics of accommodation', to use Lijphart's term, was set. I shall explore the nature of this accommodation process in detail later on.

A great deal of Dutch social, cultural, political, and educational life is organized on a sectarian basis, in blocs, or pillars of society, called *verzuiling*. Each bloc has set up a whole array of organizations encompassing every sphere of social life. Schools and universities, newspapers, radio and television corporations, trade unions, health and welfare agencies, and sports associations are organized on a bloc, or religious basis. The nation is deeply divided by religious differences. At the time of the last decennial census (1960) the religious composition of the population was: Roman Catholics 40·4 per cent, Dutch Reformed (*Nederland Hervormd*) 28·3 per cent, Re-Reformed (*Gereformeerd*) 9·3 per cent. Other smaller groups accounted for 3·6 per cent, and those without religious affiliation 18·4 per cent.

The Re-Reformed church is characterized by strict adherence to orthodox Calvinist doctrines. The so-called 'Dutch Reformed Church' of South Africa probably has a closer liturgical and doctrinal resemblance to the Re-Reformed Church of the Netherlands, than to the Netherlands' 'Dutch Reformed Church'. However, all the Netherlands' churches are extremely liberal on the racial issue, unlike the South African church.

The differences between religious blocs in the Netherlands are reinforced by geographical differences. The Catholics have their stronghold in the south, and the Calvinists (Re-Reformed) are concentrated in the west and the north of the country. But no religious group is totally isolated from any other. For example, in the two southern provinces of North Brabant and Limburg, Catholics constitute 89·0 and 94·4 per cent of the population: but only half of Catholics in the Netherlands live in these two provinces. Catholics are least numerous in the three north-eastern provinces (about 10 per cent) but in the two most heavily populated western provinces they number above 25 per cent. Gadourek (1961) has characterized the two main sub-cultures of the Netherlands thus: 'Over against the more optimistic, vivacious Roman Catholic or Southern pattern, emphasizing sexual morality, stands the more sombre and sober, more matter-of-fact Protestant–Calvinistic or Northern way of life, disapproving most of lies and theft.'

At the same time there is a 'west–rest' dichotomy. The three western provinces of north and south Holland[1] and Utrecht contain one fifth of the land, but nearly one half of the Dutch population, and most of the major cities. Industrialization and urbanization are at their most advanced in the west, and opportunities for industrial and administrative employment are more varied. There is a steady influx of migrants to the west from other parts of the country.

A Dutchman's religion has a powerful influence on who his friends are, and who he marries. A survey carried out by Lijphart (1968) of 1,570 Dutch men and women inquired about the religion of the respondent's best friends: for Catholics, 85 per cent listed as their best friend another Catholic; 78 per cent of the Re-Reformed listed as a best friend someone of a similar religion; 85 per cent of Dutch Reformed had a best friend of similar religion; and 53 per cent of those with no religion indicated someone of a similar conviction as a best friend. In other words, Dutchmen mix only atypically on intimate terms with people of another religion. An obvious correlate of this is a high degree of endogamy.

Gadourek (1961) in a survey of a bulb-growing community in Sassenheim found that 82 per cent of those interviewed objected to the marriage of people of different religions; 41 per cent objected to friends of a different religion; and 11 per cent objected to working with people of a different religion. The highest preference for social discrimination was expressed by Catholics, followed by the

[1] The Netherlands is often referred to by foreigners as 'Holland'. This is something like implying that Scotland is part of England. There is a great deal more to the Netherlands than just Holland.

Re-Reformed, the Dutch Reformed, and the 'unchurchly'. Goudsblom comments that such a pattern would be less marked in an urban area. Our own survey (*vide infra*) of residents of The Hague and Amsterdam provides a confirmation of this point. It is not surprising that mixed religious marriages are something of an issue in the Netherlands (Goudsblom, 1967, p. 56) and that there is a high degree of religious endogamy. According to the 1960 census, 94·7 per cent of all married Catholics had Catholic spouses, and the percentages of endogamy for the other major groups were only slightly lower: 89·8 per cent for the Dutch Reformed; 93·6 per cent for the Re-Reformed, and 87·1 per cent for persons without religious affiliations.

Social discrimination extends to other areas of life. Lijphart observes (p. 57): 'Though it is hard to obtain systematic evidence, observers of Dutch society agree that considerable preference is shown by buyers for stores owned by fellow-members of their bloc, especially in smaller communities and in small-scale businesses.' Sometimes this social discrimination is officially sanctioned, and in 1958 the Roman Catholic bishops issued an instruction to all Catholic institutions (including numerous Catholic schools) that were accountable to them, that for all construction projects only Catholic architects and contractors organized in Catholic associations should be employed, and as far as possible only workers belonging to Catholic labour unions. The Bishops added: 'We confidently expect all governing bodies of Catholic institutions that are not accountable to us to adhere to our stipulations too' (Kruijt 1959).

More recent information on preference for endogamy has been provided by a nation-wide random survey of 1,600 adults aged 17–70, carried out in 1965 (*Polls*, Vol. III, No. 3, 1968). In this survey, 70 per cent of Catholics stated an objection to the marriage of their daughter with a man of a different religion: 73 per cent of Dutch Reformed expressed such an objection; 77 per cent of the Re-Reformed, and 62 per cent of the 'unchurchly'. This recent evidence suggests that it is the Re-Reformed who are now the most conservative group in this respect, while Catholics were the least conservative of the religious groups. In this survey, the question on attitudes to a daughter marrying a man of a different religion was followed by one asking how they would feel if their daughter wanted to marry someone of a different race. Now, such a question immediately following one about religion is liable to carry the unspoken implication that the man of different race is also a man of different religion; that is, the answers to this question are liable to be contaminated by the question which preceded it. We would thus expect the answers to this second question to be very similar to the first, and this is in fact the case. On this, and on the religious issue men are more tolerant than women, and young people are slightly more tolerant than older people. At the two age extremes, 52 per cent of those aged 17 to 25 would object to a daughter marrying a man of a different race, compared with 83 per cent of those aged 51 to 70.

A question which was not asked in this survey was how the respondents would regard the marriage of their daughter to a man of a different race, but *whose religion was the same as theirs*. Given (*a*) the degree to which religious differences are important in Dutch society, and (*b*) the large amount of dating and marriage between people of different colour that can be observed in a city such as Amsterdam in comparison with London (Bagley, 1968), we would expect that if in fact the prospective groom, although of a *different* race, were of the *same* religion, he would be readily accepted.

In Dutch society religious affiliation seems to be an important determinant of the degree and manner of interpersonal relationships. Interaction with people of a different religion tends to be truncated. Religious differences appear to be more important than other perceivable differences, such as ethnic status. A person of the same religion will be readily accepted, other things being equal, even if he were of different ethnic status. In the survey of attitudes, reported in a later chapter, I have attempted to test this hypothesis by asking specific questions about marriage, work, and friendship with someone of a different race, but of the same religion.

## SOCIAL CONTROL AND SOCIAL INTEGRATION IN THE *Verzuiling*

Social control, unless it is entirely coercive, relies on *socialization*: on the training of an individual to accept, and internalize and make part of his belief and emotional system, the folkways, norms, values, perceptions, and assumptions of the cultural group in which he finds himself. The most important, and the most powerful period of socialization is during childhood. The child enters life without knowledge. He is physically and emotionally dependent on adults. Adults trade love and physical care for the child's acquiescence to the norms, speech, behaviour, and belief systems of his parents and their cultural system. The influence of parents, peers, and teachers—'influential others' is vitally important. The child accepts the values of those he respects, admires, and loves. He has no criteria whatever for evaluating the standards of his elders themselves. His cognitive system is largely determined by the culture in which he is born.[2] This important sociological generalization, which I have derived from Durkheim and his American followers, applies to Dutch children just as much as it applies to children in Central Africa, or in Lapland.

In the Netherlands each *verzuiling* possesses its own socialization system, which transmits the particular beliefs and values of that pillar of society, together with those beliefs and standards of behaviour which are functional for national integration and social peace, i.e. which maintain harmonious relations with other *verzuilingen*.

Religion is of the utmost importance in determining social and cultural participation. Firstly, it strongly determines choice among the prevailing types of school: public, Protestant, or Catholic. At the age of six the population is already divided into four separate blocs; the children in each bloc spend a great deal of their time in different kinds of environment from children in other blocs, and receive different kinds of instruction in subjects such as religion and history. One may receive primary, secondary, and University education to doctoral level without ever leaving one's own bloc. The divisions brought about in youth persist in adulthood: political parties, trade unions, mass media, leisure associations, health and welfare organizations all follow the principle of pillarization.

The choice of a confessional school for their children is strongest amongst Catholics and the Re-Reformed, 90 per cent of both groups sending their children to the appropriate denominational school (Kruijt, 1959). Fifty per cent of Dutch Reformed parents choose a denominational school representing their own religion for their children. An interesting example of the different systems of socialization has been provided by Gadourek's study of Sassenheim. Gadourek examined the textbooks in use in the three types

[2] It is acknowledged, of course, that there are genetic, intellectual and personality factors which interact with the cultural 'inputs' the child receives. The total interaction of these variables determines the child's personality. For a fuller exposition of this model see the final chapter of Bagley (1971a).

of elementary school in the village—Catholic, Calvinist (Re-Reformed), and Dutch Reformed. He gives extracts from history textbooks about the same events (the Reformation, Philip II, the Inquisition, William of Orange, etc.). Catholic children were given the following view of Luther:

In 1517, Luther in Germany started the revolt against the Pope. He rejected the Priesthood, the Confession, the Holy Mass, etc. His followers were the Lutherans. In our country the Protestants were mostly the followers of Calvin who broke with the Holy Church in Geneva.

Calvinist children on the other hand, were told:

On the 31st October, in a peaceful small town of Wittenburg in Germany, a simple monk nailed a paper on a church door. It contained a long list of 95 articles summing up the shortcomings and lies of the Papist church. . . . People did not trust the priests any more. The simple and holy truth was completely buried under various human inventions of the priests. . . . Martin Luther was destined to become God's servant.

Dutch Reformed children, characteristically, were given a milder account:

Many bishops and abbots began to meddle more and more in political affairs and abandoned church affairs. They thought themselves sovereigns in the first place. Even in the cloisters, the situation deteriorated. Many monks led a life that was not in agreement with their assumed reputation. . . . Martin Luther wrote down a number of objections he raised against the Catholic Church. He made an appeal to the teaching of the Bible.

On the Inquisition, Catholic children were told: 'This was a tribunal of the Church. Its members were wise and pious bishops and priests.' Calvinist children were instructed that: 'Each day, now here then there, especially in the Southern Netherlands, innocent people were tortured and murdered. The inquisition was merciless.' Dutch Reformed children learned: 'Everybody hated the Inquisition. William of Orange, while still being a Catholic, hated it too, together with many other Catholics.'

The socialization of childhood is reinforced in the Netherlands by many factors in adult life—the social pressures to marry someone of a similar religion, to work with people of similar religion, to belong to trade unions and social organizations appropriate for one's *verzuiling*, to read the appropriate newspaper, and to listen to the appropriate radio and T.V. channels. These media and organizations in turn act to socialize the individual, and subject him to social control.

There are ten national papers in the Netherlands, two 'quality' papers with liberal and secular sympathies, the remaining newspapers being with two exceptions, more or less closely associated with a political or confessional bloc.[3] Radio and television are even more closely tied to the *verzuiling* system. There are five broadcasting corporations licensed by the Government, the stations being Roman Catholic, Dutch Reformed, Calvinist, Socialist, and a general secular station. Time on the two T.V. channels is divided between these five non-commercial companies. The T.R.O.S. T.V. network, the third largest in the country, has no formal bloc affiliations.

In 1954 the Dutch bishops issued a pastoral letter forbidding all Roman Catholics to join a socialist trade union, to visit socialist meetings, to read socialist newspapers, or to listen to socialist radio programmes. The penalty for disobedience is exclusion from the Holy Sacraments, the severest sanction a Catholic can suffer. The ban on joining a socialist trade union was revoked in 1965, but the other strictures still stand. In the largely Catholic south, many municipalities ban the sale of contraceptives, and do not permit mixed bathing in public swimming baths. Similar measures can also be found in some parts of the north, in staunchly Calvinist areas. Catholics and Calvinists are united in their distaste for birth control. While one would expect this of Roman Catholics, it seems that Dutch Catholics are particularly likely to follow the teaching of the church in this respect. The Netherlands has one of the highest birth rates of all northern European countries. At 21 per 1,000 population, it is considerably higher than the birth rate in Catholic Belgium, France, or Switzerland. This pattern has been described as a 'demographic anomaly' (Petersen, 1955). Indeed, the birth rate in the Netherlands has been higher than in Catholic countries in Europe for the last half century.

The birth rate is highest, as one would expect, in Provinces with a high proportion of Roman Catholics. Van Heek (1954) found that Roman Catholic communities just over the border in Germany and Belgium all had lower birth rates than neighbouring Dutch

[3] Handelsblad and N.R.C. newspapers merged at the end of 1970. *De Telegraaf* and *Algemeen Dagblad* have no *formal* bloc links.

Catholic communities, despite similar economic and social structure. Goudsblom (pp. 41–2) comments on this phenomenon:

> The conclusion must be, then, that conditions in the Netherlands have been especially favourable to compliance with the official Church doctrine regarding birth control. The crucial factor appears to be the historic position of the Roman Catholics as a large minority with a strong organized system of control. . . . Catholics have not shunned modern methods in defending their traditional policy. Internally they have protected their following from outside opinion by setting up an effective network of communications of their own covering every medium. Externally they have exerted strong pressure upon the national government to create throughout the country a climate unfavourable to birth control. Thus Roman Catholic initiative has introduced bills forbidding the public sale of contraceptives and has strongly supported a generous scheme of family subsidies with progressive rates for larger families.

This conservatism of Dutch Catholics is accompanied by progressive attitudes in other spheres, especially the liturgical. Probably this progressive attitude, like the degree of control which the Dutch hierarchy has over the faithful, is the result of historical circumstances. For many centuries the Mass had to be celebrated in unusual places, such as private houses and workshops, and in unusual circumstances, by priests having to pose as private individuals. These are precisely the aspects of Catholic religion—experiments with the Mass, and the secularization of the clergy—in which Dutch Catholics lead the world today (Van der Plas and Suer, 1968).

Durkheim (1952) in his monograph on suicide showed that religious integration was accompanied by low suicide rates, while high suicide rates occurred in individuals who were not subject to a high degree of normative and social control. We would expect suicide rates to be lowest in the two most conservative religious groups, Catholics and Calvinists (Re-Reformed) and this is in fact the case (Kruijt, 1960). The rates are highest in minor Protestant denominations which do not fit into the *Verzuiling* system, a finding in keeping with Gibbs and Martin's derivation from Durkheimian theory (1964) that lack of status integration is associated with high suicide rates.

## ECONOMIC AND CLASS STRUCTURE

The Netherlands was dominated for many centuries by a bourgeois class of burghers, and the standard of behaviour they set—'bourgeois civility'—still dominates many areas of Dutch life. The way of life of this bourgeois elite continues to carry great prestige, even though the actual power of the old elites has diminished. Bourgeois civility is still a cultural prerequisite for social success in any national organization (Goudsblom, p. 63). Social stratification, argues Goudsblom, is not often discussed in public, and even sociologists have not made it a subject of study. Thus there are few systematic studies of the role of class divisions in Dutch society. But observers (e.g. Lijphart, Goudsblom) are agreed about the important role class plays. The population appears to be segmented by social class, with seemingly little inter-action or mobility between the classes. My own survey (*vide infra*) which inquired about respondent's occupation, and the occupation of his father, suggests that there is a strong correlation between the occupational category of a father and son. Indeed, in the *Schildersbuurt* in The Hague, a working-class area which we shall discuss in detail later, there is even a tendency for men of a similar occupation to live in the same street—the same occupation, such as flower peddler, or rag merchant, being passed from father to son.

Lijphart cites a UNESCO survey on social class carried out in 1948 in nine countries, Germany, Netherlands, Mexico, Britain, Italy, Australia, France, the United States, and Norway. The survey found a good correlation in the Netherlands between self-assigned social class and objective social class; the correlation was much higher than that in Britain, Italy, Australia, France, the United States, or Norway. Put another way, people in the Netherlands tend to objectively describe their social status, and 'know their place' in comparison with the other societies mentioned.

A second question in this survey asked, 'Do you feel that you have anything in common with your own class abroad?' and 'Do you feel that you have anything in common with people of your own nationality who are not your own class?' The answers, suggests Lijphart (p. 22), 'provide additional strong evidence of the depth of Dutch class cleavages'. The percentage of Dutchmen feeling class allegiance even across international boundaries was strikingly high: with 61 per cent, the Netherlands was in second place, being exceeded only by Australia. The percentage of Dutchmen—56 per cent—who felt that they had anything in common with other classes in their country was strikingly low. Hollan d shared the second lowest place with Mexico, Italy being at the bottom with 50 per cent feeling some community with Italians of a different class. Moreover, in all countries the percentage of national allegiance was greater than the percentage of class allegiance *except in the Netherlands*: in the other eight countries national allegiance exceeds class allegiance by at least 9 percentage points and in two cases by as much as 34 percentage points; but in Holland it is actually 5 points lower. In other words, in comparison with the other eight countries, Dutchmen have more class allegiance than national allegiance. These findings, like those in religious differences, suggest that there are deep divisions in Dutch society. In fact, class differences cut across religious ones. In the secular bloc the class line is particularly important because of the absence of cohesions provided by a common religious outlook.

'The political system of the Netherlands,' says Lijphart,

> presents a paradox to the social scientist. On the one hand it is characterized by an extraordinary degree of social cleavage. Deep religious and class divisions separate distinct, isolated, and self-contained population groups. Social communication across class and religious boundary lines is minimal. Each group has its own ideology and its own political organizations: political parties, labour unions, employers' associations, farmers' groups, newspapers, radio and television organizations, and schools—from kindergarten to university. Such a socially and ideologically fragmented system would appear to be highly conducive to dissensions and antagonism instead of consensus and co-operation, to ideological tension and extremism instead of pragmatism and moderation, and to governmental immobilism alternating with revolutionary upsets rather than evolutionary change (pp. 1–2).

The Netherlands like many other societies in the world is divided into ideological camps, which do not mix with one another very much. In many 'plural societies'—a term originally used by Furnivall (1948) in his description of society in Burma—the endogamy and social separation of the various groups of society is reinforced by ethnic differences. Many such societies exist in a state of more or less permanent tension, the sort of tension which we might expect to exist, as Lijphart says, in the Netherlands. But the paradox of the Netherlands is that this tension does not seem to exist. It is not only a peaceful, but also a democratic society. Political theorists, cited in detail by Lijphart, have suggested that pluralist societies in which the separateness of groups is reinforced by political and social organization will be weak and unstable societies. But,

The Dutch case is *prima facie* contrary to the crosscutting cleavages proposition. Expressed in the jargon of the cited writers, Dutch politics is characterized by 'mutually reinforcing', 'superimposed', 'congruent', and 'parallel' rather than 'crosscutting' affiliations and organizational patterns; class and religious cleavages separate self-contained 'inclusive' groups with sharply defined 'political subcultures'; and there is a multi-party system with considerable 'interpenetration' within each sphere among parties, interest groups, and the communication media (Lijphart, pp. 14–15).

The interpenetration of religion with political and other associations is illustrated in the following Table 1:2, which is adapted from Hofstede (1964). It shows, for example, that 90 per cent of Catholic children are in Catholic primary schools, and 95 per cent of Catholic farmers belong to a Catholic farmers' union, and 90 per cent of Catholic workers belong to a Catholic trade union.

*Table 1:2. Degree of Saturation of Denominational Organizations for Seven Activities, as a Percentage of Organized Participants per Religious Denomination*

| *Organization* | *R.C.* | *Re-Reformed* | *Dutch Reformed* | *No Denom.* |
|---|---|---|---|---|
| Primary schools 1957 | 90 | 90 | 50 | ±10 |
| Farmers' Unions 1953 | 95 | 90 | 37 | Nil |
| Trade Unions 1958 | 90 | 90 | 30 | Nil |
| Radio magazine Subscriptions 1955 | 89 | 94 | 32 | 18 |
| Voting for denominational party, 1959 elections | 84 | 95 | 32 | Limited |
| Readership of denominational daily papers, 1955 | 79 | 58 | 9 | 1 |
| Active membership of denominational association, 1955 | 71 | 73 | 36 | 12 |

*Source*: Hofstede (1964).

A similar picture can be sketched for the interpenetration of religious affiliation and membership of voluntary associations.

Seventy-seven per cent of Catholics belong to Catholic associations; 74 per cent of Re-Reformed belong to a Re-Reformed association; and 30 per cent of Dutch Reformed belong to a Dutch Reformed association.

Despite the extreme segmentation of so many aspects of Dutch life, social conflict is notably absent. All major political problems facing the Dutch during the past century have been resolved peacefully and constitutionally. Democratic government is a reality, and in fact Dutch politics seem to be not just healthy and stable, but dull and unexciting also. 'This is', says Lijphart, 'perhaps the reason why political scientists have paid so little attention to it this far, in spite of the fact that Holland is the largest (in terms of population) of the smaller West European democracies.'

A degree of consensus and social peace is maintained in Dutch society by means of a number of deeply institutionalized beliefs and modes of behaviour. It is important, in understanding Dutch society, to specify what these are. The Netherlands is not a consensual society; consensus exists within each bloc, but there is no general inter-bloc consensus, except in a number of narrow areas. One vitally important point has been agreed between the blocs: the belief that the existing system must be retained. Each bloc tries to defend and promote its own interests, but only within the confines of the total system, and without the threat of secession of civil war. There is thus a degree of nationalism in Dutch society which holds the blocs together. There has never been any question, for example, of Limburg (isolated from the rest of The Netherlands by geography and religion) seceding to Catholic Belgium. Even in the sixteenth century, some degree of fulfilment was available for Dutch Catholics within the framework of Dutch society. And the doctrine of the Catholic church in the Netherlands, like the Orthodox church in communist Russia, has been one of compromise with the existing social structure.

The most important symbol of national unity is the monarch, and the House of Orange, which dates from the liberation from Napoleon. There is a wide consensus among both religious and secular groups, and among nearly all political parties in favour of the retention of royalty. The marriage of Princess Irene to a Spanish Catholic placed the loyalty of some Dutchmen to the monarchy under strain, but its legitimacy has not been seriously questioned.

Underneath this mildly nationalist umbrella, a process of

accommodation between the blocs has been worked out. The relations between the blocs resemble relationships between countries. Diplomatic negotiations—hidden from the popular eye—take place concerning the relations between blocs, just as diplomats negotiate the relationship between countries. The tacit agreements about non-aggression, and some form of co-operation resemble relationships between one state and another. 'In Holland, . . . war is continually being averted, and the statesmen of the rival blocs have managed to achieve peaceful co-existence' (Lijphart, p. 104).

The pattern of mutual accommodation was established by 1918, and grew out of the negotiations over the franchise and the finance of religious schools, which were mentioned earlier. The process of accommodation is greatly facilitated by the form of electoral representation—that of proportional representation; thus, approximately 10 per cent of the population is Calvinist, and the Calvinist Party has a representation of around 10 per cent in the Second Chamber. The situation is similar for the other parties. A system of election by a straightforward majority would mean a parliament dominated by the majority forces in society, with minorities inadequately represented.

In Britain by comparison, the representation of Liberals in Parliament is minute, and quite out of proportion to their electoral support in the country. The British electoral system also ensures the permanent domination of one religious group over another, as in Northern Ireland.

The rule of proportionality extends to many areas of Dutch life. Schools are financed in proportion to the numbers in them and the same rule is applied to government finance for other religious agencies, such as hospitals, welfare clinics, and so forth. Governing bodies—for example, of community relations at the local level—are representative of the blocs proportionally to their numbers in the local community.

Lijphart distinguishes several other rules of accommodation. The first of these is that 'politics is a business'. Such an attitude is in accord with the long tradition of the Netherlands as a merchant nation, and with the crucial role the merchant classes have played in Dutch history. The political elite is orientated towards results. In comparison, politics in France is a 'game' with tactics of delay, equivocation, and avoidance of responsibility, regardless of the consequences for the nation. Without this result-oriented attitude, Dutch politics would look quite different. Neither the great political settlement of 1917 nor the continuing pattern of accommodation since then would have been possible without it. It is the axiom underlying all other 'rules of the political business'.

The second rule distinguished by Lijphart is 'the agreement to disagree'. The fundamental convictions of other blocs must be tolerated, if not respected. Disagreements must not be allowed to turn into either mutual contempt or proselytizing zeal. The third rule is that of summit diplomacy; this diplomacy, as we have pointed out, resembles international negotiations. An example of such diplomacy is the informal but important 'Political Council', consisting of twelve members, two each from the six major parties. This is informal and meets only intermittently. But it could assume political significance at times of actual or threatening crises. The fourth rule concerns the neutralization of sensitive issues, and justifying compromises to the rank and file. The embarrassing question of Princess Irene's conversion to Catholicism and marriage to a Catholic was, for example, translated into a technical rather than a political or ethical matter. The issue presented to the Dutch people by their leaders was whether the formal rules of the constitution allowed such an arrangement, not whether it was right or not. The fifth rule is that of secrecy. Successful accommodation by the bloc leaders requires a high degree of flexibility. Compromise and concession is extremely difficult in the context of a public debate. In this respect, the politics of accommodation again resemble international politics. The Second Chamber, i.e. the Dutch Parliament, is a forum, not for deciding between issues, but for commenting on the disclosure of political facts and decisions.

The academic world also tends to protect this secrecy. The failure to carry out any major or systematic study of elites, or social stratification, is a case in point. The communications media —press, radio, T.V.—are by and large parties to this agreement to be silent about issues that are the subject of delicate negotiation between the bloc leaders, and about issues which have been 'depoliticized'. The issue of immigration from Surinam and the Antilles is a particular case in point. I shall discuss this example in more detail below.

The final rule of accommodation concerns 'the Government's right to govern'. The Government is elected to get a job done, in the business-like tradition of Dutch politics. Once a bill is passed by the Second Chamber, both dissenting members, and the dissenting electorate accept it without question, as the rule of law.

Lijphart explores in detail an example of this. 'These informal, unwritten rules govern the political business in Holland', he says. 'They may not always be scrupulously followed, and because they are stated in general terms, they may be subject to different interpretations, but they are sufficiently salient to be regarded as *the* rules of the game. They contribute much to the success of the elite's efforts to govern the divided nation' (p. 137). Moreover, the rules of secrecy, proportionality, and depoliticization keep much of the fire and excitement out of politics. This dullness does not however mean that there are no issues and tensions in political life. The opposite is the case. Potentially divisive issues and disintegrative tendencies are ever present, but they are carefully controlled. This lack of excitement does not reflect a perfect consensus, but rather reflects the deliberate attempts of the elite to cope with the system's fragility. The apparent dullness of politics is functional for the system's survival.

### CIVILITY AND DEFERENCE

Further factors, governing interpersonal behaviour, tend to minimize conflict between members of different *verzuiling*. The ascendancy of the burgher elite over many centuries has meant that many standards of 'bourgeois' behaviour have diffused through the population as a whole. These modes of behaviour range from table manners to standards of cleanliness, personal bearing, and sexual morality. An important requirement of civility is that the individual never indulges in an open display of emotions, concealing his innermost feeling behind a restrained observance of conventional forms. The actor is expected to establish friendly relations with his fellows, while at the same time preserving distance and avoiding intimacy. Goudsblom comments:

> This prestige function of civil conduct has sometimes called forth resistance, especially in socialist quarters; nevertheless, in practically every national organization, including labour party and labour unions, the dominant code of behaviour is civil: Civility appears to present a generally acceptable set of rules for the kind of relationships that sustain a nationally integrated social structure (p. 30).

The standards of civility have obvious, and observable influences on Dutch life. In restaurants and places of entertainment dress and manners tend to be formal. Gentlemen wear ties. Ladies do not wear slacks. A lady who wears slacks in a Dutch restaurant may find it difficult to obtain service.

Civility—politeness and restraint—dominates many interpersonal relationships. Public displays of emotion, and spontaneous friendliness to strangers are not features of Dutch life. The standards of civility influence mass media. In spite of their diverging political and religious views, the five broadcasting corporations are about equally committed to the dominant bourgeois culture pattern. Everyone who appears on television professionally conforms to this pattern in dress, speech, and manners. Television thus acts as a reinforcement for the model of 'civility' in social behaviour. An interesting recent exception to this rule has been presentation of programmes by the V.P.R.O. (Protestant) network, which now places emphasis on informality.

Civility, in its most ideal and perfectly internalized form, includes not only good manners and a sense of decorum, but also more personal qualities such as self-possession and a sense of duty and responsibility. Anyone holding or aspiring to a leading position in Dutch society whether in government, politics, business, or any other organizational areas, has to acknowledge these standards. They have the effect of imbuing all conflict with some restraint, and of minimizing open conflict. Civility is thus an important regulator of inter-bloc behaviour, and serves to minimize conflict between members of the blocs at all levels. Dutch society is an extremely tolerant one; the Protestant respects the rights of the Catholic, and Protestants, Catholics, and Humanists have mutual respect and tolerance for each other. Other groups, which would be labelled deviant in some societies—such as homosexuals—are accorded a wide degree of tolerance. But homosexuals in Holland, by and large, conduct themselves with orderliness and restraint, and indeed, form their own *verzuiling*. Prostitutes and pornographers occupy similar roles, carrying on their professions with dignity and restraint. The idea of tolerance, as Goudsblom says, is matched by the idea of orderliness. Nonconformity is tolerated as long as it does not interfere with the prevailing social order. At points where the norm of orderliness is violated, the tolerance of the social system ends.

Part of the norm of civility is that of deference, deference to those in a position of authority, and deference to those older than oneself. This deference to authority, both social and governmental, is an important element in the stability of a society which, because of the ideological differences between blocs, possesses great potential for conflict. Lijphart comments on this phenomenon:

> Neither the ideologically stylized pattern of elite-mass communications nor the high degree of elite dominance of the bloc organizations can fully explain the persistent allegiance of the rank and file of the blocs to their leaders. The people must have an inherently strong tendency to be obedient and allegiant—regardless of particular circumstances. This tendency will be referred to as *deference*. This term is here used in its broadest meaning: an individual's acceptance of his position both in the social hierarchy and on the scale of political authority, accompanied by a low level of participation and interest in politics. For the masses this entails respect for and submission to their superiors (p. 145).

Lijphart carried out a parallel survey to that of Almond and Verba's *Civic Culture*, thus obtaining data on 'most admired traits' in respondents in five cultures, Netherlands (N = 1,600), United Kingdom, Germany, Italy, and the United States (N in each case 950 or slightly larger). One of the most admired traits in the Netherlands was that a man should be 'respectful, doesn't overstep his place'; 19 per cent of respondents chose this quality as their first choice, a higher proportion than in any other culture, the next highest proportion opting for this trait being in the United States, with 11 per cent, followed by Italy with 10 per cent, and Britain with 9 per cent. The proportion choosing this trait in the Netherlands is nearly twice as high as in any other culture. There were variations in the Dutch sample of proportions opting for the trait 'respect' between blocs: 16 per cent of Catholics did so, 17 per cent of Humanists and 28 per cent of Protestants.

The Dutchman trusts and respects his leaders. But the leaders themselves are imbued with a sense of propriety and deference to the opinion expressed by bloc leaders, opinion which itself is mediated by a spirit of compromise. Sometimes the leaders try to reinforce the obedience of the rank and file by moral lectures. For example, the 1954 pastoral letter of the Catholic bishops warned against the 'spirit of criticism' and admonished all Catholics not to 'overestimate their own opinions' and to recognize 'the good intentions of their own leaders' (Lijphart, p. 159).

An important determinant of status in the Netherlands is age, and the young are expected to display great deference to the old. Children and adolescents do not participate in adult culture, and even as students enjoy little participation in 'adult' institutions.

The category of youth is followed by that of the 'younger adults'; this category has a special name in Dutch: *jonger*. This term is widely used by the middle-aged to apply, collectively or individually, to those younger than themselves. The use of the term implies that the speaker expects deference from the person he is addressing.

The chief mark of the member of the *jonger* appears to be that he is a full citizen who has completed his education and has achieved adult status, even to the extent of being head of his own family; yet in the organizational structure of Dutch society still occupies a subordinate position. The *jonger* look forward to attaining within a few years the positions held by their elders. During the waiting period their attitude may be a mixture of critical detachment and ambitious deference towards the established powers. Dutch youth, and Dutch young men and women have a rather non-serious attitude to social and political affairs in their own country, though they may, through organized religious groups take an active interest in world issues such as war and famine. The life of the *jonger* (which status ends when the individual is between 35 and 40), resembles a kind of extended adolescence. Lacking in power and responsibility for decisions which may influence aspects of his daily life, the *jonger* has an attitude to life characterized by a certain dignified jollity. His behaviour somewhat resembles that of the old-style university student. The legal age at which a child could marry without the permission of his parents—at thirty—reflects the 'extended adolescence' status of the *jonger*. This law has only very recently been repealed.

Those in the age category 40 to 64 hold most of the leading positions in Dutch society, and those in senior positions may hold them well past the age of 65. This pattern of age-graded statuses applies chiefly to the middle and upper classes. Blue-collar workers can rarely hope to achieve any elevated status in later life, although the pattern of deference, of youth for their elders still holds in this class. While the middle classes achieve positions of some power by the time they are 40, there is a considerable degree of elite rule in the Netherlands. Lijphart describes this elite in some detail, showing (pp. 59–68) that in each bloc, a small number of people have 'interlocking directorates'—of labour unions, political parties, newspapers, and radio stations. This elite, by means of secret inter-bloc negotiation, is the principal source of social and political policy in the Netherlands.

A picture is beginning to emerge, of deference to one's elders, of deference to authority, of deference to the political wisdom of the leaders of one's bloc, and to the political wisdom of the leaders of the country itself. The Catholic party polls some 25 per cent of votes in the country, but has effective power since the remaining votes are split between the remaining secular and Protestant parties. But the Catholic party rules in close consultation with other political leaders, and its policies receive the acquiescence of the large majority of Dutchmen, whether Catholic or not. The case of West Irian, which I discuss below, is a case in point.

The observer of Dutch life is immediately struck by the degree to which social life is the subject of orderliness and regulation. Officials of all kinds expect—and obtain—obedience, and often give their instructions in an authoritarian manner. The stranger in the Netherlands will be treated brusquely, and often, by English standards, with rudeness. But in commercial relationships such as shopping, the customer will be treated with extreme courtesy; this is a deferential relationship, not a friendly one. Spontaneous warmth and friendliness are notable in Dutch public life by their absence. In this respect, the role of the stranger is not an enviable one. Lijphart's survey of most admired traits in five countries provides an important empirical support for this proposition. One of the items which the respondent could choose as the most admired trait was 'Generous, considerate of others'. The proportion of Dutchmen selecting this trait—12 per cent—is the lowest of all the five countries considered. The contrast with Britain is striking. No less than 49 per cent of the British respondents chose this as their most admired trait (compared with 39 per cent of Americans, 26 per cent of Germans, and 14 per cent of Italians) (Lijphart, p. 146).

While carrying out the fieldwork for the present study, the writer was based at an international institute in The Hague which provided courses for students from developing countries around the world. The writer was impressed by the strength of opinion amongst these students about the unfriendliness of the average Dutchman. By contrast, the writer was constantly embarrassed by students—many of them black, and brown—who had spent some time in England, and who were enthusiastic about the friendliness of English people towards strangers!

It is logically feasible that a people can be both unfriendly and tolerant. Indeed, the tolerance of the Dutch for diverse ideological groups is based on reserve, on stiffness, on truncated interaction. One has observed the difference between England and the Netherlands in the relationship between the sexes. In England, any man who is not wholly uncomely, and not too advanced into middle age, may catch the eye of a pretty girl and be rewarded with a smile, or, if not a smile, a certain amused disdain. Such activity in the Netherlands causes great confusion in a girl. The smile from a strange man is not an expected role behaviour, and evokes a reaction ranging from embarrassment to shame. If the cause is pressed, the *meisje* tends to fall an easy prey to the romantic suitor. The success in this field of Indonesians and Italians in winning Dutch girls, which has been a source of friction in Dutch life (see below) is not difficult to understand. The Dutch girl does not expect a romantic suit from a stranger; it is not prescribed role behaviour for a Dutch *jonger*.

Since blocs tend to be endogamous, courtship is carried out, by and large, within the confines of these groups. One does not act in an open, or friendly way with the population at large, but only with members of one's bloc, through inter-family visits, and through the activities of the appropriate religious or bloc organization. Within this context, social relations are more informal and relaxed. It is significant that, of the students mentioned above, the one who most liked the Netherlands was a Ghanaian from a Protestant background who had been absorbed into a Protestant *verzuiling*, being warmly entertained in the homes of many of the congregation of which he was a member.

Every society has in some way or other to institutionalize 'dependency relationships'; these are relationships between people who are temporarily or permanently in need with people who are currently prosperous. Most societies provide some form of assistance for the dependant—the disabled, the poor, the sick, the elderly. In the Netherlands such assistance is organized principally within the *verzuiling*. A crucial feature of interpersonal relationships in the Netherlands is that dependency relationships are not generated through interaction outside the bloc system. For example, although the stranger may buy his cigarettes at the same shop over a period of months (ceasing to be a 'stranger') a sudden shortage of cash does not give him any claim to credit with the shopkeeper whom he now knows quite well. The Dutchman is in fact very rigorous about paying his bills on time, and avoiding debt. In commercial relationships, courtesy is extended to the extent that the customer has money in his pocket. For any good or service provided, immediate payment is expected, and given. Lack of flexibility in this sphere, and the stiffness and hostility which any slight deviation from this principle caused was one of the features of Dutch life which my student informants commented on. It is a source of complaint too, for Indonesian and Surinamese immigrants who resent the Dutchman's 'obsession with money'.

There is a characteristic style of Dutch interpersonal relationships. These relationships vary with context: (*a*) Relationships in a public context are marked by formality and unfriendliness. It is this behaviour that the recently-arrived immigrant is most likely to encounter. (*b*) Within the bloc system, relationships are less formal and more friendly. Relationships are warmest within the family. The integration of the immigrant will be fostered to the extent that he can either penetrate the existing *verzuiling* system, or possesses sufficient numbers and social cohesion to form a *verzuiling* system himself. (*c*) An exception to the general unfriendliness of public relationships is that involved in commercial transactions. While the potential buyer will be treated with formality, he will also be treated with deference and respect. (*d*) Commercial relationships are governed by the prospect of the exchange of guilders; the deferential warmth does not lead to warmth in any relationships developing out of these 'exchange' roles. In particular, dependency relationships (e.g. credit relationships) are not generated from commercial interaction between buyer and seller. Dependency relationship roles are institutionalized within the bloc system, not outside it. (*e*) The curtness of everyday social relations in the Netherlands has its roots in the bloc system. It is a mode of interpersonal relationship which is functional for avoiding contact between people of markedly different ideologies, and avoiding the dangers of exogamy. Relationships in a public context will be most curt where the blocs are mixed together in more or less equal strength. Where one bloc tends to dominate (as with Protestants in the north, and Catholics in the south) public relationships will be more relaxed.[4]

[4] The writer's experience of, for example, the cities of Groningen in the north and Maastricht in the south in comparison with West Holland tended to confirm this.

## THE FAMILY

This account of socialization and family life is drawn from three sources—the Keurs' study of a Drents community (1955), Gadourek's study of a bulb-growing community (1961), and Ishwaran's study of the urban, middle-class families in West Holland (1959).

The Keurs carried out ethnographic fieldwork in Anderen, a village in the north-east of the Netherlands, in the province of Drenthe. They painted a picture of an extremely stable society, in which norms of behaviour were clearly known, understood, and conformed to by all members of the community. The system of socialization was impressive. The children were tractable, so that when parents said 'Go to bed now', they went, without demur. This tractability seemed to extend to horses and cows, which were handled with extreme gentleness.

Children in this society are taught to be polite and to be quiet until spoken to. Honesty is early inculcated. Respect for the property of another was so strong that the village schoolmaster reported that in his six years at Anderen not even a pencil had been missing from the school. Punishment of the child is rare, and will take the form of sending a child to bed without supper. The *Meester* knew of only one case of a parent striking a school-age boy. The Keurs mention the example of a child who, experimenting with fire, was in danger of burning down the yard. His father, in exasperation, hit him. The child replied, astonished, 'To think such a big fellow as you could hit such a poor little one as me.' It is rare to see or hear a child crying.

The child is indoctrinated not so much as an individual, but as part of a group. All homes in the village are open to the child, and he enters all homes happily, first taking off his clogs. Relationships are arranged on a hierarchical basis, the older protecting the younger. Love is traded for obedience. At the age of seven or eight years children are introduced to farm work, the child being responsible for the milking of one or two cows. Parental authority extends to a child in his late twenties, and a considerable degree of dependence on parents is encouraged. Children questioned in school in early adolescence were fearful about leaving home—'It is too dangerous to go away . . . I wouldn't have any friends any more.' Courting is carried out in considerable secrecy, but with the tacit knowledge and agreement of parents. Sexual relations before marriage are common, taking place in the outside buildings of the farm. Premarital pregnancy is a frequent result, but almost always results in marriage; in 1952, 51 per cent of first-born children were born less than 9 months after the marriage of their parents. There is no shame associated with such an event, nor with premarital intercourse. Young people are inarticulate about sex, but accept these relationships with great naturalness. Sexual jokes are extremely uncommon.

The strength of the family as a social unit is strong throughout the Netherlands, and is particularly strong in Drenthe, say the Keurs. Patterns of dominance in the family are muted and subtle, but undoubtedly exist. The father has a formal power, but real power lies with the mother. Grandparents of either sex have absolute authority, in keeping with the hierarchical gradings of status. These statuses are expressed by small, formal rituals such as patterns of seating, and primacy of address. Children in particular remain silent, speaking only when spoken to.

Debt is repugnant to the Anderens, who are thrifty in the extreme. In this respect their behaviour is representative, in a somewhat exaggerated form, of the rest of the Netherlands. The patterns of socialization and family life are probably an 'ideal type' of family life in the Netherlands. This is an extremely powerful form of socialization—the combination of gentleness and love with rigidity and ritualization of age and authority statuses. In Anderen 271 of the 273 inhabitants belonged to the Dutch Reformed Church; the Re-Reformed Calvinists were 'deviant' in this society (by virtue of their small numbers) and tended to emigrate. This lack of the need for inter-bloc relationships meant that the warmth of family relationships could spill into the community, which in turn acted as an additional socialization agent for the child. Social control by the community is strong, and a hard word is long remembered; the adult is dependent on the love of his peers, just as the child is dependent on his parent's love.

Gadourek's study of Sassenheim is of a bulb-growing village community within travelling distance of The Hague and Amsterdam. Unlike Anderen, the village is marked by religious diversity. Just over half of Gadourek's sample of 404 residents were Catholic, the remainder being divided between Dutch Reformed and Re-Reformed churches. Despite differences in religious teaching in the family, there were many similarities in methods of child rearing. Children are treated, as in Anderen, strictly but gently.

In both Catholic and Calvinist families the father has ritual functions as head of the family; in Protestant families he reads the Bible before meals. When the father is not present, a period of silence is observed. Nevertheless, both parents share in household tasks and in training and care of the child. There are also similarities with Anderen in courting patterns. Premarital intercourse is common, among Catholic couples as well as Protestants, and Gadourek calculates that one in six pregnancies in Sassenheim in every year are conceived before marriage. Despite a high frequency of forced marriages, illegitimacy is rare. There is strong family loyalty. Family units are set up, in other words, when there are children to care for—'Marriage', in Westermarck's term, 'is rooted in the family, and not the family in marriage.' The fertility of married couples is high.

Ishwaran studied not a community, but the parents of a sample of 415 students at the University of Leiden. His study gives a profile of the urban, middle-class family in West Holland. A quarter of families were Dutch Reformed, 17 per cent Roman Catholic, and 40 per cent had no religion. Ishwaran found that the strongest figure in socialization in the early years was the mother, while the father exercised more authority when the child entered secondary school. Older siblings also adopted socialization and authority roles in relation to younger family members. The families were described as overtly 'compassionistic', but covertly patriarchal. The father's authority is implicity recognized by the mores of the family. The father does not punish in anger, and only in relation to specific transgressions. The causes of punishment are failure to meet the parental expectations of 'promptness, cleanliness, honesty, and industry'. Ishwaran, an Indian ethnographer, was impressed by the strong element of gratitude and love which children showed to their father. A child, punished by his father, told Ishwaran, 'It hurt him more than it hurt me.' The parents exercise a strong control over the development of ideas concerning religious ideology and endogamy.

These three pictures of socialization and family life—in Anderen, Sassenheim, and Randstad Holland—show that, despite differences in geography, religion, and occupational class, there are many similarities in the families studied. The father is a kindly but authoritarian figure. He takes a great interest in his children, and is concerned for their welfare and conduct; rare transgressions by the children are punished sternly and with sorrow. Love, and the denial of love, are the most powerful elements in the socialization process. The unity of the family is reinforced by ritual elements, especially of a religious nature. Deference is built into the pattern of socialization, deference being shown to parents, grandparents, and older siblings.[5]

My interpretation of Dutch society will be that these elements—authority, affection, and deference—extend to many areas of Dutch life. The extent of deference and authoritarianism in public life has already been mentioned. But he who obeys is treated kindly, with genuine affection. His environment is highly structured; his place is ordained; his welfare is assured.

This pattern of society is particularly interesting in relation to Dutch colonial rule in Indonesia. This rule, unlike British colonial rule, has been paternalistic and kindly. The British have treated native peoples as economic and legal units, as instruments for exploitation and control. The Dutch have treated native peoples like their children, who must obey and love, and who are loved in return. I shall return to this theme in the chapter on Dutch policy in Indonesia.

These conclusions about authoritarianism, deference, and affection may well extend to the treatment of immigrants in the Netherlands. Immigrants in the Netherlands will most probably be accepted and treated with kindliness to the extent that they conform to the standards of behaviour laid down for Dutch citizens, and show the proper deference in the face of authority. (The degree to which immigrants are deferent, and obey Dutch norms of personal and inter-personal behaviour will also be connected with their appreciation of, or membership of, the bloc system.

HOUSING

The Netherlands is one of the most crowded countries in the world. The population per square kilometre—352—is exceeded only by that in a number of small islands. The five most crowded

[5] Cf. Pinner's interesting finding (1965) which compared the relationships between parental over-protection, and distrust of political figures in children of such families, in Belgian, Dutch, and French samples. Pinner found that over-directive parents bred a feeling of political distrust and dissatisfaction in the high school and university students sampled; but this tendency was much less marked in the Netherlands sample. This may well be due to the special combination of authoritarianism and tenderness displayed by Dutch parents.

countries in the world—Hong Kong, Singapore, Malta, Barbados, and Mauritius—are all, curiously enough, former British colonial possessions, and areas of potential immigration to Britain. Sixth in the list of rank order of population is the Netherlands. The population density of Britain at 217 per kilometre, is much less than that of the Netherlands (Russett, 1964).

A second index of population density is the number of people per square mile of arable land (Ernst, 1967). On this index, the population of the Netherlands is 3,220 per square acre, compared with 1,890 in the United Kingdom. The Netherlands ranks nineteenth in the world in this index of population density.

The population problem in the Netherlands—and the subsequent pressure on housing—is aggravated by the high birth rate, the high rate of infant survival, and the low death rate in later middle age. These last two factors are a function of the excellence of medical facilities. In the Netherlands in 1966 the average family size was 3·7, compared with 3·1 in France, 3·0 in England and Wales, 2·9 in West Germany, and 2·8 in Sweden (U.N. *Statistical Yearbook*, 1967, Table 109). The annual average percentage increase in population in 1958–65 was 1·4 in the Netherlands, compared with 0·8 in England and Wales.

A further factor having a bearing on the population problem in the Netherlands has been the large influx of immigrants in post-war years, especially from Indonesia. The Netherlands ranks eighth in the world statistics of immigrants per 1,000 population in the years up to 1958 (Russett, 1964). The number of immigrants per 1,000 population in this period in the Netherlands was 4·04. Britain ranks seventeenth in this list, with 1·47 immigrants per 1,000 population.

In England and Wales a little under half of the population live in houses they own or are buying by mortgage, while a further 26 per cent of the population live in rented housing provided by the local authority (Donnison 1967, p. 186). In the Netherlands only about 5 per cent of householders live in houses they own or are buying, while a much higher proportion of housing than in Britain is owned or directly controlled by the local authority. In 1960, 46·4 per cent of all new dwellings were built by local authorities (under the terms of the Housing Act) and 53·2 per cent were built by the private sector (de Yanes, 1962).[6] The cost of 'Housing Act'

[6] See Milner Holland (1965) for a comparison of housing policies in London, Amsterdam, and five other European capitals.

dwellings is subsidized by the state, the amount of the subsidy depending on the number of occupants the house is to contain, and the price of the land. In the letting of both private and local authority dwellings, the number of occupants is strictly controlled. Building by the private sector is also subsidized. Such housing is usually let for rent, and this rent too is subsidized. Subsidies are not given for new housing units of over 500 cubic metres, and such housing falls into an expensive 'luxury' class.

One of the most distinctive features of Dutch housing policy in comparison with Britain is the control of lettings by the local authority. All private lettings with the exception of the letting of furnished rooms, and luxury housing, are in the control of the local authority. Housing is either allocated to an applicant who has approached the local authority, or his tenancy is recommended to the local authority by the owner of the housing. Very often the housing is owned by a local church association, a firm, or a trade association.

Two crucial rules are operated in the allocation of housing. Firstly, the number of rooms in any dwelling allocated is related to the size of the family given the dwelling. In one local authority a young married couple are given a 'paper' child in their first year of marriage, and are expected to produce the child for which space has been allocated within a couple of years! Indeed, one way of getting sympathetic consideration in local authority housing is to show evidence of fertility. The second important rule is that the rent of the housing allocated shall not exceed one-quarter of the family's income.

Because rents are subsidized and the number of rooms occupied is strictly controlled, for many people the most expensive municipal housing appropriate for their size of family is less, sometimes considerably less, than a quarter of their salary. If the professional wants more spacious housing he must enter the very expensive housing market of private, unsubsidized lettings. In practice, the large majority of the population live in housing (which takes the form of flats) where the rent is controlled, or where the purchase price has been subsidized by the Government.

Since 1945, 1,100,000 new dwellings have been built,[7] a little under half of the total number of existing dwellings in the Netherlands. The majority of new housing has been built in the

[7] Ministry of Housing and Building, *Housing in the Netherlands* (The Hague, 1964).

Randstad area including Amsterdam, Rotterdam, and The Hague. This part of the Netherlands contains 48 per cent (5·2 millions) of the population, but covers only 24 per cent of the land area. Its present rate of expansion, too, is much faster than that in the rest of Holland. De Yanes, viewing the contrast between 'the Rest and the West' from the point of view of the town planner, advocates a policy of greater industrialization of the rest of the Netherlands, the provision of new towns, and of additional social, educational, and recreational facilities. The attraction of the West is illustrated by the fact that in some areas an applicant may have to wait as long as five years to be allocated an apartment by the local authority, while in parts of the rest of the Netherlands the waiting period is as short as two weeks. In contrast to Britain, it cannot be said that there are pockets of unemployment in areas analogous to Tyneside, Scotland, or Northern Ireland; the pull of the West probably lies in the recreational facilities it offers, and in the diversity of employment.

Donnison (1967) has commented favourably on the Netherlands' housing policy: 'Some countries—notably Holland, Norway and Denmark—have also compelled landlords . . . to seek municipal approval for their selection of tenants, thus ensuring that homes are found for poorer families with children and for other groups who might otherwise be neglected, and the space available is efficiently used' (pp. 343–4). One measure of the efficient use of housing in the Netherlands is that of 'housing slack'. This is the difference between the supply of dwellings available, and the number of dwellings actually occupied. In time of housing shortage a large number of unlived in dwellings is of political significance (at the time of writing there is a 'squatting' movement in some London boroughs, whereby homeless people occupy empty housing). A calculation using the statistics for 1966 given in the U.N. *Statistical Yearbook*, 1967 (Table 199), shows that in 1966 the 'housing slack' in Britain was 314,141 dwellings, or 2·15 per cent of the total number of dwellings. The comparable figure for the Netherlands was 0·59 per cent of the total number of dwellings. This comparison does suggest that the system of housing allocation in the Netherlands is associated with an efficient use of housing in this respect. My overall conclusion is that in response to extreme pressure on housing resources (certainly a much graver problem than the British one) the Dutch have provided efficient and largely equitable solutions.

## POPULATION AND EMIGRATION

In her study, de Yanes calculated that in the period 1930–60 the population of the Netherlands had increased by 47·6 per cent; the population increase over a similar period was 14·2 per cent in Britain, 13·3 per cent in Belgium, and 10·7 per cent in France. This spectacular increase in population received considerable publicity in the period of reconstruction after 1945. It was calculated (Hofstede, 1964) that jobs for an average of 45,000 new workers would have to be found every year between 1947 and 1963.

There were frequent articles, according to Hofstede, in newspapers, magazines, and journals complaining that 'the Netherlands is becoming too crowded'. Discussion of a solution in terms of birth control was taboo, since there was a consensus between Catholics and Calvinists that such policy was unethical. The discussion of solution took the form, instead, of pressure for industrialization, and for a vigorous policy of emigration. The official estimate of population was that the twelve million mark would be reached by 1970; in fact, this figure was already reached in 1963.

Hofstede said of the Dutch concern with emigration that, 'the Netherland people became acutely aware of the population problem—and the consequences to the community of the rapid growth of the population immediately after the Second World War. *The fear of over-population had almost become a psychosis*' (p. 57, emphasis added).

In the early 1950s the possibilities of industrial expansion were viewed with gloom; the Government's solution to the problem was to pursue a vigorous emigration policy. Emigration offices, financed by the Government, were set up in many areas. In addition subsidies were given to the emigration activities of the churches. It was the Catholic and Re-Reformed churches whose birth control policy had largely contributed to the population problem, who showed the most interest in emigration. In 1956 for example, the three largest of the private emigration associations were given a government subsidy of *Fl* 600,000 (about £60,000 each).

Emigration was very efficiently organized. The ground was carefully prepared in Canada, Australia, and New Zealand. Emigration was a group process, denominational groups emigrating together and to the same area. They were accompanied on their voyages by a priest or minister whose passage was subsidized by the Dutch Government. There was concern that the emigrants should give the Netherlands a good name overseas, and the emigrants were socialized accordingly. The churches continued this socialization with the aid of specially recruited full-time personnel in the major centres of Dutch settlement in Canada and Australia. The way in which Dutch emigration policy was conducted at all stages is an example of the efficiency of Dutch social organization.

When it is decided by the Government or a bloc that something shall be done, there is the minimum of dissent or debilitating discussion. The task in hand is attacked with great energy, efficiency, and imagination. The impressive Dutch emigration policy was matched, as we shall see shortly, by the efficiency of the policy for the reception and integration of immigrants from Indonesia.

Emigration was at its peak in the period 1953 to 1957, but declined somewhat after that period with the advent of industrial prosperity about which economists and politicians had been so gloomy in the late forties and early fifties. It was estimated as a result of public opinion surveys carried out in 1948, that between three and four million Dutch people—over a quarter of the adult population—wanted to emigrate; in the event, 500,000 people did so.

The phenomenon of public concern and action over population growth and overcrowding, and the consequent pressure on available housing supply is of great importance in the consideration of race relations, and attitudes to immigrants in the Netherlands.

The problems of housing shortage and extreme population pressure in the Netherlands are factors which might well give grounds for hostility to immigrants, who could be perceived as exacerbating the population problem. In comparing hostility to immigrants in Britain and the Netherlands, the fact that population problems and pressure on available housing are much greater in the latter country must be taken into account.

## TRADITION AND SOCIAL CHANGE

A slow rate of social change has been a feature of Dutch society. The German poet Heine remarked that if the world should perish he would go to the Netherlands: there everything happened fifty years later. True, in the nineteenth century there was little sign of an industrial revolution until the 1870s. Railways were not developed until after this date. In another sphere Dutch society has been remarkably conservative—'the annual birth rate has never dropped below 19 per thousand inhabitants, not even during the economic depression of the nineteen thirties. This fact appears to indicate that Dutch society had not undergone an abrupt break with tradition. In this respect the zuilen system may have served as a mitigating factor, restraining the social and cultural impact of modernisation' (Goudsblom, p. 33). Until the mid-1960s the birth rate in the Netherlands at 21·2 per 1,000 was the highest in Western Europe, including traditional Catholic countries such as Eire (Russett, 1964).

Lijphart (1968) commenting on his survey of political and social attitudes carried out in the Netherlands in 1964, suggested that, 'Especially the November 1964 survey showed that while religious and ideological cleavages have been diminishing, social cleavages have remained deep. Moreover, according to this survey, those belonging to the postwar generation were not notably less allegiant to their own bloc or less committed to their bloc organizations than their parents' (p. 186). Lijphart suggests that the strongest indication of the continuation of the bloc system is the evidence on religious endogamy; both the 1947 and 1960 censuses show no decrease in this practice. 'Instead', Lijphart comments, 'the already high degree of intramarriage even increased somewhat between 1947 and 1960' (p. 189). Ishwaran, in his 1959 study of urban middle-class families, argued that there was no evidence at all to suggest any change in family structure or in traditional patterns of authority. Nor was there very much evidence at all of upward mobility of the working classes into the middle classes. There is in fact a structural barrier to upward mobility in the form of the 'Middestands-Diploma'. This is a diploma showing competence in book-keeping and commercial practice and law which is required before undertaking entrepreneurial activity on any scale. It is thus virtually impossible for any working-class boy who has not had a high school education to enter the middle classes by virtue of entrepreneurship.

This evidence suggests that the pace of social change is slow. But social change there is, and a number of my informants specifically stressed changes taking place in the relationship between different religious groups. One man, a ministry official, had recently married a Catholic girl, while he himself was a Protestant. Ten years ago, he said, the match would have been met with severe opposition and possibly ostracism from their respective families. But today the marriage was accepted, if a little uneasily.

Experiments with Catholic liturgy have included the admission of Protestants to Communion; the oecumenical movement manifest in many countries has not left the Netherlands untouched. We might expect, over a period of years, that the bloc organization will become less rigid, and might eventually disappear. But for the present analysis, bloc organization is a very real phenomenon.

There are some signs too, from the results of the 1971 General Election that traditional party allegiances on sectarian lines are not as strong as they were; but despite the proliferation of small political parties, it is still the church parties who form the essential coalition through which the Netherlands is governed.[8]

Thurlings (1972), in a study of 'the tottering column'—the decline in solidarity of the Catholic bloc—indicates that in 1966 the Catholic People's Party polled 30·1 per cent of votes; in 1967, 26·5 per cent of votes; and in 1970, 24·2 per cent of votes. These figures indicate that a number of Catholics are either not voting for their party, or are actually voting for other parties. The most striking index of secularization amongst Dutch Catholics is the decline in the number of priests ordained (227 in 1966, falling steadily to only forty-eight in 1970), and in resignations from the priesthood (seventy-four in 1966, rising steadily to 243 in 1970). Figures for religiously mixed marriages are increasing, though not at this spectacular rate. In 1966, 8·7 per cent of marriages involving a Catholic partner were mixed, compared with 12·4 per cent in 1969. In 1966, 64·4 per cent of Catholics regularly attended at Sunday Mass, compared with 47·2 per cent in 1969. Clearly the changes which are affecting the priesthood are not affecting the laity with such speed.

The cause of this crisis is undoubtedly the difference of opinion between Catholic priests and the papal hierarchy, on such issues as birth control, and the marriage of priests. A 1970 survey which randomly investigated the opinions of 1,500 of the 3,500 priests in the Netherlands found that virtually all were in favour of contraception. This compared with about a half of American priests

[8] In the 1971 election the governing coalition of four parties (Catholics, Dutch Reformed, Re-Reformed, and Conservative Humanists) lost overall about 8 per cent of the votes which had previously supported them. A progressive combination (Labour Party, D 66, and P.P.R.) gained about 6 per cent more of the electorate's support, but not enough to form a government. In this election the Farmers' Party was eclipsed. A new party, D.S. '70 (a splinter group from the Labour party), gained some 8 per cent of the votes. The anarchist candidates, based on Amsterdam, obtained virtually no support from the electorate (*Handelsblad N.R.C.*, 19 April 1971).

who were similarly surveyed, and one-third of priests in the conservative climate of Colombia. 'The picture', wrote the authors of the report of this survey, 'is one of division, confusion, inconsistency, and strain, and portends change rather than stability.'[9]

Thurlings discusses the possibility that one reason for the decline in bloc cohesion amongst Catholics is the fact that bloc rigidity declines once problems of equitable distribution of power and resources have been solved. According to such a view, blocs (like the state in Marxist theory) should wither away when full bloc equality is achieved. But other factors have contributed to the particular decline of solidarity in the Catholic bloc, and in particular the ideological debates with the official hierarchy. Thurlings has commented,

> One of the greatest difficulties here [concerning birth control, etc.] is the difference between the Roman (i.e. Italian or Latin) and the Dutch cultures. To the Roman, a norm is a formula on which further discussion, more or less interesting but in any event free from obligation, is possible. To the Dutchman, a norm is a rule which has to be observed. The former therefore feels free to discuss the value of that norm without this being of the slightest consequences for his behaviour. The latter, unacquainted with this lack of obligation, either accepts the norm and observes it, or rejects it and becomes deviant in his behaviour.

For the Dutchman, moral rules derived from religious principles are accepted (or rejected) with profound seriousness. This applies to areas other than marriage and family life, as we shall see.

[9] 'Catholic Parish Priests and Birth Control: A Comparative Study of Opinion in Colombia, U.S., and the Netherlands,' *Studies in Family Planning* (Vol. 2, 1972), pp. 122–38.

CHAPTER 2

# THE DUTCH IN INDONESIA

Between 1945 and 1963 the Netherlands absorbed over 300,000 refugees from Indonesia.[1] The large majority of these were a Eurasian group, descendants of various types of intermarriage:

> This Eurasian group is compounded of many different physical types. The colour of the skin ranges from white to dark brown, the features are sometimes distinctly mongoloid, and there are also considerable differences in hair growth, etc. This is accounted for by the fact that mixed marriages were not restricted to those between Dutch and Indonesians, but also included unions of Dutch persons with other, non-autochthonous inhabitants of the islands, such as the descendants of Spaniards, Portuguese, Chinese, Arabs and Negroes (Ministry of Culture, 1965, p. 5).

The remainder of the refugees fell into two groups, the 'totoks' or Europeans without Indonesian ancestry, and Indonesians without European ancestry.

In order to understand the circumstances which led to the hurried migration of these people, their attitude to the Netherlands and of the Dutch towards them, we must consider the history of Dutch rule in Indonesia in a little detail. My account is drawn from various published sources, and the authors have various backgrounds and biases—Furnivall (1944 and 1957), a distinguished British colonial administrator in Burma; Kennedy (1942) an American anthropologist writing a book for a political, rather than scholarly market; Vandenbosch (1944) a Dutch scholar working in the United States; Chaudhury (1950) an Indian Marxist; Van der Kroef (1954) a Dutch scholar under Indonesian patronage;

[1] About 280,000 of these refugees were 'brown Dutchmen', the remainder being 'totok' Europeans. There were also a few thousand Chinese among the refugees. By 1972 the number of 'coloured' Dutchmen from Indonesia in the Netherlands had risen to half a million, because of the high rate of intermarriage with the white Dutch population (Van Amersfoort, 1972).

Fischer (1959) an American political journalist, and friend and confidant of Sukarno; Wertheim (1955) a Dutch scholar; and Palmier (1962) a New Zealand scholar.[2] Each of these authors brings a different conceptual system to bear in their analyses of Dutch colonial policy. Some, like Furnivall, are sympathetic to the Dutch; others, like Fischer, Van der Kroef, and Chaudhury are distinctly anti-Dutch or pro-Indonesian. Inevitably, my interpretation of their accounts and the events of history are influenced by factors such as my own ethical predispositions, and the further knowledge available. I hope to steer a course—largely sympathetic to the Dutch, largely unsympathetic to the British, and somewhat unsympathetic to the Indonesian nationalists—which is fair in the light of the evidence available.

The East Indies archipelago—the vast areas of Sumatra, Java, Borneo, Celebes, Moluccas, New Guinea, and numerous small islands—covers an area of land and sea equivalent in size to that stretching from Madrid to Moscow, and from Athens to Glasgow. It is the sixth most populous country in the world, with over a hundred million people. Colonization of the East Indies for the Dutch was carried out by the Dutch East Indies Company, whose motives were commercial gain, and whose policy was exploitation. The situation changed remarkably in the latter half of the nineteenth century. The opening of the Suez Canal, coinciding with an economic depression in the Netherlands, led to much greater numbers of Dutchmen emigrating to the East Indies.

In this period too, a change of policy occurred. The policy had its roots in a Dutch characteristic which is highly relevant for our study of race relations; a combination of dogmatism and authoritarianism with an unshakable belief in the rightness and worth of the ethical teachings of Christianity. In the final analysis the Dutch are not a pragmatic people, motivated by desire for economic gain, moulding ethics to expediency. Their behaviour is guided by ideology, and in particular, an ideology derived from Christianity. Fischer, discussing Dutch policy in Indonesia has described this trait: 'Toughness with oneself and others and a dogmatic demarcation between good and bad are basic to the national behaviour of the Dutch. They are not exactly flexible. They feel duty-bound to

[2] I have also consulted the Human Relations Area Files study on Indonesia edited by McVey (1963) for information on the culture of Indonesia. This volume contains surprisingly little about Dutch colonial policy. An additional source on Dutch colonial history has been Coolhaas (1960).

extirpate evil. Once they fix a goal not even their common sense, love of tidiness, and obedience to regulations will stop them' (p. 62).

The increase of Dutch emigration to the East Indies was accompanied by a growing criticism of traditional colonial policies. This led to a large number of reforms, notably the introduction of primary education, and land reforms which allowed natives to own land. But Dutchmen, including Eurasians, were forbidden such land ownership.

The change in colonial policy culminated with Queen Wilhelmina's declaration in 1901 of 'the ethical policy'. In her pronouncement she said that, 'As a Christian power the Netherlands is obligated in the East Indian archipelago to regulate better the legal position of native Christians.' But at the same time, the rights and welfare of the large Moslem population were also respected, especially after 1920. In the *verzuiling* tradition, Moslem law and schools were respected, and Moslem schools subsidized by the state. Such behaviour is explicable in a tradition of religious differences in the Netherlands. Protestants had agreed, finally, to state support for Catholic schools; and if Catholics, whose liturgy and dogma were so strange and anathemous, could be supported, why not Moslems?

The system of education introduced in the late nineteenth century more or less ensured that in many parts of the archipelago three years of primary education were available to those who wanted them. Further primary and secondary education was organized by various sectarian organizations, including Moslem groups. Dutch tolerance of the autonomy of native institutions may well have been an important factor in the rise of a militant nationalism in Indonesia, a point expanded on below.

From the beginning, the Dutch conceived of marriage with the native populations as a means to achieving good relations with the conquered populations, and as an instrument for creating a harmonious climate in which colonial exploitation could take place. A law of 1617 encouraged such marriage with the inhabitants of the East Indies. The rate of these mixed marriages did decline in the present century as more Dutch women came to the colony.

By 1930 there were about 220,000 individuals in Indonesia classified as European, but who were descendants of mixed marriages. The 1931 census of India and Burma located 119,000 'Anglo-Indians', the official term for descendants of mixed marriages in the British colonies. These people, however, were given the legal status of 'natives' by the British administration (Cressey, 1935).

Kennedy, writing in 1942, observed that one of the most striking differences between Dutch and British colonies appeared in the treatment of people of mixed European and native descent. To the British, such people were beyond the social pale. They seldom rose high in governmental or business positions, and were excluded from white clubs and social circles. In the Indies, however, they were formally treated as Europeans and were accepted everywhere as equals—

Some of the highest posts in government were held by persons of mixed blood, and no legal or social impediment stood in the way of Dutchmen wishing to marry one of them. Most of them, however, occupied a middle class status, working as minor officials, as school-teachers, or in clerical positions. This fact itself shows that some discrimination did exist, but their lot in the Dutch islands was better than in any other colonial area of the world (Kennedy, 1942).

Kennedy reports that when Dutch liners on the way from Batavia to Holland docked at Singapore, the travellers would go uptown for dinner and dancing at the Raffles Hotel.

On every ship there would be several Eurasian families of high status 'going on a visit to the mother country', usually government officials on leave. In the Indies they were accepted everywhere, and thought nothing of going with their friends to the Raffles. Here they might obtain dinner, but if any of them started dancing the manager would slip over and quietly explain that Eurasians might dine, but not dance in the hotel. This, perhaps, to the Governor of one of the Indies provinces! . . . The Americans, with their unfortunate tendency to ape the British, took over the same attitude, although not to such an extreme degree, in the Philippines. . . . I once took a *mestizo* school-teacher, a very fine gir lby any standards, to a dance. One of the 'grand old lady' social leaders of the community warned me never to repeat the performance if I wished to get on in white Philippines society (Kennedy, p. 162).

Kennedy continues:

Some of the mixed-blood families were very ancient in the Indies; and certain old towns, notably Padang on the west coast of Sumatra, had great numbers of them who intermarried among themselves or with Dutch people whom they met in the islands or when they went to Holland. . . . They were very handsome and healthy people, the Dutch heavy physique and blondness mixing nicely with the slender, dark-skinned native type.

The Dutch, 'realist to the core', saw in intermarriage a good means of cementing friendly relations between themselves and the island people through the creation of a mixed-blood intermediary group.

Besides marriage, concubinage was common, and this fitted well into the traditional culture patterns of Indonesia, where sex norms are liberal. The cultural form of Islam condones the institution of 'Nikah-mut-ah' or temporary marriage. There is, as a result, a high divorce and separation rate among the population. Divorce is based on the mutual repudiation of marriage by the parties involved. In 1950, according to Fischer, for every hundred marriages contracted in Indonesia, forty-seven were repudiated.

Dutch soldiers were allowed to house their temporary wives in barracks. Children of such unions, if not wanted by either party, were sent to an orphanage at Semarang in Java, and many of them followed their fathers into the army. Twice a year a great Indonesia lottery was held, the profits going for the support of the orphanage. Everybody played the lottery, says Kennedy, both from a desire to win money and from an obligation to 'help the soldiers'. On the plantations, concubinage was also common, an attractive native girl being selected as a housekeeper. The girls ran their masters' households effectively and economically. It was, Kennedy suggests, a 'moral process' since no betrothed or married women would be chosen. Children were sent to the girl's mother. Either the couple married, or the girl was discharged with a large gratuity. Her 'interesting past and her bit of capital' made her a sought-after bride. Kennedy concludes:

> The Dutch have done very well to treat the children of mixed matings fairly. In them they have had a generally loyal intermediary group, appreciative of the consideration shown them especially when they have heard of the status of Eurasians in British possessions. Except for the Chinese, the half-castes were the only middle-class element in the whole Indies. In this intermediate position they had an intimate knowledge of both Dutch and native society; and they made up a large part of the school teaching force in the islands.
>
> If the Indies ever rise from the desolation of the dark days of 1942, the intelligent, well-educated and temperamentally sound Eurasians will surely take their place among the leaders of reconstruction. And the Dutch, with this living proof of their tolerance and liberalism in the vital question of race relations, will have earned the right to a major voice in future plans for the orient. When East and West meet on equal terms, as all the democratic peoples of the world now bitterly realize they must, the Dutch will have done their part in showing the way to a new era of tolerance and the brotherhood of man (pp. 167–8).

The Dutch were not to fulfil the role in the east which Kennedy cast for them. Instead, the Dutch were to establish a lead in tolerance in their treatment of coloured people in the Netherlands and not in Indonesia.

## A COMPARISON OF THE STATUS OF EURASIANS, AND ANGLO-INDIANS

For the Dutchmen, to have heirs who were of mixed European and Asian race was an honourable, and a desirable thing.[3] For the Englishman such an event was covered with shame and contempt. In 1931 there were 119,000 Anglo-Indians in a population of 338 million; in 1930 the number of Eurasians in the East Indies was 220,000 in a population of 70 million (Cressey, 1935; Hurwitz, 1955). In other words, taking population into account, there were nearly ten times as many census-defined Eurasians in the Dutch Indies as there were in British India and Burma.

A consideration of estimates based on non-census information (Van der Kroef, 1954, p. 275) suggests that there may in fact have been many more people in Indonesia of mixed descent. The sources cited by Van der Kroef suggest that 90 per cent of individuals defined in the 1930 census in the East Indies as 'European' did in fact have native ancestors. Further sources suggest that in 1940 there were between 8 and 9 million Indonesians census-defined as native, who had European ancestors.

The Anglo-Indians, as we have noted, were officially classified as natives, and were not admitted to membership of European Clubs or other social organizations. Neither were they accorded any place in traditional Hindu society. Their position was, as Hurwitz put it, one of pure marginality. Despite the constant rebuffs from the British in India they strongly identified with British institutions, adopting English language, and customs of dress, food, and housing. They were urban dwellers, and often lived in conditions of extreme poverty in the cities of Calcutta, Bombay, Madras, and Rangoon. The accounts of Bhattacharya (1968) and of Murari (1971) indicate that there are still a large number of Anglo-Indians in Indian cities, and that they still occupy disadvantaged and marginal roles in Indian society.

The Anglo-Indians, unlike the Eurasians, were by and large denied admission to the British Army (though largely descended

[3] On this point, see Van der Veur (1960).

from army personnel).[4] But they formed about two-thirds of the volunteer auxiliary force. They were reviled by native Indians, and in turn treated the native population with contempt. They disdained manual labour, and instead sought employment as clerks in the British administration and commercial houses, and in the transport services. Chronic unemployment was common. They had to live with the stigma of illegitimacy, rejection by both colonial and native societies, and had to endure appalling material conditions. It is little wonder that this led to feelings of resentment, and psychological instability. This mixture of servility and resentment in the Anglo-Indians led the British to deduce that the products of inter-racial marriage were 'inferior stock'.

When the British left India after the war, the Anglo-Indian community were in a very vulnerable position. The 'Indianization' of government enterprises in many cases left them unemployed. Indian entrepreneurs would not employ them. Hurwitz says that, 'The British, before they withdrew from India, did nothing to help those Anglo-Indians who wished to leave the country.' The loyalty of the Anglo-Indians was treated, in the British colonial style, with contempt. It is thought that a number of Anglo-Indians—Hurwitz suggests as many as 50,000—did manage to emigrate to England in the 1940s.

Vandedbosch has compared the lot of Eurasians (the official term for individuals of mixed race in Indonesia) with that of the Anglo-Indian and suggests that:

> Another important factor in explaining the large number of Eurasians is the relative absence among the Dutch of race prejudice. The Dutch attitude is in marked contrast with that of the British in their dependencies. Eurasians have held the highest positions in government and business. There is very little social discrimination, though even Dutch people complain of a change of attitude in recent years. This is most marked where British influence is greatest, as in the East coast of Sumatra (p. 8).

Many Eurasians lived, more or less permanently, in the Netherlands. In 1930, there were an estimated 30,000 of them in the Netherlands, not including the Moslem community of seamen and domestic servants from Indonesia. The largest concentration of Eurasians was in The Hague, 12,000 being resident there in 1930. The Hague is a city very heavily influenced by the culture

[4] They were recruited to the R.A.M.C.; and to the Infantry when recruiting in Britain was difficult.

and civilization of Indonesia. In Indonesia there was no taboo (although there were some barriers) on Eurasians reaching the highest positions, and some of the wealthiest families in Indonesia were Eurasian. Many Eurasians sent their children to be educated in the Netherlands, and some went to retire in The Hague like their European counterparts in the Civil Service. Anglo-Indians were never wealthy enough to have their children educated in Britain.[5]

## THE DUTCH ADMINISTRATION

A most careful and detailed account of Dutch colonial administration in the East Indies has been provided by Furnivall (1944 and 1957), who contrasted the Dutch administration with the British administration in Burma with which he worked.

Before the 'ethical' or 'welfare' policy in Indonesia, rule was 'liberal' in the sense of adopting a *laissez-faire* policy towards economic activity and social change. The rise of the welfare system meant a much closer administration of native affairs in which, 'people come to civil servants, European or Native, as friends, for the amicable arbitration of disputes, which in British India would come as a matter of course into the Civil Court and be settled by strict law.' British and Dutch colonial policy were founded on quite different principles. Two basic principles of British colonial policy were the rule of law, and the primacy of economic freedom, whereas Dutch policy aimed at imposing restraints on economic forces, by strengthening personal authority and by conserving the influence of custom.

In modern Burma Furnivall distinguished a number of 'notorious evils'—(i) the failure of Western self-governing institutions; (ii) the growth of debt and agrarian distress; (iii) the rise of disaffection and unrest in Buddhist clergy; (iv) wide corruption in judiciary and administration. These had a common cause, the disintegration of social life through the inadequacy of law to control the working of 'anti-social economic forces'. The Dutch system of rule had its faults, yet in all these features Netherlands India provided a notable contrast.

The Dutch welfare policy largely retained native forms of administration with a policy of 'like over like' in a dual system of

[5] Wertheim (1955) although critical of Dutch colonial rule in Indonesia, suggests that there was certainly less colour-consciousness by the Dutch than on the part of the British in India.

administration, with a European or Eurasian retaining links with the larger society, and being responsible for the overall administration of the welfare services, finance for which was derived from Western capitalist enterprises. The results of the welfare system, according to Furnivall (1957) meant a good, universal system of elementary education, and a library system with some 3,000 branches, including motor vans distributing books. The population were enthusiastic users of these libraries.

In 'like over like' the Dutch aimed at conserving villages and village systems of customary law, and at the retention of native land in native hands. The agrarian reform acts of the 1870s allowed natives to own land they had leased for centuries. 'The new arrangement', says Fischer, 'had the virtue of defending the village, the heart of Indonesian life, from disintegrating factors. This is one reason why the Dutch won the reputation of being good colonizers.' Dutch administrators specifically intervened to protect the small peasants from landlord exploiters, action which would have been unthinkable in British India and Burma. In Burma, Furnivall documents, the fate of the people was at the mercy of entrepreneurial activity, which was only loosely regulated by law.

Village administration in Indonesia was paternal but kind, 'establishing clinics, planting flowers, building stout houses'. Furnivall summed up the policy of the two colonial powers in an address to a meeting of Dutch public administrators:

Your policy is, professedly, ethical; ours, practical. These are not mere catchwords. You try to give the people what they ought to want; we are to give them what they pay for. Your method is one of personal influence, *zachte* ('gentleness') . . . we rely on the economic motive, the desire for gain, working within the limits of the law. The results, I admit, are not quite the same. Our villages compare with yours in respect of hygiene and roads. . . . On the ethical system you aim at organizing social demands; on the practical system we neglect such wants until they threaten to create a public nuisance. Your system works very differently from ours. . . . Our officers are magistrates; yours are policemen and welfare officers. Our methods are repressive; yours are preventive. Our procedure is formal and legal; yours, informal and personal. Our civil service is an administrative machine; yours is an instrument of government. Our aim is negative—to suppress disorder; yours is positive—to maintain order. . . . You try to keep a man from going wrong; we make it unpleasant for him if he does go wrong. You believe in protection and welfare; we believe in law and liberty (Furnivall, 1957, p. 273–4).

Furnivall concluded his comparison of Burma and Indonesia:

> The Dutch, by strenuous endeavours, have succeeded in maintaining an astonishingly high level of material welfare, far above the level in those parts of India which are comparable in respect of population, and about the same level as in Burma[6] with much fewer mouths to feed. Yet if the Dutch have protected the people against those factors which have caused agrarian distress and fostered crime, corruption and clerical unrest in Burma, the price has to be paid in other ways.

The 'price' Furnivall points to is 'a lack of dynamic spirit' in the Indonesian population. But on this rather curious assumption Furnivall offers no evidence. We shall argue otherwise, that the Dutch administration, being unrepressive, and allowing the autonomy of native culture and educational institutions, fostered a powerful, grass-roots nationalist organization, which was to be the final undoing of the Dutch as a colonial power.

There were strong and definite stirrings of Indonesian nationalism in the early part of the twentieth century, and Fischer interprets the Dutch policy of allowing native autonomy in many spheres as a reaction to this movement. Kennedy commented on this policy with surprise:

> One of the most remarkable evidences of Dutch toleration of native culture appears in the sphere of religion. It is indeed surprising that a nation so deeply religious as the Christian Hollanders should have protected the pagan and Mohammedan religions of their subject peoples more than any other colonial power. Nowhere in Europe is Christianity, whether Protestant or Catholic, taken more seriously than in the Netherlands. One would have expected, therefore, that wherever Dutchmen went they would have tried with all their might to convert the natives. But the people of Holland have displayed throughout their three centuries of independence a strong regard for religious liberty. They have shown it at home in their treatment of Jews and other minority groups. Holland has rightly been honoured as a sanctuary of religious tolerance, never once violated by persecution of minority faiths, even when all other European countries were torn by church conflicts. This spirit the Dutch carried over to their oriental possessions; and, almost alone among the colonial powers, they went out of their way to safeguard the traditional beliefs of their native subjects. They never

[6] In 1964 Indonesia's gross national product per capita of $131 ranks eightieth in the world; that of Burma at $57 ranks 113th; that of India at $73 ranks 101st and that of Pakistan at $70 ranks 104th (Russet, 1964). The literacy rate in Indonesia (Ernst, 1967) is 43 per cent; in Burma 58 per cent; in India 28 per cent; and in Pakistan 19 per cent.

showed any favouritism among the various Indonesian faiths; they took great pains to investigate the religious beliefs of every native group, so as not to offend unwittingly; and they carefully controlled the well-meaning but sometimes over-zealous missionaries (pp. 143–4).

The colonial government granted licences to missionaries, and minutely prescribed the terms of their activities, anxious that existing social patterns should not be destroyed. Protests from the native people meant the likelihood of the immediate cancellation of the missionary's licence. This meant that in Mohammedan areas missionaries were extremely rare.

The Dutch system in Indonesia clearly parallels the situation in the Netherlands, in which religious conviction was firmly and deeply held, but the religious beliefs of others were respected. One of the *verzuiling* rules is the forbidding of proselytization. The Indonesian religious *verzuiling* were allowed religious autonomy. They were allowed to develop their own secondary and higher education system. But they were denied one crucial freedom: membership of the ruling elite. In the Netherlands all religious groups share in the business of government at the highest level. But the ruling elite in Indonesia was exclusively Dutch and Eurasian. At the same time, tolerance of the autonomy of Indonesian culture allowed a sophisticated and well-educated nationalist movement to arise.

The Dutchman in Indonesia retained a firm belief in the superiority of his own way of life.[7] The brown children he begot had to become Dutchmen. He treated them with a most powerful kind of socialization, a combination of authority, gentleness, sternness, and love. His brown children became Dutch because of the love of their father. The brown children of the Englishmen in India wanted to be English because of the moral arrogance of the Englishmen who projected his way of life as the most superior. But he treated his native subjects with coldness and distaste. He disapproved of their traditional organization and culture. His rule was ruthless, and was motivated by very little else but desire for economic gain. Fischer has contrasted British and Dutch attitudes to the colonies in the following way:

[7] See Wertheim (1956) and Schrieke (1955) on this point, and for a general account of the early Dutch domination in the East Indies. Wertheim suggests that 'colonial stratification based on race was merely superimposed on the original Indonesian class system'.

> Love of the Indies is widespread among Netherlanders who have lived there. The British went to India for centuries and performed their duty as they saw it, but they never, or rarely, loved India. They dreamt of green England to which they would retire when their work in the colony was done. But the Dutch grew deeply attached to Indonesia. Many married Indonesians. Many would have been happy to live out their lives on a mountain or a plantation in Java or Bali or Sumatra or some other tropical isle. When India won her freedom the British left with regrets, perhaps, but with no personal heart pangs. The chapter had ended, the tie was cut. But the Dutch had never had a divorce from Indonesia. The Indies are still in their blood. They long for them. They suffer from the separation. . . . They have been deprived, spurned by a beloved. Their homes are full of batiks, Bali wood sculptures, wayang masks, and other Indies mementos. Their hearts are full of nostalgia. It all hurts, and pain often turns to hate (p. 79).

The Dutch lost Indonesia after a bloody and humiliating struggle. Never before, during, or immediately after the Second World War had they maintained any notion that in the foreseeable future Indonesia might be a self-governing independent state. The rise of a militaristic nationalist movement took them by surprise, and in the face of Japanese occupation of Indonesia they could do nothing.

Indonesia has penetrated deeply into Dutch consciousness, and has interpenetrated Dutch lives and institutions. When Ishwaran undertook his survey of the Dutch middle-class family in the late 1950s, he drew a random sample of students at Leiden University. Of the 415 located no less than 15·7 per cent had been born *in Indonesia*. The parallel—nearly 16 per cent of English students at Oxford in 1958 having been born in India—is difficult to imagine. It has been estimated that only about 0·5 per cent of the ethnically British population was born in India. It is possible too, that at least half of these 100,000 Englishmen are Anglo-Indians.[8]

It is commonly said that 10 per cent of Dutchmen can trace an ancestor who is a full-blooded Indonesian. The writer was astonished by such a claim, and asked many of the middle-class Dutch people he met whether this might be true. His respondents have convinced him that this claim may well be an accurate one. In the fieldwork interviews with a cross section of the Dutch population I

[8] See Rose, et al. (1969). Palmier (1962, p. 139) points out that the Dutch community in Indonesia was relatively much larger than the English in India, and included not only a ruling elite but professionals and trades people at all levels. Moreover, in contrast to the English in India, some 70 per cent of the Dutch in Indonesia were born in the East Indies. Many of these had intermarried with the native population.

was not infrequently assailed with the comment, in reply to questions about treatment of coloured people, 'Why, you are talking about *us*, Dutchmen.' The Dutch have so strongly identified with Indonesia that they seem to have absorbed not only many of its customs, but also the dark brown skin of its people. 'I love that country as one can only love a woman,' Charles Welter, a former Minister of Colonies told Fischer. 'It is beautiful and fertile. Now those priceless islands have fallen into the hands of revolutionaries. . . . Throughout the world Dutch colonial rule was regarded as the best on earth. But today that great country has succumbed to famine, disease, and rebellion.'

## THE LOSS OF INDONESIA

In the years before the Second World War, a sophisticated nationalist movement had grown up in Indonesia. The movement was at times uneasily tolerated and at times suppressed, as the communist uprising of 1926 was suppressed. A kind of democracy was introduced, but the form of its constitution meant that Europeans (including Eurasians) had a permanent majority on the People's Council.

One factor which aided the development of nationalism was the system of education. Indonesian autonomy in the sphere of education resulted in the emergence of a large number of highly trained people. But the elite jobs in the colonial administration were denied them, so that there developed a large underemployed and disaffected intellectual elite. Many of these graduates themselves set up schools, thus further increasing the numbers of the educated.

This 'alienation' of the Indonesian educated elite was tragic, and it can be counted as one of the major factors which led to the rise of extreme nationalism and the eventual expulsion of the Dutch from Indonesia. Palmier comments on this aspect of Dutch–Indonesian relations:

> Indonesia had absorbed the Western way of life, at least in her higher circles. Except in the native principalities, there was no longer any national pattern of life. The same customs were observed as in European households, down to the habits and even to the meals eaten. In consequence, Indonesian hatred of the white man differed from that of the Chinese, Arabs, Indians, or Japanese. Indonesian hatred was superficial, because the haters had assimilated the patterns of living and thinking of the white man. The hatred was therefore traceable to the Indonesian's feelings of impotence towards him (p. 38).

Japan invaded Indonesia in February 1942. The Dutch—men, women, and children—were sent to concentration camps, and many perished. The Japanese tried to incite the Eurasians against the Dutch, offering them privilege in a Japanese-ruled Indonesia. Instead, they chose the fate of the Dutch, and shared their internment in the Japanese camps. The Japanese set up an all-embracing nationalist organization called the *Putera*, and established Sukarno as President of a representative council for Indonesia. Sukarno was given the task of arousing the population, using the wireless transmitters the Japanese had established in the archipelago. The people were compelled to listen to these broadcasts. Not unnaturally, Sukarno had to preach nationalist propaganda of a type which pleased the Japanese. Palmier comments: 'The Japanese of course established the *Putera* to further their own war aims. They were undoubtedly successful in this, though the price paid was the encouragement of Indonesian nationalism. In addition, however, the various youth organizations succeeded in instilling authoritarianism and a liking for violence' (p. 42). In addition the Japanese established and trained an Indonesian 'home-guard' which was to form the back-bone of the Indonesian army which expelled the Dutch.

After the defeat and capitulation of Japan, the allies were in control of areas in the Far East which Japan had temporarily occupied. Holland herself had only just been liberated from German occupation, and her strategic power was negligible. There was no possibility of the Netherlands exerting any authority in Indonesia in 1945. The Indonesians declared their independence in August 1945, with Sukarno as President. The Indonesians were well-equipped with Japanese arms.[9]

The period between 1945 and 1949 was one of bitter negotiations, and bitter fighting. The Dutch had to defer to the wishes of the Mountbatten administration in 1945, and could do little about his *de facto* recognition of the republic. Counter proposals by the Dutch allowed the Indonesians full access to the Civil Service, a major cause of dissidence in pre-war days. But the

[9] Between September and October large numbers of Indonesians and Eurasians who sympathized with the Dutch were slaughtered, including women and children (Van der Veur, 1960). Kraak et al. (1957) cites, as an example of the legacy of this incident, a Eurasian immigrant to the Netherlands: 'Between us and the Indonesians lie thousands of murdered and maltreated family member's (p. 92). See too Wehl's detailed account (1948, Ch. 5) of torture and murder of Europeans and Eurasians in 1945.

republic would not be recognized and the Indonesians therefore rejected these proposals out of hand. By 1946 the Dutch had been able to establish an army in the Indonesian theatre, and took control of East Indonesia, West Borneo, and West Java, while the Dutch navy blockaded the republican ports.

However, by June 1947, Britain, the United States, Australia, China, India, Egypt, Syria, and Iran had all given *de facto* recognition to the republic. The situation became such that the Dutch had nothing to gain from negotiation. Unsupported by any world power of standing, they invaded the republican territory in July 1947. In the U.N. Security Council the Netherlands was opposed by both Russia and America, and a ceasefire was arranged in August 1947. Dutch military action in the archipelago was thus contrary to the wishes of both the republic and the U.N. Pressure was strong in the Dutch parliament for an unyielding line in the East Indies, and after further military pressure the Dutch launched their second 'police action', in December 1948. In the United States an increasingly strong body of opinion advocated the application of economic sanctions to the Netherlands if it did not carry out the Security Council resolutions.

Under such pressure, the Netherlands Government negotiated the withdrawal of Dutch troops in the shortest possible time after the transfer of sovereignty to an all-Indonesian federal government. But Dutch economic rights and privileges in Indonesia were reaffirmed. The Netherlands insisted on the retention of western New Guinea, the implications of which I shall discuss in detail. One clause in the agreement was a tactical blunder on the part of the Dutch. They forced the Indonesians to accept a debt of 4,300 million guilders[10] in payment for the police actions! This was, in effect, a strong inducement to the Indonesians to reject the whole settlement as soon as they were in a position to do so. The republican Government of Indonesia was neither democratic nor stable and in the face of Dutch military action, it was impossible for any kind of relaxed social organization to develop. The continued existence of Indonesia meant the maintenance of a spirit of extreme nationalism and intolerance of dissenters. The situation was made more difficult by the ethnic heterogeneity of Indonesia. Non-Javanese, especially in the Moluccas, wished to be self-governing, and this movement was put down as harshly as the Dutch had put down Javanese nationalism.

[10] At this time, 10 guilders were approximately equivalent to £1.

In 1953 witchhunts began against Dutch nationals in Indonesia, and a number were arrested and held without trial. One individual, Captain Jungschlager, was brought to trial. But this trial and that of others, had all the features of a political, show trial, in which the guilt of the accused is taken for granted in the absence of reliable evidence, and where finding of not guilty is unacceptable to popular opinion. For example, in the trial of Jungschlager, the defence counsel was arrested and intimidated, and eventually fled the country. Further counsel were not allowed to enter the country. Palmier reports that, "The proceedings in the court-room were relayed to the crowd outside; but the loudspeakers were switched on only when the Prosecutor-General or one of his witnesses was speaking. The Communist-led Trade Union Federation (S.O.B.S.I.) sent messages to both the Judge and prosecuting counsel "supporting the demand for the death penalty" on behalf of the 2,600,000 members of the organization' (p. 88).

The final breaks between the Netherlands and Indonesia centred around the control of West New Guinea (West Irian). The Dutch steadfastly refused to relinquish their presence in the country. In April 1957, a new government took office, and set up a Western New Guinea Liberation Committee. This committee organized a boycott of Dutch enterprises in October that year, and more drastic action was threatened. This took the form of the physical take-over of Dutch firms. In addition, shopkeepers, hotel employees, and taxi drivers declined to perform services for Dutch nationals (including Eurasians). Dutch families were refused food as part of the 'economic blockade'. On 5 December 1957 the Indonesian Minister of Justice ordered the expulsion of 50,000 Dutch nationals. As Palmier points out, 30,000 of these were Eurasians who knew no home but Indonesia.

The Dutch, aghast at the situation, sought help from their NATO allies. None was forthcoming. The only support for the Netherlands came from Australia, who warned Indonesia, 'that her actions against the Dutch minority in reprisal for a United Nations decision [refusal to condemn Dutch presence in west New Guinea] struck at the very foundations of international order' (Palmier, p. 105). One result of the Indonesian action was the cessation of Dutch-run shipping between the various islands, which meant that by 18 December famine conditions existed in thirty areas of Java. Diplomatic negotiations were severed with the Netherlands in August 1958 because of the 'persistent refusal' of the Dutch to transfer West New Guinea to Indonesian sovereignty. In 1959 and 1960 the 'nationalization' of Dutch property was formally enacted, since the 1957 take-overs had been illegal under the existing constitution.

## THE CHINESE IN INDONESIA

The Chinese in the East Indies are a manifestation of that phenomenon described by Fallers and his associates (1957)—the movement of ethnic groups into other cultures where they establish themselves as trading groups. Like the Jews in many parts of the world, like the Chinese in Malaysia, like the Lebanese in West Africa and like the Ibos in Calabar they have fulfilled the role of the 'stranger' carrying on commercial liaison with unknown areas of the world.[11] In times of difficulty the 'stranger' is cited as a cause of society's ills, and provides a convenient scapegoat for vicarious attack.

The Chinese in Indonesia were subject to such occasional pogroms, and in Batavia in 1740 some 10,000 Chinese were massacred. It was Indonesian custom to confine the Chinese to ghettoes, which they could only leave with special passes issued by the local administration. Such a system was tolerated by the Dutch under their system of 'culture tolerance', but in 1900, with the advent of the ethical policy the treatment of the Chinese was radically altered. Their functions, as suppliers of credit and opium to the native Indonesians were abolished, such functions being taken over by the Dutch administration. In consequence the Chinese entered other fields, as merchants in sugar and timber. As such they were in direct competition with the Dutch. Relations with the Dutch were however, amicable, and in many places schools were established giving education to Dutch and Chinese children together. By 1930 the Chinese population of the Indies was about one and a quarter million and by 1960 had grown to 2·45 million (Skinner, 1963). The system of close confinement in ghettoes had broken down, and the Chinese were now established as a wealthy, middle-class group, loyal to the Dutch and lacking sympathy for Moslem nationalist organizations.

Palmier cites the treatment of the Chinese by the Indonesians in the period after World War II as of special interest, since it

[11] See Mol (1963) for a development of this notion in terms of 'the function of marginality'.

illustrates the treatment the Dutch might have received if they had been pliable and co-operative to Indonesian political demands. He comments: 'By no means all Chinese are well provided for, but enough are in circumstances to excite envy. Many Indonesians believe that if it were not for Chinese competition they would be able to make a better living in retail trade. In this they are probably right: if, for example, the Javanese had to compete only against other Javanese, they could no doubt all make more money for less work' (p. 171).

It was agreed, after talks in The Hague in 1949, that the Chinese population of the East Indies (then about two million) should be given the option of acquiring Indonesian nationality, but half a million did not, retaining allegiance to mainland China. Now, one might have expected that the expression of loyalty to Indonesia, manifested in taking out Indonesian citizenship would have saved such Chinese from the vilification reserved for Dutch businessmen who retained their European links. This was not the case. A campaign was initiated against all Chinese, whether or not they held Indonesian nationality and the businesses of many Chinese were taken over despite the fact that these businessmen were Indonesian citizens. In 1959 300,000 Chinese traders in rural areas were forced to close their businesses, and the Chinese People's Republic, which was adopting an extremely conciliatory line to Indonesia made protests on behalf of Chinese with C.P.R. citizenship. Large numbers of rural Chinese who had refused to leave their homes were arrested and put in 'detention camps'. Chinese language schools were closed, and Chinese newspapers suppressed.

Despite this treatment of the Chinese, the Chinese People's Republic continued its conciliatory line and accepted the ban on traders in rural areas. Palmier concludes that the contrasts and similarities between the treatment meted out to the Dutch and that given to the Chinese, in particular those who were nationals of the Chinese People's Republic, speak for themselves. 'Not only had the Chinese People's Republic been accommodating where the Dutch had been obdurate, but President Sukarno had professed to admire Chinese Communist institutions far more than the Western variety, whilst he had no time for the Netherlands. All this helped the nationals of Communist China not at all' (pp. 177–178).

The implication of Palmier's analysis is that there is probably very little the Dutch could have done to defend their interests in

Indonesia, and establish amicable relationships with the Indonesians. If their policy of obduracy and military action had not been employed, but instead a policy of conciliation and concession, like the Chinese People's Republic, their fate would have been the same.[12] A recent report suggests that the Chinese are still an untolerated group in Indonesia, subject to various persecutions.[13] The process of forced absorption into Indonesian culture—involving the loss of language, traditional religious and family loyalties, and even the individual's name, seems to be following the official Indonesian policy towards the Chinese set forth by Muaja (1958). One is struck by the similarity of this policy with the treatment of Jews in communist countries. Skinner (1963) in fact draws specific parallels between anti-semitism and anti-sinicism:

> It is significant, however, that the Indonesian view is based on the conviction, so often symptomatic of a prejudiced mind, that the minority in question is somehow immune to change: 'Once a Jew (read Chinese), always a Jew.' The form which this thinking takes is that Chinese of whatever stripe, being clannish and perduringly faithful to their native land, have remained unaffected by however many years or generations they have spent in Indonesia, and that they play every situation for what it is worth without regard to ultimate loyalties. In the view of many Indonesians, the WNI Chinese differs from the foreign Chinese essentially only in that he found his self-interest best served by the opportunistic assumption of Indonesian citizenship. Indonesian business groups, in fierce competition with WNI Chinese as well as with aliens, are eager to perpetuate the view that all Chinese are the same and, in congruence with their typically Islamic orientation, to define that sameness in religious and moral terms.

## THE DUTCH AND WEST NEW GUINEA

Dutch attitudes to West New Guinea (West Irian) are of great interest for they illustrate both Dutch attitudes to Eurasians, and important features of Dutch society itself. My account relies quite heavily on Lijphart's important study, *The Trauma of Decolonization* (1966).

In signing a treaty with the Indonesians in 1949, the Dutch

[12] One must bear in mind, of course, that this speculation about historical events is incapable of being proved, like 'final cause' explanations in anthropology.

[13] *Race Today* (December 1969), 241–2. See too the London *Observer* (18 February 1968), 'New Pogrom looming in Indonesia', which gives an account of a pogrom in West Borneo in which at least a hundred Chinese were executed, and many thousands made homeless.

insisted on retaining sovereignty over West New Guinea, power they held until 1962 when the country passed to Indonesian control, after a brief administration by the U.N., as West Irian. Lijphart examines the Marxist argument that the force underlying colonialism is the desire for economic gain. He argues that this proposition does not hold in the Dutch case, suggesting that 'emotional attachment can be exclusively responsible for colonialism'. The Dutch insistence on retaining control of West New Guinea was a major factor in the Indonesian vilification of the Dutch, leading to the expulsion of Dutch nationals in 1959.

When, in 1946, the Dutch future in Indonesia became uncertain West New Guinea was proposed as a new home for 'brown Dutchmen'—the Eurasians and Christian Indonesians. At that time it was never considered that Eurasians might migrate to the Netherlands. The Dutch argument was that New Guinea was not an integral part of Indonesia. Its people—the Papuans—are ethnically distinct from Indonesians. From Merauke, the most southerly port in West New Guinea (W.N.G.) the distance to Australia (Somerset, N. Australia) is 220 miles. The distance from Sorong, the most westerly port in W.N.G., to Banjuwangi, the most eastern port in Java is no less than 1,250 miles. Not only are the Papuans geographically distinct from the rest of Indonesia, but they are also linguistically and culturally distinct. Eastern New Guinea is in fact under the control of Australia. Lijphart suggests, 'On balance, the dispassionate observer can only conclude that West New Guinea is more Australian than Indonesian or Asian in character' (p. 27).

After 1949, anxious to maintain their world image as just colonialists, the Dutch established an impressive programme for the social and economic development of the area, particularly in the fields of education and health. At the same time the Papuans were rapidly prepared for self-government, which was partially introduced in 1960. The administration of the Dutch compared favourably with that of the Indonesians in underdeveloped parts of the archipelago. In traditional fashion the Dutch were fostering considerable loyalty on the part of the Papuans. But in 1962 the Indonesians invaded Papua, and the Dutch found themselves in a militarily weak position. Under pressure from world opinion which was now concerned in both East and West with a renunciation of the old colonial ideals, the Dutch withdrew from West

New Guinea after agreement from the United Nations to administer the territory for a period of ten months before handing over to Indonesia.

The Russians, among others, had accused the Dutch of carrying out their New Guinea policy for hope of material gain. Lijphart produces evidence which effectively disproves this claim. West New Guinea had a continuing budget deficit, which by 1961 stood at Fl. 91·5 millions. The economy was maintained by large subsidies from the Netherlands. It provided no outlet for Dutch exports. The principal export of New Guinea between 1945 and 1961 was scrap, salvaged from World War II wreckage! Crude oil had been discovered, but the yield was too low for commercial exploitation. Oil production in the Netherlands itself was in fact ten times higher than in West New Guinea. The soil of the country is poor and plantations are not feasible. Nor does New Guinea have very much strategic value for the Dutch (though it may have such value for Australia). The case with which the Indonesians overran the country in 1962 illustrates this point. Holding West New Guinea also cost the Dutch many millions of florins worth of investment and trade in Indonesia itself. Lijphart concludes that 'There is no alternative to the conclusion that objective economic, strategic, and political factors were completely absent in the motivation behind Dutch colonialism in Western New Guinea. Dutch behaviour can only be validly explained in terms of subjective and psychological factors' (p. 66).

The New Guinea problem had its origins, Lijphart suggests, in the inter-war period. At its root was the Eurasian desire to establish a fatherland in New Guinea. With the rise of nationalism and of native education they were faced with increasing job competition in the commercial and lower professional spheres. Forbidden land ownership as a result of the ethical policy, Eurasians began to look elsewhere for a permanent home, and in 1919 the Indo-Europeesch Verbond (I.E.V.) was formed, with the aim of maintaining some of the privilege and autonomy of the Eurasians. I.E.V. supported the idea of New Guinea as a national home for Eurasians, and in 1923 a specific organization (Vereniging Kolonisatie Nieuw Guinea—V.K.N.G.) with this aim was set up. The V.K.N.G. proposals were for communes, Kibbutz-like, which would be ethical and self-supporting, and would not exploit native labour. A number of pioneer groups did settle in New Guinea, consisting mostly of Eurasians, but with some Europeans and Asians.

New Guinea was to be a second Holland, as Australia was a second England. Increasingly strong Eurasian pressure on the Netherlands led to the setting up of a Colonization Council in 1937, which gave information and advice on settlement, and subsidies which in 1937 amounted to Fl. 300,000. Nevertheless, by 1938 the number of permanent settlers in West New Guinea was only 600. These 600 were either killed by the Japanese on invasion, or perished later in concentration camps.

There was a curious involvement in the thirties of the Dutch Nazi Party with the New Guinea scheme. This involvement was quite separate from the V.K.N.G. involvement. Settlement in New Guinea was seen as a solution to the chronic Dutch problem of overpopulation. The leader of the Dutch Nazi New Guinea movement said he naturally included Eurasians in the settlement plan because they were Dutch and declared, 'In this case "white" means not so much the colour of the skin, as a settlement within Dutch culture.' This attitude of the extreme right in the Netherlands is of great importance in our consideration of Dutch race relations since it illustrates the very great emphasis, even at this extremist level, not on colour or ethnic characteristics but on the maintenance of particular cultural standards. Even for the Dutch Nazi it mattered more that a man was Dutch in spirit and outlook than that his skin was dark brown. The involvement of the Nazis in the New Guinea settlement movement was embarrassing for the Dutch Government, and in 1938 official subsidies to all schemes, including that of V.K.N.G., were withdrawn.

The Indonesian declaration of independence in 1945 confronted the Eurasians with a problem of previously unknown magnitude. Their middle-class status depended on the continued Dutch presence. But Eurasians had been born in Indonesia. 'Leaving the Indies for Holland', says Lijphart, 'was not an attractive solution, and emigration to many other white countries was precluded because of the colour bar. It is not very surprising, therefore, that they looked for a place within the Dutch East Indies where they might be able to retain their Dutch identity and escape domination by the Indonesians' (p. 90). The obvious solution to this problem for the Eurasians was the adoption of New Guinea as a national home. The V.K.N.G. was re-established after the war, and set about applying vigorous pressure on the Dutch. The demand of the V.K.N.G. was for: 'A fatherland, where our group will be able to maintain itself, where we will be able to stay Dutch, where

3*

we will be able to keep thinking, speaking and feeling Dutch, and where the Dutch rhythm of life will govern our manifestations.'

Pressure group activities extended to the Netherlands, where various organizations advocating settlement in New Guinea for the Eurasians had thousands of members. A frequent point made by these groups was the extreme population pressure in the Netherlands, and the necessity of finding a new home for Eurasians. Implicit in this propaganda was the notion that the Netherlands itself was too crowded to accommodate Eurasians. The strongest support for the New Guinea settlement came from Dutch conservatives and nationalists. The Eurasian pressure groups were, Lijphart says, able to command the attention of individuals close to the centre of government in The Hague, and had members in key positions in the East Indies Government, and successfully harnessed the nationalist movement in the Netherlands.

The Dutch policy-makers themselves saw New Guinea as a means of maintaining a stronghold in the East Indies, to which so many Dutchmen were strongly wedded. There were powerful psychological motivations making the Dutch want to cling to New Guinea. The loss of the Indies was a great blow to Dutch pride, a kind of political castration, a bereavement. By contrast, the Dutch West Indian possessions were small, and their existence was only briefly considered in Dutch geography books. The East Indies were *the* colonial possession. The feeling of shock at the loss of the East Indies was coupled with the belief that the Dutch were one of the most enlightened and progressive colonizing states of the world. Indeed, the praise which foreign observers had given the Dutch administration in the inter-war years justified the pride. But the Dutch, occupied by the Germans at home and interned by the Japanese in the Indies, had failed to make a realistic adjustment to the changed political circumstances in the Far East. They had failed to realize the changed attitude to colonialism in many quarters of the world. They were now no longer praised as good colonialists, but merely condemned as colonialists. The Dutch were hurt and outraged.

Lijphart's comparison of English and Dutch attitudes to India and the Indies is similar to other authors we have cited.

Dutch withdrawal from the Indies was especially painful because their attachment to both the country and the people was deep and personal. In this respect, the Dutch were strikingly different from the English who did not very often develop a sentimental attachment to India. . . .

The idea that Holland was engaged in a mission of service to the native population was sincere and was more than merely a shallow rationalization. The Dutch felt duty bound not to interrupt their mission. Again, when this appeared to become unavoidable after all, New Guinea offered the opportunity to continue the mission in at least one part of the Indies (p. 89).

To the Dutch, they seemed alone in the world in their stand. The Indonesians had co-operated with the Japanese, and in the imprisonment and suffering of the Dutch in concentration camps. Britain's Far Eastern army denied help to the Dutch in 1945, and the U.N. showed a considerable lack of sympathy for the Dutch position. Yet the Dutch regarded their cause as a right one, and morally justifiable. Nay, more: it was seen as a crusade, an enterprise of moral duty which they could not shirk. The Indonesian republic was seen as a brittle Japanese creation which had to be put down. True, the Indonesian state rose on Japanese suppression of the Dutch, but it proved not to be a paper structure. A betrayal of the Eurasians would have seemed to the Dutch centre and right to be indication of the Netherlands' moral bankruptcy. The Netherlands was not morally bankrupt. She was, and is, a nation dominated by moral notions which are derived from the ideologies of the religious groups which dominate the Netherlands. Lijphart stressed this point which is similar to one made by Fischer:

The tendency to view the Republic as an evil force was strengthened by a trait in the Dutch national character. The Dutch think of themselves as a sober and hard-headed people, but this national self-image is far from accurate. The Dutch are strongly imbued with principles rather than pragmatism. Their hardheadedness consists of sticking to a line of conduct based on deduction from principles rather than induction from experience. Unyielding adherence to conviction rather than compromise is highly valued. This attitude easily results in an interpretation of events in terms of a moral dichotomy (p. 109).

The Dutch stand was aided by their intensely legalistic outlook on life. The rule of law has been stabilizing influence in Dutch domestic politics, since as shown in Chapter 1, the seeds of potential conflict are inherent in Dutch social organization. The rules of accommodation include a legalistic interpretation of political process, and a rejection of unconstitutional means by all the blocs of Dutch society. The relative claims of Indonesia and the Netherlands to West New Guinea were examined by the U.N. in 1954, and in the face of considerable world pressure the Dutch evolved the idea of self-determination for the Papuans. This notion itself 'was elevated to an absolute moral principle which the Netherlands was bound to carry out'. The Dutch stand on New Guinea was, at all stages, an intensely moralistic one. In this light one can understand the subsequent response to the forced Eurasian emigration to the Netherlands. The Dutch treated this 'invasion' in a typically moral fashion, as a call upon the moral principles they had evolved of just reward for loyalty.

In 1956 Lijphart suggests that there was a well-nigh perfect unanimity in all sections of the Netherlands' population on the New Guinea issue: Dutch policy was regarded as a lofty moral principle, while the Indonesians were seen as deceitful and Machiavellian. At this time New Guinea as a home for Eurasians was still a very real option in Dutch eyes, and in debates about the fate of Eurasians it was hardly ever mentioned that they would make the Netherlands their home. At the same time the Netherlands' population problem was continually stressed, and West New Guinea as a settlement area was seen as the only solution to the Eurasians' problem.

There were a few dissident voices. Van der Kroef (1954) writing in a book published in Bandung, took a line which was sympathetic to Indonesian nationalism, and was scornful about both the possibility of the emigration of Eurasians to the Netherlands and of settlement in West Irian:

> . . . even without the Indonesian minority Holland is a severely over-populated country, where hundreds of native born seek emigration visas annually. The poverty stricken Indonesian immigrant merely swells the labour movement, and since his training has in the majority of cases not been on a par with that of the average Hollander, he is inevitably becoming a public burden, a hindrance to the post-war reconstruction of the country. . . . Some will succeed in leaving the country, thanks to the pressure exerted by their class-conscious fellows in the Netherlands, but for the most there will, through various circumstances, be no such opportunity. Their only hope will lie in a psychological adjustment, an assimilation of mind and culture, as well as an eventual racial amalgamation (pp. 289 and 296).

Van der Kroef's view accorded with the ideology of Indonesian socialism of that period, and is an interesting example of the views of the small, radical minority of Dutchmen who were opposed to any Dutch action on behalf of Eurasians.

After 1956 the Netherlands' policy over Indonesia was increasingly frustrated. Recognizing the power struggles going on in Indonesia between left and right, the major world powers were anxious to win support for their particular ideologies, and Indonesia was supplied with armaments by the United States, Russia, and Britain. By 1962 Indonesia had enough military and diplomatic power over West New Guinea to force the Dutch to compromise. The increasing strain on relations between the Netherlands and Indonesia over New Guinea led, as we have seen, to the persecution of many Dutch citizens (including Eurasians) and in 1959 to their expulsion. In these conditions the movement of this population to New Guinea was impossible: the difficult work of pioneering settlements could not be carried on under conditions of military threat, and so the large population of 'brown Dutchmen' had to leave for the Netherlands. How they fared there we shall see in the next chapter.

Despite its military defeat in 1962 the Netherlands still tried desperately to influence world opinion over New Guinea, and was successful in obtaining United Nations agreement on a period of interim administration by the U.N., and the promise of a plebiscite on the part of the Papuans on whether to be self-determining or remain under Indonesian rule, before the end of 1969. Lijphart commented that, 'The plebiscite is to be held after many years of Indonesian administration. In the light of Indonesia's consistent and firm opposition to self-determination, it is highly doubtful that the Papuans will actually get a completely free choice' (p. 21).

Lijphart's prediction, it turns out, was somewhat optimistic. Far from curtailment of 'a completely free choice' it does not appear that the Papuans have had any choice at all. It is now clear that no form of political organization which favoured independence was allowed at all when the Indonesians took over. There was wide-scale arrest and transportation to Java, 2,000 miles away, of the advocates of independence. Those who resisted were hunted down, slaughtered.[14] Many Papuans have fled to Australian New Guinea. By 1969 far from a free plebiscite being possible, anyone who wished to vote for independence was either in a concentration camp, or had been murdered, or had fled the country. There has been remarkably little condemnation of this

[14] See 'Tribes wiped out in secret war' and 'West Irian: thousands of tribesmen killed', London *Observer* (1 June 1969).

policy by any world power, or by the U.N. The reason, as the London *Observer* pointed out, is probably that Indonesia is a prize jewel in the battle of ideologies between East and West. At one time the prize of communism, Indonesia is now adopting a somewhat pro-Western position having put anyone with any communist connections into prison or to the sword. The world powers are anxious not to offend Indonesia by protests about her West Iranian policy. The minds of a hundred million people, and £200 millions worth of investment are at stake. These are not worth risking as the *Observer* put it, 'for the sake of a few million blacks'.

The Dutch have been defeated in West Irian. They have been defeated by Indonesia, the United Nations,[15] and the combined efforts of the world powers. The ethical policy has been defeated. Since 1940 Dutchmen and Dutch aspirations in Indonesia have suffered scorn, vilification, and persecution.[16] They have striven in vain to bring self-government to West Irian. It is a manner of some irony that the Indonesians, such keen advocates of their own self-determination, should have denied it so vigorously to others. The Dutch, since 1962, have remained silent on West Irian. It is, says Lijphart, not the silence of indifference, but the silence of shame, a shame that their moral purpose for West Irian has not been fulfilled.

## INDONESIA TODAY

On 30 September 1965 a communist coup was attempted in Indonesia. The coup was unsuccessful, but during its course six generals were murdered in Jakarta. As a result, communists and alleged communists were sought out in all corners of the archipelago and were murdered with knives, bullets, scythes, and home-made guillotines. By the end of 1965 something like half a million Indonesians had been slaughtered (Hughes, 1968). Following this event Indonesia showed a less partisan attitude towards communist

[15] See Taylor (1960) for an account of attitudes to Dutch policy in the United Nations.

[16] There is evidence that some elements of the Dutch army over-reacted in an extreme manner in the defence of the South Celebes. A report was delivered to the Second Chamber in The Hague in June 1969, alleging atrocities by 150 soldiers. See 'Dutch atrocities in Indonesia in 1947 bared by The Hague', *International Herald Tribune* (4 June 1969). See too Van der Veur's account (1960) of Westerling's private military action in the Celebes in 1946–7.

countries. Indeed, in President Nixon's Far Eastern tour of 1969, Indonesia was cited as a successful case of a country finding its own path to righteousness, unaided by American troops as in Vietnam.

Those fortunate enough to survive the massacre of 1965 were interned in camps. By 1968 there were about 110,000 prisoners of all kinds in internment camps.[17] These included Papuan nationalists as well as suspected communists. An official publication of the Indonesian Government[18] was at pains to discount any analogy between these camps and the Nazi and Japanese concentration camps.

It does not appear that the Dutch banishment from the Indies, brought about by all sectors of world opinion, has been followed by stability or enlightenment. It is difficult to lay the blame for present events on Dutch colonial policy in the pre-war years, or on her ineffectual attempts to retain territorial interest there after 1945.

Indonesia at the present time appears to be an unstable country. In part this is due to the pluralistic nature of Indonesian society, which is stratified not only by rival political and national factions, but also horizontally by *alirans* or 'streams'. There are also vertical divisions in Muslim society between those termed *santris*, the devout and dedicated, and the non-*santris*. There are important regional differences. West Sumatra is fiercely Islamic in a puritanical way, which is entirely different from the synthetic Hinduized Islam of Java. Many of the inhabitants of Ambona are still Christian. The task of welding together this geographically huge, highly-populated, and socially diverse archipelago is very great,[19] and one cannot be confident about the efforts of the present regime in Indonesia. The Dutch lessons of accommodation in a plural society were insufficiently demonstrated in Indonesia for them to be emulated by any Indonesian administration.

The events of 1965—the slaughter of the communists, and the subsequent decline in power of Sukarno—have been followed by increasing repression. Dahm's verdict (1971) is that,

[17] See the annual report of *Amnesty International* (London), for 1969; and the report by Peter Schumacher in *The Guardian* (5 January 1972).

[18] 'Indonesia's Political Prisoners', *Indonesia* (January–February 1969), pp. 6–7.

[19] Cf. Liddle's account (1970) of ethnicity, party, and national integration in Indonesia.

Whatever may be said against Sukarno's use of political power—and certainly there was much to criticize, especially his neglect of economic problems for the sake of an increasingly fantastic ideology—it must be admitted that in his time . . . there was no serious internal security problem and the only political enemies were a few irreconcilable enemies who spurned his attempts at compromise. Whatever may be said in favour of Sukarno's use of power—and there is much in it to praise, such as his efforts to stabilize the economy and his sense of political reality—it remains true that the new order has a grave security problem on its hands and the country's prisons are full to bursting.

In our opinion Dahm underestimates the political repression during Sukarno's regime of the Ambonese and Papuan nationalists, and the Chinese. But we must accept his interpretation that political repression in Indonesia has increased.

## CONCLUSIONS

My conclusions are as follows: A pervasive trait underlying Dutch social and political activity is an ideological basis for action which is derived from religion. It is this ideology, rather than pragmatic experience, which guides Dutch activity. Issues tend to be seen in the light of this moral ideology, and action is based on loyalty to a tenaciously held moral ideal. These ideals tend to be uninfluenced by the criticism of others, or by adversity in economic fortune which may result from such action.

The *verzuiling* system of a society divided into blocs or pillars which are separate from each other, but nevertheless support the society as a whole, existed in Indonesia as well as in the Netherlands. In line with this policy the cultural autonomy of Moslem and of traditional society was maintained. Nevertheless, Indonesians were not allowed to occupy elite positions, and this was a major source of strain.

The manifest Dutch tolerance of colour has deep historical roots. For many years the Dutch have intermarried with the Indonesian population, and have accorded European status to 'Eurasians'. The opposite applies to the British. The history of their rule in India suggests that they have been intolerant of 'Eurasians', and that this intolerance is based not on cultural differences, but on skin colour. In addition, the British in India have been intolerant of native culture, in contrast to the Dutch in Indonesia.

The Dutch system of 'cultural tolerance' allowed the growth of sophisticated nationalist organizations in Indonesia with strong linguistic, religious, and cultural autonomy. One of the reasons for the strong rejection of European culture when the Indonesians were in a position to do so was the fact that they possessed a coherent social organization on which the nationalist movement was based.[20] A major factor in the downfall of the Dutch colonial system was the fact that it had been *too* tolerant of the existing culture of Indonesia. Nevertheless, despite their tolerance on grounds of colour, and tolerance of native culture, the Dutch did hold up the European model as a superior one; while the native culture was tolerated, there was no secret that Dutch culture was regarded as very much preferable. This was reflected by the one important detail in which the Indonesian *verzuiling* system differed from the Dutch system: although Moslem culture was tolerated, its leaders were not admitted to the ruling elite. The *verzuiling* system in the Netherlands works because all of the pillars have access to the elite group of leaders. The Indonesians had no such access, and this was a fatal error on the part of the Dutch. Moslem autonomy in the sphere of education meant that a sophisticated and educated elite emerged. It was inevitable that such an elite, in a situation of 'status dis-equilibrium' would take vigorous activity to change the existing system.[21]

The issue of Indonesia and of West New Guinea had absorbed Dutch energies and emotions since 1945. The issue had been seen in moral terms, and there was a considerable consensus about the legitimacy of Dutch activity in West New Guinea. The most powerful, conservative elements of society were strongly sympathetic to the plight and aspirations of Eurasians. The specific idea of *colour* had in fact failed to pervade even the most right-wing ideologies. Dutch chauvinism has treated colour as irrelevant, and cultural loyalty as all important.

[20] Cf. Van der Veur's account (1969) of education and social change in Indonesia, which concludes: 'Dutch education had strongest appeal among the lower strata of Indonesian society, and not among the traditional elite, as intended, a fact that was to have significant implications for the subsequent character of Indonesia's nationalist movement.'

[21] Cf. Geschwender's description (1968) of situations of status dis-equilibrium, e.g. an inbalance between an individual's rank on one status, such as education (high) and occupation (low), as a precursor of radical or revolutionary activity.

CHAPTER 3

# THE IMMIGRANTS FROM INDONESIA

Human migration can take several distinct forms, ranging from the most passive or involuntary movement of people (as slaves or convicts) to the most aggressive (as military conquerors). In between are varying categories of voluntary migration, ranging from indentured labour to the most voluntaristic category of economic migrant, i.e. the modern migrant worker. Another distinct and less voluntary movement is that of political refugees. Some of these types of migration can fall into two sub-types. The migration can be of individuals or of groups. And migration can be pioneering in the sense that migrants to the old colonial territories were pioneers; and it can be conservative in the sense that the migrants wish to preserve their traditional culture in a new land. An example of this is the post-war migration of Dutch Calvinists to Canada and Australia (Hofstede, 1964).

The relationship between immigrants and the native population has been variously categorized by social scientists: acculturation, accommodation, adaptation, adjustment, assimilation, absorption, amalgamation, fusion, and integration are some of the terms used (Heeren, 1967).

These concepts imply various kinds of behaviour on the part of the host and migrant cultures. Adaptation and adjustment have been used in a one-sided way, as indicating what behaviour is necessary from the migrant's point of view in order to become acceptable to the host's society. The term 'assimilation' is often used to describe the degree to which a migrant has become part of his new culture and has absorbed its norms and behaviour patterns as his own. This is not an easy process for the individual, and studies of people with a very strong orientation to the receiving culture, as in Israel (Eisenstadt, 1954) or in the case of British migrants to Australia (Richardson, 1961), have shown that the process of assimilation in such cases can take years rather than months. For the migrants, the process of divesting themselves of the trappings of their previous culture and becoming part of a new culture (as in the case of British migrants to Canada) can be one involving a period of acute insecurity (Richmond, 1967). The difficulties of adjustment in these cases are illustrated by the study which showed a higher rate of mental illness in English-speaking migrants to French-speaking Quebec than in those migrants to English-speaking Ontario (Malzberg, 1967).

I have cited these examples of the difficulties experienced by British migrants to Canada and Australia, and by Jewish migrants to Israel, to illustrate the following proposition: whatever the initial similarities in culture and ideology between immigrants and their hosts, the process of settling down in the new culture and establishing a satisfactory relationship (by extinction or accommodation) between one's traditional ways of thinking, feeling, and acting, and those customary in the host culture, is extremely difficult.

The study of migrant behaviour is very complex. Heeren has identified the following factors which can influence what he calls the 'fusion' process:

(a) the number and rate of entry of immigrants;
(b) the immigration system and type of immigrants;
(c) the composition of immigrants in terms of wealth, economic skills, and ethnic categories;
(d) the territorial distribution of the immigrants;
(e) the interaction of cultures of migrants and hosts.

We can apply this model to the relationship of Normans and Saxons, of slaves and colonizers in America, and to the more recent experience of Poles in post-war Britain and of West Indians in Britain. In every case the dimensions of these five aspects of migration are different. Often the differences are profound.

Heeren's own study of Javanese migrants to Lampong, for example, showed that the relationship between migrants and hosts was influenced by the following factors: (a) the migrants outnumbered hosts, but they lived in enclosed societies; (b) the migrants were poor and had little prospect of gaining sufficient wealth to become socially accepted, but had a marked status consciousness which was accentuated by their present situation.

One of the most interesting situations is that in which there is a dis-equilibrium between the outlook and behaviour of the host culture and the migrant individual or group. As Eisenstadt suggests, this can take several forms:

(a) The migrant culture is generally apathetic to the chief values and symbols of the new society and is not disposed to maintain any communication with the bearers and transmitters of those values, and there is a consequent 'enclosure' within the most private spheres of social life.
(b) The migrant culture adopts a rebellious attitude to the host society and does not accept the primary claims to loyalty. As a result, there is inter-group tension.
(c) The migrant culture has a 'verbal identification' with the new culture without acceptance of the institutional premises of such identification; the individual migrant indulges in a certain ritualistic over-emphasis on certain collective symbols and behaviour patterns.
(d) The migrant group accept the formal premises of the host culture and behave accordingly. But despite the formal emphasis on equality and universalism, various discriminatory practices are employed against the immigrants, which seem permanently to stand in the way of their realizing their aspirations. This is, as Eisenstadt says (p. 261), especially conducive to disorganization in the second and third generation of immigrants.

From the array of concepts available, those of integration and assimilation have been chosen; those represent two kinds of relationship between migrant and host cultures which are not alienating[1] for the individual. The two states represent opposite poles of a continuum. Assimilation takes place when the migrant is absorbed, more or less totally, in his new culture—for example, when the Jewish immigrant in Israel speaks Hebrew and is absorbed totally into the life of new culture, or when the British immigrant to Australia becomes totally Australian. Integration, on the other hand, takes place when the migrant group retains a considerable cultural identity in terms of norms and folkways which are different from those of the culture in which they find

[1] Alienation is defined as a condition in which a state of social structure interferes with, or prevents, an individual from attaining some fulfilment of his personality. See Bagley (1967) for a fuller discussion of this concept.

themselves. The group may also have a religion which is different from that of the host culture, and may also be largely endogamous, social and familial relationships being more or less exclusively generated within the migrant group rather than within the society as a whole. At the same time the migrant group's cultural identity is accepted by the host culture, since the migrants perform certain elementary civic functions in a satisfactory manner—they do not offend the norms—legal and informal—of the larger society, and they contribute economically, as workers and tax-payers, to the host society.

Integration has been defined prescriptively in the British context by Mr. Roy Jenkins, a former Home Secretary:

> I define integration therefore, not as a flattening process but as equal opportunity, accompanied by cultural diversity, in an atmosphere of mutual tolerance. This is the goal. We may fall a little short of its full attainment, as have other communities both in the past and in the present. But if we are to maintain any sort of world reputation for civilized living and social cohesion, we must get far nearer to its achievement than is the case today (Quoted in Patterson, 1969, p. 113).

The perspective of this chapter will be to examine how various immigrant groups from the Far East—Javanese, Eurasian, Ambonese, and Chinese—have fitted into Dutch society. In examining the behaviour of both hosts and immigrants we will use as a frame of reference the two 'ideal' concepts of integration and assimilation.[2] It is worth mentioning that Banton (1955) uses the terms 'accommodation' and 'adaptation' in a rather similar sense in a British study. Pakistanis are seen as non-assimilating, or accommodating, while West Indians are seen as adapting, for example by intermarriage.

## JAVANESE IMMIGRANTS IN THE HAGUE

The Javanese community in The Hague has been studied by an American anthropologist, Joan Schutzman Wilder (1967). Her fieldwork was carried out in 1965 and in 1966. Wilder, who spoke Javanese, set out to study not the recent Eurasian immigrants to the Netherlands, but the long-established Javanese community

[2] Both integration and assimilation can take place at different speeds in particular institutions of society. Assimilation may occur, for example, in the economic but not in the religious sphere.

who retained both Indonesian nationality and cultural identity. This study is valuable because it shows very clearly the difficulties of a group with its own cultural identity making an adjustment in a larger culture which they serve and depend upon for support, but with which they do not wish to be merged.

The Javanese community in the Netherlands grew as a result of the frequent sea journeys to and from the East Indies by the Dutch. Javanese seamen and male servants often spent considerable periods of time working in the Netherlands. Females were employed by Dutch families as cooks and nursemaids, and were called 'Ibu', a Javanese word meaning 'mother', and used towards any respectable older woman. The Javanese community is concentrated in The Hague, and it is here that Wilder's fieldwork was carried out. Because of the changed relationships between the Netherlands and Indonesia there are no more immigrants of this type. Of Wilder's sixty-one informants, 90 per cent had been in the Netherlands for periods ranging from 30 to 50 years.

The concentration of the Javanese in The Hague is the result of the activities of a Dutchman, Mr. Stuyvesant, a convert to Islam. This gentleman established the *Persingahan*, a large house where Javanese could stay for a little cost while they were looking for work. It also acted as an employment agency. The *Persingahan* closed in 1948 on Mr. Stuyvesant's death. The institution was receiving at this time a government subsidy of Fl. 75,000 per annum (about £7,500).[3]

Because of the liking of many Dutch families for Indonesian food, there was a considerable demand for resident Indonesian cooks. Jobs were fairly easy to come by; an Ibu who was tired of the Netherlands could easily obtain a passage back to the East Indies as a nanny to a returning Dutch family. When the money they had earned ran out, they would return to the Netherlands. One informant said of The Hague: 'We felt at home here—our own coterie, cultural and social clubs, the beautiful woods. The Hague is a little like Indonesia: the woods, greenness and parks, walks and the sea.' But there were also disillusionments. The Dutch colonists had built up a picture of the Netherlands as some kind of heaven, an ideal which did not match reality.

[3] This piece of Dutch social policy is rather typical: when a project has been established through voluntary effort, and is seen to be fulfilling a useful purpose, it receives government support. Further examples of this are the emigration and the community relations organizations. The financial support is given on an *ad hoc* basis, without the need for specific parliamentary enactment.

The social and cultural organization of the Indonesians in The Hague remained distinct from that of the Dutch. Geographical concentration in The Hague meant that some form of community and social and economic co-operation could be established. A co-operative effort was made to buy land for an Islamic cemetery, since the large majority of the Indonesians were Moslem. A crucial part of the community life is the meeting for *Slametan*, an Islamic ritual meal. This is celebrated at any important life event. A *Slametan* is held, for example, on the first, third, seventh, fortieth and hundredth day after a death, and also after one year, two years and 1,000 days. The form which Moslem ritual takes is very similar to that described by Malefijt (1963) in Surinam. Religion offers common societal values for the migrant community, and these help to maintain the culture as a whole.

Not only the ritual meal, but food itself, is a crucial factor in social solidarity in the Indonesian community. Among the Ibus, food is constantly being prepared, eaten, or talked about, and is constantly offered. Time is elastic, as in the East Indies; 'rubber time' means that for an appointment at 10 a.m., the visitor will arrive any time up to 3 p.m. The Ibus have taken over the Dutch custom of birthday parties, which is unknown in the East. It provides, Wilder says, another excuse for visiting, and the preparation and eating of food. The Indonesians began to own their own homes in the 1930s, as opposed to living with Dutch families as servants.

It was during this period that the convention of holding birthday parties began; they were marked by lengthy bouts of eating and card playing. The Ibus have developed an institution called *Por Satuan Wanita*, an intervisiting group which looks after the sick and elderly.

Feeding of children is informal and on demand, a pattern continued throughout life. Anyone who is hungry helps himself; there are no regular mealtimes, and food is always prepared in abundance. Children are generally indulged: 'When one asks an Ibu about traditional family life, she will discuss with pride how different the Dutch and Indonesian families are. The main divergence comes with regard to *harnat* (respect): "The Dutch children do not respect their parents. They speak back to their parents with a loud voice . . . ."' Indonesian children are loved, wanted, indulged, but at the same time they are trained to show great respect for their parents. The respect which Dutch children have for their elders is different, and is based on a different kind of warmth. The life of the Dutch child is closely regulated, but at the same time his behaviour outside the family is boisterous and often uninhibited.

The values with which Javanese children are imbued are co-operation, quiet behaviour, and above all avoidance of conflict—never losing one's temper; always listening to an elder; and never voicing a disagreement. But Javanese children in The Hague, educated in Dutch schools, inevitably acquire some of the jollity and 'Dutch humour' of Dutch children.[4]

Wilder observes of the Javanese family: 'Thus, there is no freedom for children. The compensation is increased love at home. This is not to say that there is a lack of love in Dutch homes, but the air is different—more sobriety, coldness, and less sentimentality. But according to Dutch norms these Indonesian children are spoiled because they get material things easily; almost everything they want is bought for them.'

There are points of strain in the contact of the Indonesians with the Dutch, but there are also valuable and rewarding contacts. The Dutch family which first brought the Ibu to the Netherlands may still pay annual visits for many years—sometimes for thirty years or more. But contact with Dutch neighbours is small. Mutual help in times of stress does occur, and this seems to be the product of proximity over a lengthy period—perhaps twenty years—rather than of any cultural similarities.

Few of the Indonesians in The Hague spoke Dutch with any proficiency, and there was in fact some pressure not to learn Dutch. The Dutch, Wilder reports (and confirms from her own experience) react with 'mockery, sarcasm and vexation' to mispronunciations and mishandling of the Dutch language.[5] An Indonesian woman in New York told Wilder, 'Americans may

[4] There is a special brand of Dutch folk humour which takes great delight in 'banana-skin' situations. It is a rough and rather boisterous kind of humour—for example, the tram driver may close the tram doors after a small child has boarded, leaving the child's mother on the pavement. This situation will be treated with great mirth by the passengers of the tram car. The child's confusion and bewilderment at apparently losing his mother will only add to the roars of laughter. Norman Wisdom films have a large following in the Netherlands, but have little following in other European countries. A visit to a Norman Wisdom film is the highlight of a Dutch Christmas!

[5] The writer, a rather indifferent speaker of Dutch, can also confirm this point from his own experience.

laugh with you at a mispronunciation but the Dutch laugh at you and not politely.'

The Indonesians found the smell of cabbage cooking in Dutch households particularly hard to bear. They could not understand, either, the Dutch reluctance to bathe themselves. In the tropics one bathes several times a day; in Holland this is translated to several times a week, especially in summer. Moreover, they could not hide their distaste at Dutch toilet habits; being Moslem, their toilet habits were of a much higher standard than those of the Dutch.[6]

The Indonesians, as we have seen, like to entertain often and generously, and without regard for strict keeping of appointments. Dutch habits are quite the opposite. They expect guests to arrive on time, and to depart after a decent interval. They serve tea or coffee with one cookie, after which the lid is put firmly back on the tin. The Dutch housewife has strict work schedules—washing on Monday and cleaning all day Friday. But the Indonesian housewife takes a day off or works when she feels like it, and is not endlessly scrubbing and polishing. The Indonesians claimed that the Dutch are dirty and smell, but at the same time are obsessed with household cleanliness. One informant summed up her feelings about the Dutch, 'The Dutch say our hospitality is a waste of time and money. They are a cold people, we are warm. . . . When I had company my landlady could not understand how I could invite friends on Friday. That was the day to clean the house. They schedule their days. I cannot live like that.'

Another informant, a student, told Wilder: 'I did want to interact with my neighbours but I can understand why the Ibus did not. During the first winter here, my child was playing outside with Dutch children. Dutch mothers leave milk and a sandwich on the doorstep for the children's lunch. It was freezing and I asked them all to come inside, to play in a warm room and have some warm food. The next day the Dutch mother called and was very angry. "I want my children to play outside." I never asked them in again.' Wilder comments,

[6] It is for this reason that in some English factories Pakistani workers have separate toilet facilities. The main toilet rules are (i) one's body shall not touch a toilet that has touched the body of another; (ii) after going to the toilet, one must wash oneself thoroughly—the use of toilet paper is definitely not enough; (iii) one may not wash oneself with the hand with which one eats food.

To the Ibus, food and hospitality are intertwined and indispensable. They discuss the strange Dutch customs, tea for tea, coffee for coffee; inform the host in advance or the door will remain shut; lack of personal cleanliness, while having a rigid housekeeping schedule. How can it be that a person will not answer a door? How can one not have time for another human being . . . ? How can one admire a people who close their doors against each other?

The counter stereotype of the Indonesians which the Dutch hold is that they are dirty because of the disorder in their homes, and the mess in their kitchens from continual preparation of food. The Indonesians, it is said, are lazy and do not take life seriously, and their children are always laughing.

The Indonesians in The Hague constantly talk about their home country, and always say they will go back; yet always, something prevents them, and the changed political circumstances in Indonesia make this increasingly unlikely. The economic position of the Indonesians in the Netherlands is very favourable compared with their earning power at home. The demand for Indonesian food has in fact risen with the influx of expatriates from Indonesia. In 1959 there were 204 Indonesian restaurants registered in the Netherlands; in 1965 there were 339, and in 1966 there were 358. As one informant told Wilder, 'Here I can work. I cook delicious Indonesian food, but in Indonesia everyone can cook. What would I do there?'

Wilder concludes that: 'The Ibus have achieved integration through accommodation, not assimilation. They have derived security and maintenance of their homeland's cultural values. This results in estrangement from the host culture.' But we must conclude, too, that over time there are pressures towards assimilation of the Indonesians, especially those born in the Netherlands. Inevitably these brown Dutch men and women will be absorbed more closely into Dutch society, and they may especially identify with the Moslem bloc of recent political refugees from Indonesia. The refugees, both Moslem and Christian, as we shall see, have some rather similar objections to the Dutch culture into which they have been more or less absorbed.

### POST-WAR IMMIGRATION FROM INDONESIA

After 1945 the immigrants from Indonesia came because of political changes in that country, unlike the pre-war Javanese immigrants who came for economic reasons. The immigrants came, not in a steady flow, but in several distinct 'waves', following events in the East Indies. On several occasions, therefore, several thousands of immigrants arrived in the Netherlands in the space of a few weeks or months, requiring immense organization, energy, and goodwill on the part of the Netherlands administration, and of the people as a whole.

The first wave of immigrants—45,000—left Indonesia after liberation from the Japanese. A further number, about 65,000, spent a period of temporary leave in the Netherlands before returning to the Indies. The majority of immigrants in this phase were 'totoks'—a group of wholly European ancestry. The second influx occurred in 1950–1, following the handing over of sovereignty to Indonesia. The Royal Netherlands East Indies Army was disbanded, and some thousands of ex-soldiers and their families departed *en masse* for the Netherlands. They were joined by others who had been in government service or private employment, and retired persons. The total number arriving in this period was 90,000. These were followed by a steady trickle between 1951 and 1957. It was the 50–1 influx which first taxed Dutch resources, ingenuity, and goodwill. The country was still struggling to recover from the effects of war, the devastation of many cities, and the disorganization of the economy.

The third phase began at the end of 1957 when the Indonesian Government proclaimed all Dutch nationals still in Indonesia to be 'undesirable aliens'. The entire Dutch population, including the sick and elderly, was forced to leave the country at very short notice. Four thousand people arrived in the Netherlands in December 1957, and more than 35,000 in the first half of 1958. A steady trickle followed, of people who had taken Indonesian nationality but who had found life in that country too difficult for anyone with connections with the Netherlands. The fourth phase began in July 1962, as a result of the decision to transfer sovereignty of West New Guinea to Indonesia. During the following three months, 15,000 people were evacuated to the Netherlands. The final phase of emigration was less dramatic. In order to round off the whole question of repatriation, the Government decided at the end of 1963 that (i) Dutch nationals still in Indonesia must arrive in the Netherlands no later than 31 March 1964, and that (ii) those who had opted for Indonesian nationality and those in receipt of benefits from the Dutch

Government must apply for permission to settle in the Netherlands before 1 April 1964. The numbers in the last category who eventually settled in the Netherlands was a little over 19,000.

## SOCIAL POLICY

How did the Dutch view these waves of coloured immigration? de Boer-Lasschuyt (1959) has described the Dutch perception in poetic terms. Dutch people saw:

> Melancholic brown big-eyed nowhere belongers, in cotton dresses, serpent green woollen gloves (too big for the small fingers) and little white socks on brown legs; with a basketful of kropok lombok and emping, which are protected as their most beloved possessions; small delicate dark children like pathetic little birds, all clothed alike in their dark blue or red 'training-pakjes', children so moving and beautiful that many Dutch school-children ask for having such a baby-child ('zo'n kindje') in their class.

Indonesia, as we have seen in the previous chapter, occupied a major place in Dutch public life during the post-war period, and at an official level and in many sectors of the Dutch as well, there was warm sympathy for the displaced residents of Indonesia accompanied by a firm resolution to help the immigrants.

Once it had been established that the Dutch would accommodate these coloured immigrants[7] the first urgent problem was one of transport, and ships and aeroplanes had to be commandeered and hired for this purpose. The cost of this was borne by the Dutch Government. The large majority of immigrants arrived by ship, and this presented problems of social organization; but the long sea passage also provided an excellent opportunity for the counselling and interviewing of the migrants. The social services for the care of migrants evolved in 1949; their emergence followed the whole-hearted decision of the Dutch Government, supported by all sections of intellectual and business opinion, to accept the migrants. Further, these social services were generously financed

[7] The decision to accept the Eurasians in 1949 was by no means a foregone conclusion. As we saw earlier, the notion that Eurasians would come to the Netherlands had hardly been considered before 1949, and West New Guinea was the official area of settlement for Eurasians. It would have been possible for the Dutch, as the British abandoned the Kenyan Asians in 1968, to have repudiated responsibility for the Eurasians. Holland's urgent population problems would certainly have given her some subjective justification for following this course.

and there was no shortage of full-time personnel. There appears to have been the minimum of muddle, and the maximum of speed in implementing decisions. Critics of the Government's policy based their objections on grounds of the over-rapid and perhaps forced assimilation of Indonesian migrants into Dutch life, and on the grounds of hyper-efficiency, rather than lack of it. The process was super-efficient, and the administration was superb.[8]

On the ship details were taken of skills, family size, religion, and special wishes about area of settlement and type of job. These details were then sent on ahead by air to The Hague, and the details co-ordinated with data on the availability of employment, accommodation, and schooling in particular areas of the country. On the boat journey the process of orientation and socialization began, a training in what to expect in Dutch society and what was the most appropriate behaviour in various situations. At the same time individual counselling was carried out in cases where it seemed likely that the individual would have difficulty adapting to Dutch life. Opportunity was taken on board ship too, to equip the migrants with warm clothing.

The next major requirement was housing the migrants once they arrived in the Netherlands. At a time of great housing shortage it was, in the majority of cases, impossible to accommodate the family in a house of their own. Therefore, a large number of 'contract boarding houses' were established, boarding houses and other buildings being taken over by the Government for the purpose of providing temporary accommodation. These boarding houses were in all parts of the country, and provided full board and lodging. In addition, some camps and army buildings were taken over during the 1950–1 phase of immigration. The largest number of individuals in all kinds of temporary accommodation at any one time was 30,000. The concentration of individuals in the boarding houses allowed the authorities, both governmental and religious, to carry out further socialization and social control of the immigrants. At the same time, clothing and financial assistance was provided for families where the wage-earner had not yet found work.

In 1950 there were 600 contract boarding houses containing some 4,000 families (17,500 persons); the numbers accommodated in these boarding houses during the 1958 period was, at its highest

[8] My information on Dutch social policy is drawn from: Ministry of Social Work (1965); de Boer Lasschuyt (1959); Kraak et al. (1957); and Ex (1966).

point, 3,900 families (16,250 persons). By the end of 1962 there were 1,900 families (6,500 individuals) in the boarding houses. Today all of the immigrants from Indonesia have their own accommodation, with the exception of certain special groups such as the infirm, elderly, and the Abonese whom we shall discuss in detail later on. The cost to individuals in the boarding houses was Fl. 3·50 (7s.) a day in 1952, and by 1965 this had risen to Fl. 4·90 (9s. 6d.). Where the immigrant did not have any income, or only a small income, such costs were waived.

Families moved out of the boarding houses when a house, and accompanying job, had been found for them in an appropriate area. This meant, for a Catholic family a Catholic area, for a Dutch Reformed a Dutch Reformed area, and so on. The large majority of the immigrants fitted into the Dutch *verzuiling* system, somewhat less than 5 per cent of immigrants belonging to religions other than Christianity or 'Humanism'; the majority of those belonging to other religions were Moslem.

In addition to homes coming on to the market in the ordinary way, a special allocation was made of 5 per cent of all new houses built and subsidized under the Housing Act.[9] This 5 per cent amounted to approximately 2,000 new houses a year. In addition, the Ministry of Housing made available an additional supply of new housing in times of urgent need. This was the case in 1954, 1955, and 1958. In all, 28,700 new dwellings were allocated to immigrant families between 1950 and 1964. Taking into account the comparative number of households in Britain and the Netherlands, and the comparative proportions of coloured immigrants in the two populations, this would amount to the allocation in Britain of 115,000 *new* houses to coloured immigrants over a 14-year period—enough new housing to accommodate over a third of Britain's coloured immigrants. The Dutch policy must also be read against the fact that housing need (measured by population pressure upon available housing supply) is much greater in the Netherlands than in Britain.[10]

The vast majority of immigrants lacked the means to furnish

[9] See Chapter 1 for a description of the system of housing allocation in the Netherlands.

[10] In a study of council housing in a London Borough (Bagley, 1970g) we found that 103 of 6,000 coloured families in the Borough had been allocated council housing—but much of this was pre-war housing of low quality. See Rex and Moore (1967), Burney (1968) and P.E.P. (1967) for discussions of British local government policy in allocating houses to coloured immigrants.

their new houses adequately. For this purpose, credit was granted to the family by the local authority who were in turn reimbursed by the Ministry of Social Work. The amounts lent (which were free of interest) ranged from the equivalent of £219 10s. for a family of two to £465 10s. for families with eight children, with an increase of £29 10s. for each additional person. Single persons were also given a furniture loan, of £53 10s. The loans had to be repaid over a period of years, but the debt was cancelled in the cases of families whose income was small. Credit for furniture during the period 1950–64 was given to 25,000 families, and amounted to the British equivalent of £6,500,000.[11] A further subsidy took the form of free transport from the contract boarding house to the immigrant's new home.

Old people are cared for in twenty-two homes, run by various voluntary organizations, containing some 1,500 inmates. In these homes considerable effort is made to recreate as far as possible Indonesian conditions, with the serving of Indonesian food, and the wearing of Indonesian dress, such as the sarong and kabaja.

In the earlier stages of migration from Indonesia many children were sent on ahead, and these were placed either in boarding schools or with Dutch foster families. Between 1950 and 1964, 1,275 such children were placed. It seems that there was no shortage of Dutch families wanting to foster coloured children.[12] There is an interesting parallel to this willingness of Dutch people to accept coloured children into their families in the case of the movement to adopt Korean children in the Netherlands described by de Hartog (1969).

A further group of immigrants was given special care—these were the mentally and physically handicapped. The mentally handicapped were housed in 'Waringen', in the north, and the physically handicapped in the 'Tamarinde' centre in the pine-wooded area in the centre of the country. These two centres are named after sacred trees of Indonesia. On arrival in the Netherlands all immigrants were given a special health check and free treatment was given where necessary, including treatment of people with T.B., asthma, and chronic bronchitis, which are liable to be

[11] Surie gives a figure of 26,000 furniture credits (value Fl. 55 million) in the period 1952–6.

[12] Again, it seems that the situation in Britain is unfavourable compared with that of the Dutch. See Raynor (1968) for an account of the number of coloured children whom children's authorities and societies are unable to place with foster or adoptive parents.

aggravated by the Dutch climate. A number of people with chronic chest disease are accommodated more or less permanently in the 'Tamarinde' centre. It is interesting that, in contrast to the vigorous efforts which were made to assimilate various individuals into society, groups such as the elderly and handicapped were housed in institutions in which a specifically Indonesian cultural atmosphere was maintained.

Once the immigrant had moved from the contract boarding house to his new home, a new stage of socialization began. Qualified social workers—Catholic, Protestant, or Humanist, according to the denomination of the family—were attached to each family, and gave assistance with various social problems and difficulties in relating to the community, difficulties at work, and so on. At the same time these social workers acted as agents of socialization (extending the training in Dutch norms) and of social control (providing 'negative feedback' for non-compliance with Dutch norms). The various schools of social work provided specific training for social workers in the problems of immigrant families, and at the peak period of migration sixty-one full-time and thirty-five half-time social workers were employed in this work.

These social workers also co-ordinated the work of numerous voluntary organizations concerned with immigrant families. I shall mention these voluntary organizations in more detail below.

Not all heads of households allocated a new home had a job to go to. Some, used to clerical or administrative work had to take manual jobs, since the large number of immigrants, especially in the 'influx' years, often exceeded the number of suitable jobs available. Fortunately, the late 50s was a period of industrial expansion in the Netherlands as it was elsewhere in Northern Europe. The immigrants were required to register their skills with the government employment office. A little over 1,900 individuals spent some time at regional centres training for new skills, but for the rest, the absorption of the immigrants into the economy seems to have been remarkably painless. The Ministry of Social Work commented (1965): 'Considering the small number [322] of repatriates still registered as unemployed in 1964, a tremendous problem for the Netherlands, with its high population density may be said to have been solved. The number of persons still seeking employment at that date represented less than one-quarter per cent of the total repatriates seeking employment in the period 1946 to 1964.'

For heads of households who had not found work a maintenance allowance was provided, calculated on the basis of a fixed percentage of the income which the immigrant, in view of his qualifications, could earn in his occupation in the Netherlands, plus a family allowance, and free health insurance.

In their review of the assimilation of the migrants from Indonesia into Dutch society, Kraak et al. conclude with the dictum 'aanpassen kost geld'—assimilation costs money. Just how much money is difficult to calculate, since assistance was provided in so many ways, and from so many different sources. The Government, too, did not start a specific accounting procedure in relation to the cost of social services for immigrants from Indonesia until 1952. The cost of the contract boarding houses between 1952 and 1964 was estimated to be in excess of £20,000,000, while the cost of retraining, maintenance whilst unemployed, and settlement in new houses during the same period amounted to £14,800,000. In addition, the 'opportunity cost' of the various interest-free loans has not been calculated in this total, nor the various subsidies in the form of services provided by voluntary organizations. In addition, too, there is the non-accountable cost, in terms of services foregone, to the Dutch population of the allocation of a large number of new houses to the immigrants, and the diversion of capital which could otherwise have been invested in more economically productive ways. In comparison with Britain, taking into account population size and the proportion of immigrants in the two populations, this represents an expenditure of approximately £140,000,000 over a twelve-year period. One must read this amount, too, against the comparative gross national products of the two countries. In 1957 (Russett, 1965) the G.N.P. per capita of the United Kingdom was $1,189 compared with $836 in the Netherlands. The Netherlands was, in fact, the *least* wealthy of the group of Northern European countries comprising Britain, France, Belgium, Sweden, Denmark, Norway, West Germany, and Luxembourg. Comparing the G.N.P. of Britain and the Netherlands in percentage terms, it can be seen that Britain had some 25 per cent more national wealth than the Netherlands, taking population size into account. One must make this 25 per cent adjustment, in comparing the expenditure of Britain and the Netherlands on the integration of coloured immigrants.

How much, in fact, has Britain provided in terms of the cost of special services for the integration and assimilation of immigrants?

We just do not have sufficient data to provide this figure: the detailed and comprehensive study of British race relations by Rose et al. (1969) for example, does not attempt such an estimate.[13] But we can compare the services Britain has provided with the Netherlands: in the period 1952–64 these services in Britain were so minimal that we are hard put to identify them—we can only identify expenditure on welfare facilities for workers recruited abroad by London Transport on temporary unemployment benefit; certain classes in schools; and on establishing the National Committee for Commonwealth Immigrants. The cost of these amounted to less than £1,000,000, and probably much less, although the proportion of coloured immigrants coming in to the two countries in this period (about 2·0 per cent of the total population) has been similar.

In the period since 1964 certain special services have been provided in Britain for coloured immigrants, notably in education, in special area subsidies and in support for community relations. But since 1964 Holland has been active on behalf of *her* West Indian immigrants, and on behalf of foreign migrant workers. Expenditure in the Netherlands in this area, as we shall see in a later chapter, again outstrips the British expenditure.

How, we may ask, did the Dutch people accept such a large invasion, and such a large apportionment of their national budget? Two factors underlaid the tolerance and good will shown by large sectors of the population. The first, as we have already indicated, was the involvement of the Dutch people in the loss of Indonesia, and the feeling that the role of the Netherlands was a righteous one, a role unrecognized by the world powers. The Dutch people had a strong psychological orientation to Indonesia, and to Indonesians who remained loyal to the Netherlands. The second factor was the example set by the *leaders* of Dutch society, and the use of traditional authority networks to gain a concensus on the way the immigrants should be treated.[14]

[13] But see the Chapter by Peston in Rose et al. on the beneficial economic effects of immigrants for Britain's economy and social services.

[14] A study of the treatment of 'repatriation' in the Dutch press has been carried out by Baschwitz et al. (1956). This study examined a sample of seventy-three weekly and daily papers published in 1955–6, and showed that the Dutch press treated the immigration in a rather formal manner, giving prominence to statements by prominent individuals, and to debates in the Second Chamber. The Dutch press implicitly accepted the repatriation programme as an obvious and valuable exercise demanding uncritical support.

Queen Juliana herself visited the incoming migrant ships, and spent the night in a contract boarding house, so as to establish a common feeling with the immigrants. She also gave up a large part of her palace for the purpose of accommodating the immigrants. It is difficult to imagine Queen Elizabeth doing the same for Asians expelled from Africa![15]

The impetus and example of the Dutch leaders was followed by numerous voluntary organizations. Some of these had been active since 1949 but, as Boer-Lasschuyt suggests, 'The terrifying shock of mass-repatriation in 1957 called for a mobilization of all these forces.' This was carried out by an organization called C.C.K.P. ('Central Commission of Denominational and Private Initiative for Social Care for the Benefit of Repatriants'). The assistance, help, and guidance to immigrants was organized by C.C.K.P., in association with the Ministry of Social Work. C.C.K.P. co-ordinated the work of the following organizations: the National Catholic Foundation for Repatriants' Care; the Commission for Spiritual and Social Welfare of Repatriants (a Protestant body); the Dutch Israelitic Denomination; the Association for Social Work on a Humanitarian Basis (Humanists); the Council of Labour (Socialist); the Dutch Red Cross; the Foundation of Labour; the Domestic Council; the Dutch Women's Council; the Foundation for Domestic and Family Information, and the Dutch Youth Council.

We see that the traditional *verzuiling* sectors of society were represented, working separately, but nevertheless in close co-operation. Many of the social workers employed by the various organizations were professionals, and many had experience of life in Indonesia.

## THE ABSORPTION OF THE IMMIGRANTS: STRUCTURAL AND PSYCHOLOGICAL ASPECTS

An official study by Kraak, Ellemers, Wittermans, Ploeger, and Tjeong (1957) studied aspects of the absorption and adaptation of the immigrants from Indonesia in Dutch society. For the purposes of their study they divided a sample of immigrants into three groups: I. Those who had only been temporarily resident

[15] In February 1971, Queen Juliana made a personal gift of several thousand pounds to the World Council of Churches' fund for aid to anti-racist groups in Africa. Again, it is difficult to imagine an Elizabethan counterpart.

in Indonesia, and were very largely of European origin (n=503); II. Those who had lived in Indonesia for most of their lives, including some Europeans (n=262); III. Those who had lived all their lives in Indonesia (n=211). The last group contained many more coloured immigrants than the first group, and the middle group contained an intermediate number. The numbers in the study do not, however, reflect the actual proportions in these categories in the total number of immigrants before 1957. Table 3·1 shows the geographical distribution.

*Table 3:1. Geographical Distribution of Immigrants in the Study by Kraak et al.*

| *Province* | *% of the Sample* | *% of all Dutch Population* |
|---|---|---|
| Groningen | 2·8 | 4·9 |
| Friesland | 2·5 | 4·8 |
| Drenthe | 0·9 | 2·5 |
| Overijssel | 3·6 | 6·1 |
| Gelderland | 7·7 | 11·0 |
| Utrecht | 8·4 | 5·7 |
| Noordholland | 21·4 | 20·6 |
| Zuidholland | 40·1 | 25·7 |
| Zeeland | 1·9 | 2·8 |
| Noordbrabant | 7·7 | 10·2 |
| Limburg | 3·0 | 5·9 |

Although this distribution of immigrants shows a concentration in Zuidholland, the final distribution was probably much closer to the general population distribution, since the process of distribution to various parts of the country was not complete when Kraak's study was carried out. A report published in 1964[16] said that between 1960 and 1963 council houses had been allocated to immigrants from Indonesia on the following basis: in Amsterdam, 553; The Hague, 243; Rotterdam, 349; Groningen, 236; Gelderland, 548; North Brabant, 966.

In their employment in Indonesia and in the Netherlands the distribution by occupation of Kraak's sample is as shown in Table 3·2.

[16] *Digest of the Kingdom of the Netherlands—Social Aspects*, Supplement (The Hague, 1964).

*Table 3:2. Distribution by Occupation of Immigrants, from Kraak et al.*

| *Occupational group* | *% in Indonesia* | *% in Netherlands* |
|---|---|---|
| Highest professional | 0·4 | 0·2 |
| Professional | 17·7 | 8·7 |
| Lower professional | 49·6 | 13·3 |
| Clerical and lower white-collar | 26·0 | 60·0 |
| Skilled and semi-skilled manual | 4·9 | 7·7 |

It will be seen that for many individuals migration was associated with occupational down-grading. This was the inevitable result of the absorption of a large influx of individuals into a relatively crowded labour market. Over time, we would expect individuals with particular kinds of professional training to move into the appropriate occupational categories. This assumption, of course, involves the supposition that discrimination on grounds of colour is largely absent in the Netherlands. I will discuss this feature of Dutch society in a later chapter. It should be noted that this aspect of migration—downward mobility—may have had an alienating effect on the migrants. But against this, we must also remember that many of these immigrants had experienced life in Japanese internment camps, and had also been living in a climate of insecurity prior to migration.[17] In other words, the reference orientation of these migrants may not have been a previous state of security and higher status, but one of insecurity and disorganization.

At the time of the inquiry of Kraak and his colleagues, approximately half of the immigrants had been permanently housed. There was, as expected, a rapidly diminishing number of individuals in contract boarding houses according to the time spent in the Netherlands. Of those permanently housed 93 per cent of those owning their houses said they were 'very satisfied', compared with 68 per cent of those renting accommodation. It was found that 8 per cent of subjects were still looking for work.

[17] Zinkin (1964) estimated that 10,000 Eurasians had died in Japanese prisoner of war camps. This was a voluntary fate, emphasizing their solidarity with the Dutch.

An inquiry was made into how the immigrants perceived the behaviour of the Dutch hosts, and experience of 'ungracious behaviour' and 'discrimination' was recorded. Most of the complaints referred to 'coldness' and 'rudeness' on the part of the Dutch—behaviour which became easier to understand over time. This 'coldness' is similar to the unfriendliness of Dutch public behaviour which we commented on in Chapter 1. Some evidence of discrimination in housing was produced—for example, a woman complained that on several occasions accommodation which the local authority housing bureau said was vacant was denied her by the owner, who said that the house was now let.[18] Fortunately, since the letting is in the hands of the local authority, the grounds for denial of accommodation can be checked, so that there are powerful structural factors discouraging discrimination.

*Table 3:3. Classification of 'Discrimination and Ungracious Behaviour'*

| | *Category I* | | *Category II* | | *Category III* | | *All* | |
|---|---|---|---|---|---|---|---|---|
| | %*m* | %*w* | %*m* | %*w* | %*m* | %*w* | %*m* | %*w* |
| No discrimination | 70 | 70 | 55 | 65 | 55 | 80 | 65 | 65 |
| Some discrimination | 28 | 23 | 43 | 31 | 41 | 17 | 32 | 32 |
| Don't know | 2 | 7 | 2 | 4 | 4 | 3 | 3 | 3 |

It is interesting to note that although males in the European category I reported less 'discrimination', there was no difference between males in the categories II and III despite differences in the proportion of coloured people in these two groups. It seems that it is lack of familiarity with the culture, rather than colour as such which accounts for reports of discrimination.

The choice of partner of the male subjects, and the expressed choice of marriage partner of their children reveals an interesting pattern. Of the 'full-blooded Europeans' (mostly Category I) 27 per cent of the males had taken an Indonesian wife (i.e. born in Indonesia), whilst 37 per cent of the children of these couples expressed a preference for a partner who had been born in

[18] In the Dutch system all unfurnished lettings have to be notified to the local authority, who then sends a tenant from its list to view the property. See Chapter 1 for a discussion of the Dutch housing system in more detail.

Indonesia. Of the male subjects born in Indonesia, 72 per cent had married a partner born in that country. But only 38 per cent of the children of those couples expressed a preference for an Indonesian Netherlander as a partner. This last finding suggests that, in terms of partner choice, the Indonesian Netherlanders (a largely coloured group) were rapidly being absorbed into Dutch culture. The children of the all-European group, however, expressed a *higher* proportion of preferences than their parents for an Indonesian partner, suggesting a quicker rate of acculturation amongst the Indonesian Netherlanders than among the all-white group.[19]

A special study of 162 subjects found that fifty-one were Catholic, sixty-one were Protestant, seventeen belonged to 'foreign churches' and five to minor Protestant sects. In seventeen cases a Protestant and a Catholic were married. The evidence suggested that the majority of immigrants were taking an active role in the life of the denomination to which they belonged.

Kraak's study, carried out with a sample of immigrants from Indonesia who arrived in the Netherlands before the 'great wave' of 1958, suggests that although there were some difficulties of adjustment, the process of absorption was taking place. Absorption meant that the immigrant was treated in every respect like a Dutchman. He was fitted into the sectarian bloc system, and expected to behave, in relation to his fellows, like any other Dutchman. But there was a price to pay for this policy of absorption, as de Boer-Lasschuyt points out. Topaas de Boer-Lasschuyt, a Dutch anthropologist specializing in Indonesian culture, was resident in that country from 1952–9. Her thesis is that absorption or assimilation had been carried through too quickly, and without regard for the traditional culture of many of the immigrants. First of all, she argues that the immigrants still have a strong attachment to Indonesia. Indeed, in some cases the decision to migrate was a painful one, and families were split, some taking Dutch nationality, others taking out Indonesian citizenship. She characterized the initial reaction of the Dutch people thus:

Coming ashore in the cold Netherlands they offer the traditional picture of helpless children with big brown eyes and shivering grannies in 'sarong and kebajas'. This picture has aroused a stream of warm

[19] 'de hypothese geformuleerd, dat kindern van ouders behorend tot migrantie catorie II en III even snel of nog sneler hun partners in kringen van niet-gerepatrieerden zouden zoeken, dan kindern uit migratie categorie I' (Kraak et al., p. 303).

compassion and sympathy among the 'Hollanders' for these poor immigrants. Especially when the Minister of Social Work, Miss Marge Klampé—in a now famous radio speech—on account of the 1957 happenings, made a strong and heart-stirring appeal on the Dutch to help and assist their poor compatriots from the tropics, an immense wave of hearty well meant tenderness and pity swept the country.

The Government evoked both the spirit of nationalism, and the Dutch sense of moral duty in enlisting sympathy for the immigrants. But nevertheless, de Boer-Lasschuyt argues, points of tension existed. First of all, there is a Dutch stereotype of the Indonesian: he is said to be unreliable, supine, listless, lazy, lacking in initiative and economic sense, prodigal, suspicious with an inferiority complex, a chip on his shoulder. The Indonesian view of the European is that he is slothful, a profiteer, exploiting the native people, short-tempered, rude and unhygienic. Who, held this stereotype of the Indonesian? It was probably most prevalent amongst the working classes, and especially those in positions of least wealth and authority. Amongst these, de Boer-Lasschuyt suggests, occurred hostility not only to the Indonesians but to the Dutch colonialists as well—'They've benefited from colonial exploitation, and now they remember they're Dutch.' In 1958, in the Schildersbuurt, a working-class quarter of The Hague, there were disturbances—a 'youth war'—in which Indonesian youths were attacked because, it was said, of the ease with which they attracted Dutch girls.

These events were a considerable embarrassment to the Dutch authorities who were very anxious that the assimilation process should be smooth and complete, and that 'ghettoes' or sub-cultural groups of immigrants should not form; de Boer-Lasschuyt commented:

A well-organized society like the Dutch simply cannot permit the disorder and tensions which certainly spring from the lack of assistance. The spontaneous national feeling of acute compassion and sympathy with the migrants cannot be overlooked. The aim of Dutch policy is very simple and straight: it aims at complete absorption of this 'out-group'. The absorption-principle knows only one thing: as soon as possible the Repatriant group should disappear and dissolve into Dutch society, lose its typicalities, segregational tendencies, its being different and apart.

But, the author argues, the assimilation has been one-sided. The contemplative and ascetic values of the Indonesians have been lost in the process. Indonesians lack the materialism and the concern over time of the Dutch. Their gentleness and good manners have had to be replaced by Dutch ruggedness:

Dutch life is so regulated, so organized and ruled even in the smallest details, that it would become unbearable if not everybody stuck to the instructions and regulations. The fact that everybody lives according to the same restricted patterns of life, is the only consolation [for the Dutch]: consequently 'being different' is hated and jealously disliked.... The Dutch way of life is good, yes the best. Consequently 'being different' is very near to 'being less good'.

In the face of very strong pressure to conform, to be like the Dutch, assimilation may be 'feigned': according to the author's argument the immigrant will show an interest in the appropriate *verzuiling* to please the social worker, attending services, social activities, and religious talks because of social pressure to do so, rather than because of their intrinsic interest. The immigrant will adopt certain 'ritual' norms which imply acceptance of Dutch culture—eating potatoes rather than rice; washing clothes on a Monday; offering only small helpings to a guest because 'one should not overdo things'; and 'cutting one's coat according to one's cloth'. The points on which there are culture conflicts are very similar to those outlined in Wilder's study of the earlier immigrants from Indonesia.

The Dutch complaints about the recent immigrants from Indonesia reported by de Boer-Lasschuyt are also very similar to those reported in Wilder's study: these recent arrivals were said to be:

bad housekeepers, debt-makers, party-loving, irresponsible neglectors of the necessary floor and staircase scrubbing; playing the generous hosts to baker boys, window cleaners and the milkmen, by giving these people (too expensive) coffee, instead of using this money for coal; and inviting these people into their living room to warm their hands; giving lemonade and sweets to all the children on the street on an ordinary winter's day (no birthday party!); and having at the same time no carpet on the floor and no money for next week; their houses are real children's paradises, and the children are spoilt; the neighbourhood children all want to play in the Indonesian houses and seem to prefer to clean strange Indonesian vegetables for these people rather than helping their own mothers to dust and clean rooms; but you never know what they learn, the children, in such surroundings; the Indonesian men are not good workers like the Dutch—they are very willing and not lazy or elusive, but they simply don't have the stamina.

De Boer-Lasschuyt's thesis is that in absorbing the immigrants the Dutch have been too one-sided: the Indonesian aspect of immigrant culture has been ignored, steam-rollered, and trampled on; yet many of the elements of Indonesian culture are valuable and could be absorbed by the Dutch. She points with approval to one area of assimilation—the increasing indulgence in Indonesian food by the Dutch. Her conclusion is that Dutch society has, at a formal level, a set of high moral standards about racial equality and the dignity of man, and there is a conscious effort to put these principles into practice: 'Living up to these standards and criteria, (even mentally and psychologically) means a constant struggle, an unceasing struggle for the soul of the individual citizen.' The Dutch have an unshakable belief in the high standards of Dutch hospitality to oppressed aliens and refugee groups, and secondly a firm conviction that no race prejudice exists in the Netherlands. These assumptions have been built into the Dutch value structure over a period of many years. But at the same time there exists a tension between the ideal of duty, and the xenophobia or hostility to coloured people which has psychological roots, or an origin in the pressures of social structure (e.g. through housing shortage). Those most likely to depart from the official norm are the young, those aged between 16 and 26 years who are hypercritical of the exercise of authority on the part of the older generation. The fact that Dutch youth were involved in 'race riots' in The Hague in 1958 (and again in Twenthe in 1962) provides some support for de Boer-Lasschuyt's hypothesis.

Further detailed information on the processes of the assimilation of the immigrants from Indonesia have been provided by Ex's study (1966). Ex carried out interviews with a sample of forty families three months, one year, two years, and three years after arrival in the Netherlands. The interviews were semi-structured, and lasted some three hours, during which the respondents developed 'spontaneous themes'. The requirements for inclusion in the sample were both husband and wife born and bred in Indonesia and having two to four children; in the Netherlands for the first time in their lives and in the country for less than two months; the husband aged 25–40 and occupying a lower technical or administrative occupation; and the family living (at the first interview) in contract boarding houses in or near two specified towns.

The sample was ethnically heterogeneous, and was made up of four groups, (*a*) autochthons—Javanese, Madurese, Sumatrans; (*b*) Asiatic foreigners—Chinese, Siamese, Japanese; (*c*) 'Europeans' —Dutch, Germans, Arabs; (*d*) various ethnic mixtures of (*a*)–(*c*). Ex's study is typical of Dutch studies on the adaptation of immigrants in that colour of skin is not isolated as a variable of special interest, cultural differences being seen as the crucial variable accounting for difficulties in assimilation.

The 'spontaneous themes' developed by the subjects were as follows: *Theme I*, 'The people and their behaviour'; e.g. 'The girls in the shops, the butchers and bakers all have a special kind of uniform; it's much nicer than in Indonesia. Even the lower classes are neatly dressed here . . . the Dutchman here is not like the Dutchman in Indonesia; here they are much more friendly and ready to help . . . the Dutch are coarse, but they don't cherish feelings of hatred.' Ninety-two per cent of respondents spontaneously expressed this kind of theme. *Theme II* (expressed by 90 per cent): 'The Environment'; e.g. 'Housing is so cramped, just like a doll's house, and there is very little, if any garden. People live on top of each other.' *Theme III* (expressed by 85 per cent): 'Freedom of action and amusement'; e.g. 'There is no entertainment, no variety here. It's so monotonous! There you had all those friends and acquaintances and those homely parties which brought some variety, nearly every week. Sundays especially are dreadful here; no street vendors, nothing! Here every day's the same. . . . Here you're not allowed to cut down trees just like that. And if you want to keep chickens you have to have a permit . . . we miss the freedom.' *Theme IV* expressed by 77 per cent, was 'Job-finding'. *Theme V* (60 per cent): 'Regulation of the Community'; e.g. 'Everything is regulated and organized. There are set early closing days for tradesmen . . . there's a special wash day and a day for ironing. We in Indonesia don't have those obligatory days. The people in the Netherlands are insured against everything. Social welfare is excellent. In the Netherlands it's the general neatness that strikes you, everything is so clean and beautifully cared for . . . you wonder what they do with all the dirt. You don't see any beggars in the streets; in Indonesia it's simply swarming with them.' *Theme VI*, expressed by 47 per cent, was 'Making ends meet'. *Theme VII* (45 per cent): 'Contact with others'; e.g. 'All my family is still in Indonesia. We're often homesick, and write home every week. . . . What we need very badly here is contact with the outside world. We don't even have contact with the neighbours. But still, the Dutch are like that; they keep more to themselves.'

Interviews held with the same family at different points in time provided useful information on the degree of their adjustment, and their changing perception of Dutch society and behaviour over time. Ex's findings are given in Table 3:4.

*Table 3:4. Ex's Findings on Adjustment and the Immigrant's Perception of Dutch Society*

| *Variable* | *Stage I After 3 months* % | *Stage II After 1 year* % | *Stage III After 2 years* % | *Stage IV After 3 years* % |
|---|---|---|---|---|
| Subject does not feel at home in his environment | — | 95 | 77 | 50 |
| Head of household often feels bored | 68 | 59 | 54 | 43 |
| 'My work is satisfactory' | — | 28 | 38 | 52 |
| 'The Dutch look down on one' | 39 | 36 | 38 | 34 |
| 'The Dutch see us as intruders, taking jobs and benefits' | 37 | 24 | 20 | 12 |
| 'The Dutch are friendly and helpful' | 70 | 20 | 25 | 20 |
| 'Doctors hardly ever examine the patient thoroughly | 21 | 13 | 0 | — |
| 'On inter-visiting terms with at least one Dutch family' | — | 23 | 56 | — |
| 'I have good relations with workmates' | — | 95 | 88 | 90 |
| Families with a private dwelling | 0 | 7 | 53 | 83 |
| Median age of children | 3·6 | 4·2 | 5·0 | 6·1 |

These results show the changing pattern of adaptation of the immigrants over time. Although 'feeling at home in one's environment' increased over time, nevertheless, after three years half of the subjects did *not* feel at home. Adjustment to work increased over time, and relations with workmates were good at all stages of the inquiry. The proportions believing that 'the Dutch look down on one' did not change over time, although there was a significant decrease in the numbers who thought that the Dutch held negative attitudes about them ('the Dutch see us as intruders, taking jobs and benefits'). The initial impression of the Dutch as a friendly and helpful people was not maintained over time, and this may be because of the decreasing support given by special social services for immigrants.

Ex reports that many of his subjects were fearful at leaving contract boarding houses, and the support of their former countrymen, for the larger society. He found that 75 per cent of the immigrants had obtained information on Dutch jobs, shops, houses, and customs from fellow refugees. This had the unfortunate effect, in Ex's opinion, of perpetuating the stereotypes the immigrants had of the Dutch. On the perpetuation of the stereotypes held by the Dutch themselves, he comments:

> The Dutch population too was repeatedly kept informed, via the press and the radio about the living conditions of the Indonesian Dutch and their flight too and their rehabilitation in the Netherlands and about ways in which one might lend a helping hand, both by one's attitudes and by actual assistance, in building up a new existence. In spite of this, many remained ignorant, distrustful and only passively benevolent. Moreover, they were a little put out by these people, characterized by their Eastern pliability and consequently easily forgot the very tragic circumstances which encompassed them through no fault of their own.

The 'stereotypes' held by the immigrants were similar to those mentioned by Wilder and de Boer-Lasschuyt—the lack of hospitality in Dutch households, and meanness and over-careful husbanding of resources, insistence on prompt payment and punctuality. All of these traits were in marked contrast to the spontaneity and generosity of the Indonesian household. As the immigrants' children grew older they inevitably mixed with Dutch children and acquired some of the outlook on life which these Dutch children had learned from their peers and parents. The Indonesians were ambiguous about this increasing similarity of the behaviour of their children to that of the typical Dutch child. They were pleased at the ease with which their children mixed with Dutch children and took the typical roles of a child. But at the same time they regretted the change in parent–child relationship that this implied. One parent commented on this situation:

> The parents teach their children to keep their eyes open and explain anything the child wants to know. But if they want something they don't get their own way as easily as our children. The relationship between parents and children is more friendly here, more chummy. We assert our authority more and punish more severely. . . . Parents here talk more with their children. Perhaps it's better; in this way the child remains more open towards you, while if you treat them harshly, they become frightened of you. . . . The method of punishment is different here than in Indonesia. They, the Dutch, punish more mildly and give fewer corporal punishments. For example standing in the corner, not playing outside, no pocket money, a week without going to the pictures, going to bed without a meal. We would never do that, sending a child to bed without a meal; that's cruel. We'd rather give a good smacking, so that at least they'd be afraid of doing it again. We're more heavy handed; here they'll talk to a child.

However, by Stage IV, after three years, markedly more mothers were conforming to the Dutch custom of turning the child out of the house to play, because he would make it dirty!

The immigrants were particularly impressed by the treatment they received in Dutch shops: 'You're served here in a more friendly, polite and obliging way than out there. Here they come and ask you if they can help you, and they'll show all sorts of things. Over here it is the customer that's right.' In Indonesia the shopkeeper tends to regard the customer, apparently, with some contempt and is apt to change the price of goods according to the look of his customer. Doctors in Indonesia tend to charge high fees and to make a great show and ritual of examining the patient, and prescribing expensive, and often unnecessary treatment. But the Dutch doctor makes only the examination which is strictly relevant to the patient's complaint, and prescribes conservatively. The data indicate that over time the immigrants understood this different behaviour of doctors between the two cultures.

Over time, the level of reported boredom of the heads of households decreased, although three years after migration 43 per cent did complain of boredom and lack of variety in social life. Ex attributes this boredom to the lack of friends whom one could visit frequently, and inhibition in participating in social organizations. In Stages II and III many families told Ex that they wanted Dutch friends—'Real trusted friends, that's what we miss. Preferably a Dutch family; with Indonesian families you only harp back to Indonesia all the time.' The evidence did indicate that over time the immigrants had more Dutch friends. However, feeling free to mix on equal terms with Dutch people was something that had to be bought by experience. During a Stage II interview (after one year) a woman told Ex: 'Why don't we feel at home here? It's because you don't fully share their point of views and ways.' Another informant said: 'What am I and why am I here? I don't belong and it's wretched. I've never been so miserable as I am here. My wife wants to go back, just as I do; we'll never stay here.'

During a Stage III interview (after two years) a woman told Ex: 'They do stare at you so here; you feel that they keep looking at you. They've invited us more than once to come and drink a cup of coffee, but we've never accepted. I'd rather they came here. You can never tell what's expected of you when you visit the Dutch.' But another informant said, in a Stage III interview: 'I feel much more at home than two years ago, but not altogether yet. Our way of doing things, our way of thinking are different, you see. When I behave as I think I should be polite, Dutch people think I'm overdoing it and being insincere.'

Ex's study suggests that the immigrants from Indonesia experienced considerable stresses and difficulties in 'becoming Dutch'. In this respect they are similar to the Englishmen who experienced difficulty in 'becoming Australian' or 'becoming Canadian', and the Jews who do not find 'becoming Israeli' an easy process. The studies which we cited at the beginning of this chapter suggest that this process of absorption into a new culture is never easy, and is often fraught with difficulty. Nevertheless, there are significant indicators that for the immigrants from Indonesia, a process of assimilation is taking place.

Ex's conclusion is that, 'The dwelling together of people suffering the same fate appears to retard rather than further their adjustment to the new way of life.' In this report his conclusion is the opposite of de Boer-Lasschuyt's, who argued that too ready a dispersion from communal living, or living in houses close to one another, deprived the immigrant of group support, and meant that he had to become, for many purposes at least, 'Dutch'. When the immigrant is the only person from Indonesia in that village or suburb he has a choice between isolation, and interaction based on acquiring similar norms to his fellows. Given that the Dutch policy was one of dispersion and assimilation at the outset, and that vigorous supportive services, both material and social, were provided for the immigrant so dispersed, it seems inevitable that a large part of the immigrant's traditional cultural background would be sacrificed.

If, however, a more or less conscious policy of *integration* is followed, in which the immigrant is left much more to his own devices, then the case for tolerating the immigrant's traditional culture becomes much stronger. It is inevitable, in these circumstances, that the immigrant will wish to derive group support from living near people of a similar cultural background to himself.

Dutch policy in relation to the immigrants from Indonesia has been of assimilation; but what if the immigrant group does not want to be integrated with Dutch society, but wishes instead to live apart and maintain traditional cultural patterns? The answer, in the Dutch situation, is that they are tolerated, and indeed supported by the Government. This is the case with the Ambonese, to whom we now turn.

## AMBONESE IMMIGRANTS IN THE NETHERLANDS

The Ambonese immigrants, unlike other immigrants from Indonesia, were a homogeneous ethnic group. The 12,500 Ambonese came from the group of islands called the Moluccas (formerly the Spice Islands). Since 1650 they had been employed as soldiers by the Dutch, since they possessed a traditional prowess in the military sphere. The Ambonese immigrants are a largely Christian group, and supported the Dutch occupation of Indonesia in 1948. Ethnically and culturally distinct from the Javanese mainland, they had no desire to be ruled from Djakarta. In 1949 when Dutch sovereignty was transferred to a confederacy of states, the South Moluccas (including the island of Ambon) were granted a degree of autonomy. But the confederacy collapsed in 1950, and the Ambonese vigorously resisted the invading Indonesian army. The Dutch, embarrassed by this situation, sought to disband the Ambonese troops in the Royal Netherlands Army. Such a move was fiercely resisted by the Ambonese, who threatened to commit mass suicide if these plans were carried out. The Dutch Government's answer to this threat was to transport the soldiers and their families to the Netherlands, where they were accommodated in several camps in various parts of the country.

A Republic of the South Moluccas had been declared on 25 April 1950. This Republic was not recognized by the invading Indonesians. A considerable number of Ambonese were left in the

Moluccas, and these carried out an intermittent but largely unsuccessful struggle against Indonesia. Many of the nationalists were imprisoned, and there have been a number of executions. Many Ambonese who came to the Netherlands have maintained the firm intention of returning to their liberated homeland.

In consequence they have taken—in their early years in the Netherlands at least—little interest in any kind of absorption into Dutch society. This was recognized by the Dutch authorities, and the immigrants were allowed to remain in the forty-five centres to which they had been allocated. By October 1953 these centres contained 2,856 families and 1,110 unmarried people over 18 years, in total 14,620 individuals. Since then the number of Ambonese has increased, largely as a result of a high birth-rate, to an estimated 25,000 in 1966 (Gwynn, 1967).[20] The religious composition of the immigrants is given in Table 3:5, taken from Wittermans (1955a), and refers to a 1953 census of all adult male immigrants:

*Table* 3:5. *Religious Composition of Ambonese Immigrants (from Wittermans)*

| *Origin* | *Protestant (Calvinist)* | *Catholic* | *Muslim* | *Total* |
|---|---|---|---|---|
| Spice Islands and Ceram | 2,700 | — | 74 | 2,774 |
| Kai and Tanimbar Islands | 659 | 194 | — | 853 |
| | | | | 3,627 |

The situation of the Ambonese has, according to Wittermans and Gist (1962) been one of 'status deprivation'. The Ambonese had always been a high prestige group in the East Indies, and considered themselves superior to other ethnic groups in the archipelago. They came to the Netherlands as soldiers of the Royal Dutch Army, a fact which contributed to their subjective feelings of status. They had too an influential pressure group of Dutch citizens advancing their cause. 'The Ambonese', wrote Wittermans and Gist, 'were given shelter, food, medical care, clothing, school facilities, even spending money at public expense. Materially they had no reason for complaints. Yet, to the surprise of officialdom a period of general unrest soon prevailed, manifesting serious dissatisfactions with the situation.' This was because, the

[20] The estimated numbers in 1971 were about 30,000, according to information given by the Ministry of Culture, Recreation, and Social Work.

authors argue, a succession of unexpected events and situations altered the status of the Ambonese radically and disfavourably.

First of all was their entirely unanticipated discharge from the Dutch Army. This was traumatic because it altered their cherished status, shattered their self-image, blighted their hopes, and spread confusion as to their identity. They felt humiliated and betrayed. Now, instead of regular army pay, they had a much smaller weekly unemployment benefit. They felt depressed, useless, and resentful. When they did find work, 60 per cent of their wages had to be paid as an accommodation charge, and in some cases this actually discouraged work finding. Their political status was uncertain; they did not regard themselves as immigrants; they retained Indonesian nationality, but did not regard themselves as merely visitors. They felt themselves rejected by both Indonesia and the Netherlands, with a consequent 'identity crisis'.

Inevitably, it seems, some tensions in camp life developed in the early stages at least, and there was strong rivalry between the two political groups, one moderate representing about two-thirds of the Ambonese, and the other extremist tending to be anti-Dutch. Both were organized on a para-military basis. The aggression of these two groups for one another, suggested Wittermans and Gist, represented a kind of 'emotional catharsis'. The women were organized into their own group called 'Kaum Ibu' which arranged entertainment for the men, and continued traditional cultural customs. Both Moslems and Christians served in this organization, religion being subordinated to the role giving ritual support for the nationalist cause. Between 1951 and 1953 at least four mass parades were held by the Ambonese. Most of these were in the parliamentary city of the Netherlands, The Hague. At those rallies both Dutch and Ambonese speakers stressed the injustice of treatment of the Ambonese both in the East Indies and in the Netherlands, and there was strong right-wing support for the reinstatement of the Ambonese in the Dutch Army.

At these and other parades the Republic was ceremoniously declared, and recent political events were symbolically re-enacted by actors in native costumes, to the accompaniment of traditional folk dances and music. Printed propaganda on behalf of the Ambonese was widely distributed, and special South Moluccan postage stamps were issued. This movement was organized by Ambonese intellectuals in association with former civil servants from the East Indies, university professors, and members of the

Netherlands Parliament. The national flag was flown in every camp, and the national anthem daily played. The slogan of the nationalist movement is 'Mena Muria' meaning 'afore and aft'. It is derived from an instruction to members of the large Moluccan canoes and means 'all pull together'. At nationalist meetings a speaker will call 'Mona' and will be greeted with the thunderous return 'Muria'. A popular theme in church sermons is that of the children of Israel who will return from exile to their promised land.

The Dutch Government in 1952 offered the Ambonese membership of a domestic Civil Guard if they would abandon their nationalist aspirations for a return to the Moluccas. But only thirty-nine out of the 3,000 former soldiers who were eligible took up this lucrative offer. Nevertheless, this nationalist unity has declined over the years as the possibility of a return to the Moluccas grows more remote, and as time goes on the involvement of the Ambonese in Dutch life and institutions increases.

The study by Wittermans (1955a) has illustrated the degree to which the life of the Ambonese is interconnected with that of the Dutch. Wittermans, an anthropologist, carried out fieldwork in four of the accommodation centres. A number of men had found jobs in the towns close to the camps, but continued to live in the camps. Others were attending retraining courses, although a number of residents did refuse to attend such courses on the grounds that their rightful place was with the Dutch Army. However, many of the men from the camps did seasonal work in the locality, helping with the corn, fruit, and potato harvests. Children attended the local Dutch schools, and there became bilingual, since the majority of the Ambonese spoke only Malay.

Contacts at work have built up friendships with the Dutch in the local community: 'A neighbouring farmer may ask his Ambonese seasonal workers in for a cup of coffee, and some workers have been invited to join the farmer's family at their midday meal.' Ambonese Christianity is strongly identified with Calvinism, and for this reason close links have been established with Re-Reformed church members. In one village the local church hired a coach to collect Ambonese attending the morning church service, and afterwards they were invited to the homes of their hosts for coffee, and the 'customary edifying discussion on the sermon'. Cases are reported of particularly frequent contact between Ambonese and Dutch families, and of a three-year-old child left with a Dutch family to learn Dutch. Ambonese flute orchestras play in Calvinist churches by invitation, and members of the orchestra, clad in traditional black silk jackets, will set out from the camps to play at evening religious meetings.

The Hawaiian style guitar bands are very popular in the camps, and are also favourites of the Dutch. One band, 'The Mena Muria Minstrels' had a regular half-hour programme on Dutch radio.[21] An outstanding individual member of a band in the Camp Almere was engaged by an Amsterdam nightclub. Ambonese volley ball, basket ball and football teams regularly play against local teams. A group of teenage Dutch girls formed an *ad hoc* volley ball team and visited the local camp regularly; but its purpose, Witterman suggests, was not sport as such, but to meet Ambonese boys. 'Two hasty Ambonese-Dutch marriages have been the result so far. . . . In these cases the initiative is usually taken by the girls, who seem to be greatly attracted by the Ambonese boys.' These ventures are accepted with apparent equanimity by both Dutch and Ambonese communities. Ambonese girls, however, don't venture out of the camps to meet Dutch boys; this is because of parental restrictions. Dutch girls who marry Ambonese boys tended, at the time Wittermans was writing, to come and live in the camps. However, with the passage of time more and more Ambonese are setting up households of their own in the community, and this is especially the case when an Ambonese boy marries a Dutch girl. The statistics for 1967[22] show that 116 girls who still hold Indonesian nationality were married in the Netherlands. Almost all of this number are Ambonese. Of this number, fifty-four married Dutchmen and fifty-five Ambonese men. In the same period 154 Ambonese men were married in the Netherlands: fifty-five of these married Ambonese girls (i.e. the fifty-five marriages indicated above), and ninety-five married Dutch girls.

A particular feature of many camps are the Calvinist choirs, each

[21] The Dutch pirate radio station, Radio Veronica, regularly broadcast concerts by these bands, as well as music from Surinam, Italy, Greece, and Spain. These programmes are specially designed for the various groups of immigrants.

[22] *Buitenlandse Werknemers* (No. 1, 1969), p. 10. Of the 458 marriages in the Netherlands between 1965 and 1968 involving an Ambonese partner, 38 per cent involved a Dutch partner (Mariën, 1971). Mariën points out that the Ambonese population contains proportionately more young people than the Dutch population.

containing fifteen to thirty members. Often there are several choirs in one camp, and performances are given both in the camps and in local towns and villages. The Ambonese Protestants have evolved an elaborate social organization; Muslims, by contrast, have only sporadic organization. Nevertheless, there is no overt inter-religious conflict. Nationalism has been an important source of social integration in the camps, and overrides all other differences, including religious and inter-village ritual patterns. This latter, called *pela*, has been described by Wittermans (1955b) and illustrates the degree to which the Ambonese community has maintained traditional forms of social organization, despite quite extensive contacts with the Dutch population.

Villages in Ambon are connected by ritual links called *pela*. In the communities Wittermans studied sixty-one villages were represented, and thirty-eight had *pela* links with from one to four villages. *Pela* is a solemn oath in which the members of one village agree to provide reciprocal help in the collection of field and forest produce, alliance in warfare, and the pooling of some resources. It was a useful device in long-distance raids, when an ally far from home is needed. But with the decline of warfare the mutual assistance given is now domestic and commercial. There is a ritual taboo on marriage between members of villages linked by *pela*.

Wittermans found that members of the same village tended to group together in camps, so that in the camp at Schattenburg there were forty-six families from the same village; this village had *pela* links with members of a village living 100 miles away in a camp at Lunetten. The ban on marriage between people linked by *pela* has the status of an incest taboo, and the traditional sanctions against breaking it have been severe. Wittermans questioned 355 married couples in the two camps, and found only one pair who had contracted a *pela* marriage. He concludes that the force of *pela* in this respect is still strong. One of the functions of *pela* is to provide group support for weddings and funerals, and one's *pela* village usually supplies the 'best man' at a wedding, and food for the wedding feast. At funerals, both sympathy and food for the wake are provided.

Some young people, especially those born outside the Moluccas expressed ignorance or apathy about *pela* matters. But fourteen students questioned said that they would not challenge *pela* marriage rules, and one had in fact broken his engagement when he discovered that his fiancée was in *pela* relationship to him. Young people being educated in local schools and universities still kept the *pela* marriage and courtship rules.

Witterman's argument is that it is not the age of an institution which ensures its survival, but the functions it performs for the social system. *Pela* has provided a very useful means of extending group support in a new and strange environment; in increasing physical contact between the camps it also enhanced the nationalist ethos and provided cultural links with the past and with the homeland. There are supernatural sanctions against breaking *pela*, and the particular purveyors of punishment are the spirits of one's ancestors. The notion of the presence of such spirits has been incorporated into Calvinist theology without apparent difficulty.

The Ambonese, until the mid sixties, provided an interesting illustration of the integration of a group of immigrants who maintained a very distinct cultural identity and whose principal orientation was to a set of values (Moluccan nationalism) which were outside the value framework of the society in which they lived. Yet they had considerable and amicable links with Dutch society. Over time these contacts increased. Large concentrations of Ambonese living together do still exist, however: in Moordrecht, for example, one-quarter of the population is Ambonese.[23]

A strong nationalist spirit survives, however. On 25 April 1969, for example, nineteen years after the declaration of the Republiek der Zuid Molukken, Ambonese from all over the Netherlands took part in a large parade in The Hague. The parade was headed by the very Dutch institution of a girl's band, dressed in para-military uniforms with short skirts, followed by a boy's bugle band, and a large, orderly procession containing many Ambonese and a few Europeans. The procession was flanked by police horses and observed by the Dutch crowd with a sober lack of emotion. The parade itself was orderly and quiet, but carried a number of banners proclaiming the rightfulness of the Ambonese claim. Finally, at a ceremony in the Malieveld in The Hague the

[23] Cf. the estimate by Krausz (1969) that some 40 per cent of the population of Edgware, London, is Jewish. Jews in Britain are another example of an integrated rather than an assimilated group. On dispersal, see the press statement of the Commissariat van Ambonozenzorg (Ministry of Culture, Recreation, and Social Work, 1967), 1366, p. 12. This indicated that Ambonese families could now be found in almost every town (in at least fifty of them) in the Netherlands.

flag of the Republic was ceremoniously raised, and a number of speeches made by people of importance. The speeches dwelt especially on the plight of individuals who had been imprisoned or executed in Indonesia.[24]

One cannot tell how long resistance will be maintained in the Moluccas themselves, and what the eventual fate of the Ambonese people both there and in the Netherlands will be. Their plight is similar to that of Polish *émigrés* in Britain who maintain a Polish government in exile and a Polish-language daily newspaper, and also maintain many Polish linguistic and cultural traditions. Such groups may maintain a separate cultural identity, with a relative degree of endogamy for many decades and perhaps centuries; at the same time they will merge quietly into the societies in which they live, accepting their role as a cultural minority contributing nevertheless to the society in which they live, and in turn tolerated and accepted by that society.

The crucial difference between the Poles in Britain and the Ambonese in the Netherlands is that the Poles are not at all identifiable by physical characteristics. But the Ambonese are a dark-skinned people, and this makes the non-assimilation of any group particularly noticeable. It seems—a theme I shall develop later on—that colour of skin is a minor factor in social differentiation in the Netherlands. But in Britain skin-colour seems to play a major role in social differentiation, taking precedence over social, linguistic, and educational factors.

In September 1970, President Soeharto of Indonesia paid an official visit to the Netherlands. This event was, in itself, a sign of increased cordiality between the Netherlands and Indonesia. At the end of August, thirty-two young Ambonese occupied the Indonesian ambassador's residence in The Hague. It was known that protests about Soeharto's visit were likely, and a police guard had been put on the ambassador's house. At the time of the demonstration the ambassador was elsewhere, but his wife and children remained in the residence. At dawn on 30 August the demonstrators, armed with stenguns and knives, raided the embassy, and shot dead one of the policemen who was on guard. The policeman, aged 28 years, had a wife and two children. The ambassador's family were taken prisoner. The demonstrators demanded that their President, Dr. J. A. Manusama should be allowed to discuss their independence claims with Dr. Soeharto.

[24] *Haagsche Courant* (25 April 1969).

They threatened that if the talks did not take place the ambassador's family would be shot dead one by one.

The official leaders of the government of the Republic of the South Moluccas in exile in the Netherlands at first disowned the young rebels, but then supported them. A statement issued from the South Moluccan leadership declared, on the evening of the day in which the policeman was killed:

> We regret very much the death of the policeman. Having heard the explanations given by the Free South Moluccan youths, we can say that 85 per cent of the South Moluccans in Holland are behind this action. It is not so serious because peace will return if the demands are met. The South Moluccan youths have decided to act because for 20 years the responsible authorities have never taken the cause of the South Moluccan Republic seriously.

The Dutch Prime Minister, Mr. de Jong, was at the scene during the day, together with his Foreign Minister Dr. Luns. The President of the Moluccan Republic spoke to the demonstrators, requesting that they give themselves up. On the evening of that day the thirty-two young Ambonese surrendered. During the subsequent visit of President Soeharto security restrictions were very stringent, and Ambonese trying to enter The Hague during this time were turned back, and some with arms were arrested. The Ambonese complained bitterly that in this respect they were being discriminated against.

The demonstrators came to trial, and were sentenced in January 1971. The most interesting thing about this trial was the leniency of the sentences. The prosecutor demanded the maximum sentence of seven years for the man accused of manslaughter of the policeman (the burst of machine-gun fire which killed him was apparently intended to frighten, rather than to murder). This man received only a three-year term, however. The organizer of the demonstration received a two-year sentence, and a number of others got lesser sentences ranging from eighteen months to three months. The president of the court said that in fixing the sentences the court had taken into account a message in 1945 from the late Queen Wilhemina of the Netherlands thanking the Ambonese for their loyalty to the House of Orange. One cannot help detecting an air of ambivalence in the Dutch treatment of these young rebels. In terms of the standards of behaviour expected of Dutch citizens, their conduct had been outrageous. It could hardly have been worse. But influential sectors of Dutch opinion have expressed tacit support for the young rebels (who had official support, after the event, from the Ambonese leaders), and the sentences passed on them have been token ones.

Nevertheless, one has detected, from an analysis of various sections of the Dutch press, and from exploratory interviews with sections of the Dutch public[25] a distinct increase in hostility to the Ambonese. These events have without doubt seriously set back the tendency towards assimilation in the less radical sections of the Ambonese, and united them to a certain extent around the old ideals of cultural integration and return to the South Moluccas (a goal which seems ever more hopeless). The manifest hostility now expressed towards the Ambonese seems most strongly expressed amongst working-class Dutchmen. The middle- and upper-class conservative Dutchmen who have traditionally given the Ambonese nationalist movement some support have been considerably embarrassed by these recent events, but nevertheless remain constant in their tacit support at least for the long-term goals of the Ambonese.

It is now clear that relationships between the Ambonese (or South Moluccans, as they are now known), and the Dutch present a major problem of group relations. Young Moluccans have formed themselves into groups of 'South Moluccan Panthers' and wear hair-styles, uniforms, berets, and weaponry strongly resembling those of the American Black Panthers. New slogans, such as 'Maak Soeharto Dood' have appeared on the walls in Amsterdam. Marien (1971) shows that there has been a resurgence of Ambonese nationalism since 1965: the slow but steady process of integration sketched by Wittermans and others has been reversed, and the overt aims of the most vociferous section of this community are now those of separatism, rather than integration; friction between South Moluccans and Dutchmen is frequent. Marien points out that this new generation of nationalists is an educated group, and education *per se* has done nothing to foster the integration process. Van Amersfoort too (1971) has shown that the young Moluccans have rejected the passive, or ritualistic adaptation to Dutch culture of their parents.

Following The Hague incidents two reports appeared on Dutch T.V. about miserable economic conditions in the Moluccas. The

[25] These events took place after my systematic investigation of public opinion of race relations issues (see later chapters) had been completed.

message of the T.V. commentators was that life for the Moluccans was a good deal better in Europe than in the Far East. Yet the response of the Moluccans themselves to these programmes was one of nationalist fervour, and the desire to return home to make things better.

Further eruptions involving South Moluccans occurred in the summer of 1971 in Weert, when a simple bar quarrel over a girl ended in a pitched battle in the streets between large numbers of Moluccans and Dutchmen. Then in August 1971 a bar quarrel in Roermond erupted into a similar incident, leading to stone throwing and fist fights between black and white groups. A Dutchman was wounded in a stabbing incident. Police fired their pistols (which every Dutch policeman carries on duty) to disperse the crowd, and in doing so shot and killed a 20-year-old Dutch soldier in civilian clothes. Press reports[26] indicated that this man was a bystander, uninvolved in the fighting. Friction between young Moluccans and the police seems to have been of long standing, and when a number of Moluccans were arrested after the rioting, a large demonstration was organized for the following day. The marching Moluccans were greeted with derisory and hostile cries from onlookers, and cries of 'maak die bruinen af' ('finish the darkies off') and 'maak ze kapot' ('tear 'em to pieces') were heard.

Buikhuizen (1971) reports that the crime rate in young Moluccans is rising rapidly; this crime is mostly of a group nature, and appears to be an expression of the general frustration felt by these youngsters at the failure of their aspirations. Buikhuizen outlines four major problems: a solution to the diplomatic problem of the Free Republic of the South Moluccas; a less sensational treatment of the activities of young Moluccans by some sections of the Dutch press; the problem of relationships with the police; and discrimination by bar-owners, youth-cafés, and dance halls against the apparently non-conforming Moluccans. Such discrimination, similar to that experienced by non-conforming Italians and Moroccans undoubtedly exists, and serves to remind one that Dutch tolerance is forthcoming only for groups who clearly conform to standards of public morality.

Buikhuizen has urged that a policy of 'enforced dispersal' should be applied to the South Moluccans, since their delinquency and

[26] See *Haagse Post Deze Week* (11 August 1971), and the editorial comments of *De Volkskrant* (2 August 1971).

deviance has an obvious group basis. This suggestion has been vigorously resisted by Wagenveld (1971). Wagenveld, Chief of the Moluccan Section of the Ministry of Culture argues that what is required is not dispersal, but a more vigorous effort to build up the sense of identity of the Moluccans, and that from this enhanced social identity a realistic social purpose will emerge. He has also stressed that more efforts should be made by the Dutch public to understand the difficult position of the Moluccans. A group called *Stichting* I.C.A.A.N.—Interchurch Agencies for Contact with Ambonese—has been formed specially for this purpose (Hansen 1971). It is obvious that in accommodating the Moluccans, and handling the relationships between them and the Dutch public the Ministry of Culture, Recreation, and Social Work has a major problem on its hands.

It is difficult to see any gleams of light in possible diplomatic negotiations over the future of the islands of South Molucca. Queen Juliana received a warm welcome on her visit to Djakarta, Indonesia, in August 1971. But in this same month a Russian technical mission returned to the country, indicating a thaw in the strained relations which followed the massacre of communists in 1965. In October 1971, many of those arrested following the coup were still held in detention camps, and a further group of political dissidents was arrested.[27]

## THAI AND CHINESE PEOPLE IN THE NETHERLANDS

The existence of Thai people in the Netherlands is largely due to the propensity of Dutchmen to marry the native population wherever they are set down. During the last war a number of Dutchmen captured by the Japanese in Indonesia were forced to work in Thailand. A number of these Dutchmen took Thai brides and subsequently settled in the Netherlands. A sample of thirty-six Thai people, twenty-two women and fourteen men was studied by Survarnatemee (1966), a Thai post-graduate student working in the Netherlands. Sixteen of the Thai women in the sample had married Dutchmen. In Dutch-Thai marriages in which the woman was Dutch, the couple tended to remain in Thailand. Half of the Thai subjects were Buddhist, the remainder being fairly equally divided between Catholic and Protestant religions. All subjects could speak and read Dutch. A questionnaire investigation found

[27] *De Volkskrant*, 4 October 1971.

that the longer the individual had lived in the Netherlands, the greater was the amount of their adaptation, indicating a clear progress to assimilation.

There are about 5,000 Chinese in the Netherlands, other than those of Chinese descent from Indonesia (de Deugd, 1970).

The Chinese community, descended from seamen, is mainly situated in Rotterdam. Its position is one of integration; little research has, however, been carried out on this group (Vellinga and Wolters, 1971).

## CONCLUSIONS

I have argued that there are two 'ideal types' of relationship between host and immigrant. These are on the one hand integration, when the immigrant group accept the major purposes of the society in which they live, but at the same time maintain a distinct cultural identity which may involve religious, linguistic, geographical, and social homogeneity; and on the other hand, assimilation which implies that the immigrant is absorbed more or less totally into the society in which he finds himself, adopting the norms, customs, and outlook of his new society to the extent of being absorbed geographically, socially, linguistically into the major society. There are deviations from this model which I shall discuss in later chapters: when (*a*) the immigrant group is deviant, and the immigrants do not conform to the norms of the society in which they live, either because of lack of knowledge, or because of a conscious rejection of them; or (*b*) the host society rejects the immigrants despite their conformity to the host society's norms.

In Dutch society the relationship of Javanese, Chinese and Ambonese (except in the last three years) has approximated to the situation of *integration*: these groups have retained a large part of their cultural identity, but at the same time they have been tolerated by Dutch society. In the case of Ambonese it is interesting that their economic contribution has, in the early years of settlement, been marginal. The relationship of the post-war immigrants from Indonesia (and of some other groups, such as Thais) has been one of *assimilation*, of a more or less total absorption. In neither situation has the process of integration and assimilation been perfect. There have been mutual misunderstandings and stereotypes based on the different lifestyles of people brought up in

Indonesia, and the Netherlands. In their early years in the Netherlands the immigrants have often felt isolated and sometimes rejected. But this isolation and rejection seems to be on the grounds of cultural differences, rather than on grounds of colour. It follows that as cultural differences diminish over time, as groups learn to be more culturally contained and understand what cultural behaviour can be overt and what covert, the degree of integration will increase. The learning process will take place too, in the case of assimilation. The evidence reviewed suggests that there is a definite relationship between time in the culture and the degree of social absorption.

My overall conclusions are as follows. Depending on the attitudes and social policy of the host culture, and the political disposition of the immigrants, the relationship between hosts and immigrants will be, *ceteris paribus*, one of *integration* or *assimilation*. In the absence of discrimination on grounds of colour, immigrants will increasingly adapt to their roles of integration or assimilation over time: this is a function of learning what the norms and folkways of the major society are.

Over time, and in the absence of colour discrimination groups of immigrants who have been integrated will tend to be assimilated (i.e. absorbed), into the host culture. This is particularly likely to happen in the second generation. Being educated in Dutch society, as a school-child and student, is a particularly potent way of learning, and internalizing the norms of Dutch culture, and is thus a pathway to assimilation. This will not take place, however, if the immigrant group retains control over the socialization of its members. This is most likely to take place when the immigrants are religiously homogeneous (e.g. Moslem) and form a separate but tolerated pillar of society, with their own schools and social organizations.

In the process of assimilating post-war immigrants from Indonesia, Dutch society has shown a remarkable degree of both altruism and efficient social organization. This has encompassed, and been assisted by, wide sectors of the population.

Deviants, those who have not accepted the Dutch norm of toleration and assistance to immigrants, but who display attitudes of hostility, are likely to be deviant in other areas, and have a low degree of participation in formal religious and social organizations. This suggestion, derived from the work of de Boer-Lasschuyt, will be tested in a later chapter.

The South Moluccans now form a deviant group of immigrants, whose aims are separatist rather than integrationist as such, and there has been considerable friction between Moluccans and Dutch in the past three years. The Moluccans pose a major problem for Dutch community relations workers.

CHAPTER 4

# THE WEST INDIAN IMMIGRANTS

Like Britain, the Netherlands has considerable colonial links with the Caribbean. Immigrants, ethnically very similar to West Indian immigrants to Britain, have been coming to the Netherlands for many decades. These coloured immigrants come from Surinam and the Antilles, former Dutch colonies which now have Dominion status in the tripartite Kingdom of the Netherlands. Since citizens of Surinam and the Antilles have Dutch citizenship, they have the right of free entry to the Netherlands, and they are migrating to the mother country in increasing numbers. Britain has placed severe restrictions on the entry of Caribbean immigrants; the Netherlands has not. In order to understand Netherlands policy, and the attitude of both Dutch leaders and public to West Indian immigration we must consider the background of such migration in a little detail.

The ethnic composition, history, and social structure of Surinam (contiguous to Guyana) and the Antilles (a group of islands near to the Venezuelan coast) are rather different. But they possess certain similarities within the framework of the development of Caribbean societies. Such societies, as Van Lier (1950) has pointed out, have been created by European initiative and are 'segmentary societies' of recent development, each society containing a number of different ethnic groups. Characteristic of such societies was miscegenation of the European ruling class with imported African slaves, resulting in a 'coloured' intermediate group sensitive about status and anxious to adopt the European view of the world. This included the ideology that a slave was 'lazy, beastlike, pagan, a being only partly human and towards which all actions were permissible'. This ideology *had* to be true for the slave-traders and planters if they were to continue in business with any conscience. The white ruling class at the same time existed in fear of slave rebellions. These were not infrequent, and were savagely suppressed. At the same time the coloured middle class was disliked because of their aspirations to status and education which represented a threat to white superiority. There was a general and mutual disrespect between the three segments of the Caribbean societies.

In such highly segmented societies any kind of national consensus did not exist, and solidarity within the segments themselves was weak. The strongest bonds holding the white group together were race consciousness, and fear of rebellion by the slaves, or the black proletariat which they became. The intermediate group had only a weak solidarity: their major motivation was to marry white, and be white, not to establish links with their fellow coloureds. The slaves themselves were not a homogeneous group. They came from various parts of Africa and had various tribal and religious divisions. In Surinam the slaves were further removed from the coloured and white segments than they were in other Caribbean colonies. The Dutch practised their system of 'culture tolerance' (which might in this context be interpreted as an extreme aloofness) to the extent that the language of the slaves was English, while that of the middle and upper classes was Dutch. In addition, proselytization was infrequent, and the slaves retained to a large degree elements of their tribal religions. Van Lier cites evidence to suggest that nowhere in the New World are African cultural elements as prevalent as in Surinam. This is illustrated, for example, by a report (Schakels, 1969) of the life of 'Bushnegroes' in the interior of Surinam. These people, descendants of slaves, have a strongly African culture with dialects, art-forms, and religious and magical practices very similar to those of the parts of Africa from whence they were transported.

Slavery in Surinam was abolished in 1863. Considerable social change occurred in the years following this event and slaves left the plantations in large numbers and moved to towns and cities in the coastal plain. Many of the white ruling class returned to the Netherlands, and they were followed by members of the coloured middle class. There has been in fact a tradition of receiving higher education in the Netherlands. This is in contrast to the British Caribbean, where the coloured middle class received higher education with the development of universities in the West Indies, and only atypically came to the metropolitan country for this purpose.

Labour for the plantations was recruited in two areas, in Java, and in British India. The migrants from Java arrived as contract labourers in the period 1893 to 1916 and the Indians in the period 1873 to 1916. A small Chinese trading class also came to Surinam in this period. After their period of contract labour was over both Hindu and Javanese groups acquired land as small farmers. Hindus, by virtue of asceticism and hard work acquired capital and power, and tend to be an educated and upwardly mobile group. The Javanese by contrast are similar in culture to the Javanese immigrants to The Hague we described earlier: they tend to be generous, unthrifty, spending money acquired from wages or crops on entertaining friends and on immediate gratification of various kinds. The ethnographic study of the Javanese in Surinam by Geertz (1960) suggests that Javanese culture survives in a very compact form. The Javanese speak, by and large, only their own language, but the Hindustani population is bilingual. Significant numbers of the Hindustani community have moved to the towns, and have also migrated to the Netherlands where they are centred in The Hague.

The changes in social structure after 1863 created a need for teachers and officials in Surinam, and these were recruited not only from the coloured middle class but also from the black lower class.[1] By the time the Hindu community was established, a number of the coloured community were occupying elite positions. Members of the Hindu community too, have risen into elite positions in the twentieth century. But among the Javanese community there is little stratification: they are a lower middle-class group of farmers and small traders, and very few have either migrated to the towns or to the Netherlands, or entered the professions. Up to 1954, when self-determination with Dominion-style links to the motherland was granted, whites dominated the elite structure (although less so after an interim agreement of 1949).

Language is still an important factor in stratification, Dutch being spoken by the middle classes and by anyone aspiring to upward mobility (which includes migrants to the Netherlands). A form of English is spoken by the African (black and coloured)

[1] Since 1876 all children living in the populated coastal belt, aged between 6 and 12 years had to attend school. This was years before the introduction of similar compulsory education in the Netherlands. Today one-third of the total budget is allocated to education. Illiteracy is virtually unknown (Gastmann, 1968, p. 7).

proletariat, and Hindi and Javanese by the other two segments of society, and of these, Hindus are most likely to speak Dutch as well.

Migration to the Netherlands has had its effects on the social structure of Surinam. The propensity of the coloured group is to be upwardly mobile; but at the same time this class underwent, as Van Lier (1955) says, 'a continuous drain of its strength because a large number of its members have left for the Netherlands and the Netherlands Antilles'. There has been, as Van Amersfoort (1968) points out, a long history of two-way traffic between Surinam and the Netherlands, especially on the part of the middle class, for both economic and educational reasons.

The evidence presented by Buve (1963) indicates that the tradition of migration from Surinam to the Netherlands goes back to the eighteenth century. House servants came with their masters to the Netherlands, a practice similar to that carried on by British colonialists in the West Indies. What, however, is distinctive about the Netherlands practice was that in addition slaves were sent to Amsterdam to be trained for a trade, or to gain a general education. Van Lier (1949) points out that the Dutch colonialists not only sent their children by European wives back to the Netherlands to be educated, but also their children by Negro wives and concubines. In this way an educated, coloured middle class grew up. Moreover, the strong tradition of obtaining further and higher education in the Netherlands meant a steady flow of blacks to the mother country. Van Lier comments: 'Colonial society in Surinam, where the coloured man was regarded as a second-class citizen in spite of his university education, had little attraction for him once he had lived in Europe. He had outgrown that society and felt more at home in Europe or in the East [East Indies] where he could forget about discrimination, than in Paramaribo' (Van Lier, 1949, p. 261).

Surinamers have been a common sight in Amsterdam for some 150 years. Van Amersfoort (1968) surveying the immigration from Surinam stated:

> The Netherlands has never experienced an influx of Surinamese immigrants, whose economic position was weak and who crowded together in ghetto-like quarters in the larger towns. Such an influx of immigrants occurred even before World War II, in the United Kingdom, in Cardiff, for instance, and in Rotterdam where Chinese immigrants lived under most unfavourable conditions as described by Van Keek

(1936). Surinamese immigrants in the Netherlands did not pose any problems for Dutch society, which indeed paid very little attention to them (p. 14).

Post-war immigrants from Surinam and the Antilles have been more numerous than pre-war and less occupationally homogeneous. Their migration is discussed later in this chapter.

## THE ECONOMY AND STRUCTURE OF SURINAM

Surinam's economy in the twentieth century has been heavily reliant upon the export of bauxite, so that a decline in world trade in the late 1920s hit Surinam badly. Such relative deprivation was accompanied by an increasing hostility to the Dutch. Van Lier says (1955):

> This antagonism was increased still further by the fact that the governing group consisted mainly of Dutch officials sent out from the Netherlands who had often to take important decisions. . . . There was also a tendency discernible in the administration to withhold important positions from Surinamese. The antagonistic attitude was reflected in the local press, which had considerable influence on public opinion. . . . Economic difficulties led to aggressive outbursts among the frustrated masses which rendered it necessary to restore order by force. Usually such national movements collapsed at the first sign of an energetic display of power.

After 1945, however, economic conditions in Surinam improved, and a special commission from Barbados which visited Surinam in 1948 (Poole, 1951) reported that in comparison with other parts of the Caribbean there was an ample supply of food, and a high standard of nutrition. The birth rate was 34·2/1,000 and the death rate 11·3/1,000. The Barbadian commission found that the school-children were 'well-nourished and healthy, with free lunches to most school-children of lower income'. This relative prosperity may have accounted for the quiet passage of independence which, after a long period of secret negotiations, was ratified by the Dutch Parliament in 1954. Population figures are shown in Table 4:1.

*Table 4:1. The population structure of Surinam at the Latest Count (Schakels, 1969)*

| | | | |
|---|---|---|---|
| Total population | 324,211 | African (black and coloured) | 114,961 |
| Hindustani | 112,633 | Javanese | 48,463 |
| American Indian | 2,979 | Chinese | 5,339 |
| European | 4,322 | Bushnegroes[2] in tribes | 27,698 |
| Indians in tribes | 4,308 | Others | 3,508 |

We can see from this population breakdown that there are three major ethnic groups within Surinam, Negroes (a generic term to include both 'blacks' or lower class, and 'coloured' being the middle class or 'Creole' segment),[3] Hindustanis and Javanese. These three groups tend to be linguistically and religiously different from one another. The Europeans and the coloured middle class belong in the main to the Dutch Reformed and Lutheran churches; the black lower class are Catholics or Herenhutters; of the Asian population the Indians are Hindu, and the Javanese adhere to Islam. The three main groups have different life styles, food, and dress. Political parties reflect these ethnic divisions: there is a Moslem Party, a Hindu Party,[4] a Surinam Progressive People's Party, dominated by Catholics, a Christian Social Democratic Party dominated by the minor sects, and a National Party of Surinam. This last party is open to all, but has its strongest support among the Negro middle class. Following universal suffrage, granted in 1949 with the gradual withdrawal of the Dutch, the National Party emerged as the strongest party. Poole, commenting on the segmentation of political parties on ethnic and religious lines, suggested that the country possessed, as a result, a great potential for political instability. But in the seventeen years

[2] 'Bushnegroes' are descendants of African slaves who escaped into the bush shortly after transportation to Surinam, and re-established their tribal life. They are, therefore, an extremely interesting group from an anthropological point of view, and a source of pride and interest for Afro-American groups in the Americas. These African tribal groups appear to be unique to Surinam, and do not exist in other slave societies in the Americas.

[3] As Hoetink points out (1967), in North America no intermediate middle class of coloureds developed, and children of plantation 'miscegenation' were assigned to the lowest class regardless of skin colour. In making the generic classification of 'Negro' we must be careful to avoid the fallacy, which Hoetink outlines, of assuming that because coloured–white relations are equable, the lot of the entire population of African origin is tolerable. In Surinam, as Van Lier points out (1955) there is still a class division on colour lines.

[4] There have recently been schisms in the Hindu party in Surinam.

following Poole's prediction, overt social conflict in Surinam has not emerged. But in neighbouring Guyana, formerly British Guiana, severe social conflict has occurred between the two major ethnic groups, Negro and Indian. This differential experience suggests that developing, ethnically heterogeneous societies may experience social conflict, but under different structural conditions this is not necessarily the case. Mitchell (1963) has in fact observed that the bitterness which marks party debates in Guyana is notably lacking in Surinam.

The idea of Surinam as a 'plural society' in the sense of Furnivall's definition has been developed by a number of writers, notably Van Lier (1950), Speckman (1964), and Hoetink (1967). Van Lier says:

> In the plural society there is no unity of race or religion and the religions differ typologically; the groups also live in different economic spheres. . . . It may be said that in the plural society the social differences between the heterogeneous groups are greater than those in the simple society, but at the same time there is a stronger feeling of solidarity within the groups of the plural society than in those of the simpler society.

These groups are bound together by their mutual interest in trade, and by loose national bonds.

Segmented or plural societies seem to possess great potential for social conflict: but Dutch society itself is segmented, as shown in Chapter 1, and it is also socially harmonious and democratic. The structural mechanisms by which social harmony is ensured are extremely interesting, for they suggest possibilities for the resolution of social conflict in other plural societies. These preconditions for harmony appear to be: (*i*) There should be as little imbalance as possible in the wealth and access to education and means of production between the segments; (*ii*) there should be at least some feelings of nationalism cutting across ethnic and religious boundaries, e.g. as a response to some external threat; (*iii*) all segments should have access to political power in proportion to their representation in the community; (*iv*) negotiations about major societal goals should take place between leaders of the segments on a secret, diplomatic basis in the same way that different countries negotiate with one another; (*v*) there should be agreement to differ on religious issues, and no group should try to convert members of other groups to its own religion.

There is some evidence that these *verzuiling* principles, evolved in the Netherlands over many decades, have influenced the development of relationships between ethnic groups in Surinam. Since Surinamers receiving higher education went to the Netherlands for this purpose, it is fair to suppose that they absorbed, to some degree at least, the *verzuiling* principles of Dutch society. Mitchell (1963), an English observer, did in fact comment on 'the strong spirit of compromise' between ethnic groups in Surinam which he found lacking in Guyana. Unity is in fact achieved, according to Van Lier (1950) through the framework of the European superstructure, and through the fact that the most educated in each group speak Dutch and have probably been educated in the Netherlands. In this respect the Javanese represent a potential threat to the stability of Surinam society, for this group has taken least interest in social mobility—into professional positions, and in its concomitant, geographical mobility, which has brought both political sophistication and middle-class status.

The national flag of Surinam is black, brown, red, white, and yellow, intentionally symbolic of the skin colour of the ethnic groups which make up the society of Surinam. On an overt level relationships between the ethnic groups appear to be equable and easy-going, and an American observer (Thompson, 1967) commented on this favourably as an indication of mutual tolerance. Van Lier (1950) was, however, more pessimistic. He saw rather,

> A weak total society, with no social ideals to inspire the individual and to stimulate his social activity. . . . Lassitude characterizes the social life of Surinam . . . the individual has a feeling of ineffectiveness and isolation. Although an easy going friendliness and willingness to help are displayed in social intercourse, the distrust of individuals to each other is always awake.

The phenomenon of the number of, and the tolerance of, mixed marriages which we remarked on in the chapter on Indonesia seems to have occurred in Surinam too. Hoetink notes that the number of such mixed unions was greater in Surinam than in Jamaica, but attributes this to structural factors—the lack of available European women—rather than to ideological ones. Poole, however, comparing the social structure of the Caribbean countries observed (1951): 'The Dutch handled the colour problem very simply. There are no colour bars or discrimination. Social barriers are based only upon the usual preference of individuals for their own kind. Negro and white children are educated in common, and intermarriage between races is widely practised.' Thompson (1967) went so far as to refer to Surinam as a 'multi-racial paradise' when contrasted with North America. She was struck both by the number of interracial marriages, and the mixed ethnic ancestry of the people, and commented that, 'If interracial marriages and unions continue at their present rate, assimilation can't be far behind.' The situation seems similar to the Netherlands, where, I have argued, religion is far more important as a factor in social differentiation than colour, but where, nevertheless, there is a movement towards increasing intermarriage between religious groups. A marriage between a Catholic and Protestant in Holland is a cause for comment, and disapproval by the most traditional; but it is a phenomenon of society, just as a marriage between say a Creole and a Hindu is an acceptable phenomenon of Surinamese society. In the main, however, religious groups in Holland and religious and ethnic groups in Surinam tend to be endogamous.

Thompson (a black American) interviewed fifty Surinamers and reported a universal acceptance—in principle at least—of interracial marriage. Moreover, fifty-five per cent of those questioned said that conflict of the Guyanese type could not happen in Surinam. There appears in fact to be a conscious ethic of 'verbroedering', an explicit acceptance of the ethical principle that ethnic groups ought to co-operate in the running of society. In line with this very Dutch ethic is a system of proportional representation which means that no party can rule without the support of the other parties, and a more or less permanent coalition government—as in the Netherlands—is the result.

Three factors affect the continuance of social harmony in Surinam. The first of these is economic: both Poole (1950) and Mitchell (1963) were struck by the relative prosperity of Surinam, and Mitchell commented that it was more prosperous than its contiguous neighbours, French and British Guiana. Mitchell also suggests that the Dutch had surplus capital for investment after the loss of Indonesia when they were anxious to justify themselves as a colonial power, both in substantive and ethical terms. For this reason they seem to have devoted far more resources to the development of Surinam than either Britain or France have done to their Caribbean territories.

We suggest that economic factors are important for harmonious relationships in a segmented society for two reasons. First of all, following Parsons's economic analogy on circulating power (1963), social conflict may result from economic deprivation. Put very simply, when resources are short, different groups of society, be they classes or religious or ethnic groups, tend to quarrel, not merely over the division of resources, but over many other issues as well. Economic prosperity is a necessary, but not sufficient, condition for social peace. Secondly, economic growth tends to be a function of urbanization and increasing trading activity on the part of members of society. In the towns, as Speckman points out (1964) the various ethnic groups are increasingly in contact. This interaction provides, in Furnivall's terms, the necessary cement of the plural society. From a Durkheimian[5] point of view, during a period of significant economic growth relatively underdeveloped societies tend to change from 'mechanical' to 'organic' societies, from brittle structures without societally agreed value systems to more organic systems, where individuals, by virtue of the technological complexity of society, take on increasingly diverse and complex roles and interact with a broader range of people, including members of other ethnic groups. There is a tendency, as Parsons and Shils have observed (1951) for individuals involved in such interaction to develop mutually agreed definitions of such interaction: in this way normative consensus begins to cut across ethnic or religious boundaries. It is possible for ethnic groups to retain a high degree of separate identity while they exist as peasant farmers, or small traders: but when the members of different ethnic groups are employed in the construction of, say, a hydro-electric plant, interethnic interaction becomes inevitable. As I have observed in another context (Bagley 1969a), such interaction leads, other things being equal, to a greater degree of tolerance between ethnic groups.

It is interesting to note that, according to Mitchell (1963), Surinam's hydro-electric scheme, which will make possible the domestic smelting of bauxite, will also make Surinam dominant over her neighbour, Guyana. In the case of Guyana it seems viable to argue that the severe social conflict in the 1950s and early 1960s had as its basis an observable imbalance in the distribution of resources and political power: this imbalance in power (concentrated in Indian hands) became intolerable when it was

[5] This argument is developed by Durkeim in *The Division of Labour in Society*.

associated with an absolute or relative economic deprivation. Racial divisions in the United States provide another such example: a few Negroes obtain middle class status, but the vast majority of Afro-Americans have neither power nor wealth, in a society which places great emphasis on the possession of observable wealth. Social conflict (violent civil rights movements) are the result of such an imbalance.[6] In Surinam, one ethnic minority—the Javanese—may in the future find themselves in such a position of observable relative deprivation.

There is a further variation to this model: if the members of the various ethnic groups are employed *at the same grade* in the hydro-electric plant, and the supervisory and managerial grades are monopolized by a single ethnic group (e.g. whites) who exploit the workers, then these workers will tend to develop a proletarian type of group-consciousness. There is some evidence to indicate that this is precisely what led to the Willemstad riots of 1969 on the former Dutch island of Curaçao. It is to the Dutch Antilles that I now turn.

## THE DEVELOPMENT AND SOCIAL STRUCTURE OF THE ANTILLES

The former Netherlands Antilles are in two groups, the Leeward Islands of Curaçao, Aruba, and Bonaire, and the Windward Islands of St. Eustatius, Saba, and the Dutch portion of St. Martin. Of these islands the most important are Curaçao and Aruba, twenty and thirty miles respectively from the Venezuelan coast. Curaçao was captured from the Spanish by the Dutch in 1634, and most of the indigenous Indians left with the Spanish for the mainland. From this time Curaçao was a 'segmented society' of the three groups each with a separate cultural identity: the imported Negro slaves; a commercial population of Sephardic Jews; and a Dutch ruling class. Curaçao was a trading island, not a plantation economy. Hoetink (1967) suggests that this fact fundamentally affected the treatment of slaves in the direction of tolerance. The Dutch elite was Protestant and exclusive, having strong links with the Dutch Reformed church and the city of Amsterdam. 'In house construction, food and apparel, style, usage and fashion of the mother country was maintained with an

[6] I have developed this argument more fully elsewhere (Bagley 1970a). See also Runciman and Bagley (1969).

obstinacy that yielded only reluctantly to the tropical climate,' says Hoetink. The Dutch community was itself stratified into a semi-aristocratic elite, emphasizing their Orangeness, and disdaining marriage with groups lower in status; and a Dutch middle-class group. The marriage partners of the elite were newly arrived women from the Netherlands, but the middle and lower middle-class Dutch strata, despite being Protestant, often had recourse to Catholic wives from mainland Venezuela. But the Dutch would not learn Spanish or Portuguese, and trading links with the mainland were maintained by the Sephardic community. Originally from Brazil, their principal language was Portuguese. The Jewish community was highly adaptable and by the mid-nineteenth century had acquired considerable wealth and had begun to penetrate elite positions. After 1870 Dutch rather than Portuguese was used in Synagogues.

The exclusiveness of the Dutch community in Curaçao meant that interethnic marriages were much rarer than in the plantation economy of Surinam, and a significant 'coloured' middle class did not develop. Africans have always been numerically the largest segment in Curaçao: in 1914 they numbered 26,000 as against 4,000 Europeans and 1,000 Sephardic Jews. The Protestant Dutch did not attempt to convert the black population to Christianity. This task was left to Catholic missionaries who were licensed, and in some cases subsidized, by the state.

The 1920s were a period of rapid social change, which saw the setting up of a giant Shell plant which refined oil from Venezuela. A similar large refinery was established by Standard Oil on the island of Aruba, where both the original social structure and development of society have many similarities to Curaçao's. A consequence of the establishment of these refineries was a large population growth, and an accompanying rise in general prosperity. The Antilles have become a centre for migrant labour, not only from Surinam but from the British Caribbean as well. The population of Curaçao rose from 30,000 in 1914 to 125,000 in 1969. The influx of capital, migrant workers, and Dutch and other European technicians meant that the traditional balance of society was changed, and the exclusiveness of the Dutch ruling class declined. The commercial position of the Jewish population was enhanced by these changes, and the position of the traditional Dutch community has changed from one of a ruling elite to that of an isolated minority group fighting a rearguard action to maintain vestiges of tradition and power in the face of a rapidly changing situation.

The traditional colonial policy of the Dutch in Curaçao has been described favourably by a number of observers. The treatment of slaves was lenient in comparison with Surinam and other islands, and manumission in times of trade slackness was common. The tolerance shown by the Protestant ruling minority for the Catholic majority (to the extent of paying the salaries of priests) reflects the tolerance of the plural society of the Netherlands. Nationalist movements, at least before the Second World War, were largely absent, and the society was marked by a high degree of loyalty to the Dutch crown and an atmosphere of social peace (Poole, 1951).

Social change in Curaçao in recent times has been in the direction of the development of a nationalist movement, unifying diverse elements in the society and putting pressure on the Netherlands for independence. Hoetink has commented, 'To put it into seemingly paradoxical terms, in the segmented society of Curaçao, this nationalist movement can be described as the expression of a wish to achieve a homogeneous society with the retention of the *status quo* of the segments; it fostered a temporary feeling of solidarity against the colonial mother country, and all who were not "natives"' (Hoetink, 1967, p. 118). The two Protestant strata in society, the traditional elite, and the middle classes, have joined to form a single Protestant party. The alternative party is led by a university-educated coloured man, with Sephardic ancestry and a Jewish name. This party has the support of the rural Negroes, and of the Jewish community. Social change seems to be moving in the direction of a value consensus among the working-class sector of the population, supported to a certain extent from a nationalist point of view by pragmatic sections of the middle class, especially the Jewish community.

In May 1969, serious riots broke out in Willemstad, the capital of Curaçao, and at the same time workers at the Shell plant went on strike. The ostensible cause seems to have been the laying-off of a number of workers employed by Shell, and the lowering of the wages of other workers. Large parts of the commercial centre of Willemstad were burned, and demonstrators marched on Parliament. Order was restored by 600 Dutch marines, invited under the constitutional arrangements between Curaçao and the Netherlands. The disturbances in Curaçao seem to have been manifestations of revolt by an exploited proletariat, rather than the interethnic clashes that have characterized Guyana. The process of industrialization appears to have broken down the traditional pattern of 'pillarization' in Antillean society.

## THE CONSTITUTIONAL LINKS OF THE NETHERLANDS WITH SURINAM AND THE ANTILLES

Following the loss of Indonesia the Dutch West Indies assumed a far greater importance. According to Mitchell (1963) immense pains were taken to ensure the stability and loyalty of these remaining jewels. Secret negotiations were begun about the future partnership of Surinam and the Antilles with the Netherlands in 1946. The settlement was announced in 1954. The negotiations were delicate and secret, but the terms of the agreement seem successfully to have accommodated the nationalist spirit in these countries. The 1954 charter was, Mitchell says, 'An intricate and subtle document designed to combine the desire of Surinam and the Netherlands Antilles for the maximum of self-government and appearance of independence with their wish to remain part of the Kingdom of the Netherlands.' Close integration on French lines was unacceptable, but the arrangements agreed gave the former colonies much closer links with the mother country than the former British Caribbean territories. On this Mitchell comments that, 'Surinam and the Netherlands Antilles had achieved a position of far greater influence in Dutch affairs than had Puerto Rico with its single observer at Washington.'

The progress of Surinam and the Antilles towards independence is an important illustration of accommodation. The changes in constitution were heralded in 1937 with the establishment of a new set of constitutional laws called the *Staatsregelingen*. These laws widened the franchise, but nevertheless because of economic inequality excluded many Javanese and Hindus from it. Representations to the governor were made on these grounds by the Hindustani and Javanese communities, and as a result five extra members representing these groups were appointed to the *Staten* (Gastmann, 1968, p. 14). From the first, special efforts had been made in the movement to independence to ensure that ethnic groups were represented in proportion to their numbers in the community. Further accommodation to the cultural autonomy of the Hindu and Mohammedan groups was made in 1940 when marriages regulated according to Indian and Islamic religious custom were recognized as legal. This action, on the part of Governor Kielstra did provoke considerable protest from African members of the Surinamese *Staten* who saw it as an action 'which would prevent the fusion of the three principal races of the country into one people' (Gastmann, p. 17). Nevertheless, after considerable negotiations, the principles of formal equality of culturally separate blocs has been incorporated into the Surinamese social and legal structure.

Demands for independence were, by and large, for autonomy within a tripartite Kingdom, and the pressures of Surinam and the Antilles in this respect were successful. The Kingdom is in itself a plural society, consisting of three major blocs, culturally and politically separate from one another. These blocs are bound together by mutual interests of trade, defence, and international relations. Relationships between them, like the relationships between blocs in the Netherlands, are conducted secretly and diplomatically. The negotiations on the Kingdom took part in the years when the Netherlands still hoped to retain links with Indonesia, and undoubtedly the Netherlands would have welcomed a Kingdom in which Indonesia was an equal partner. The doctrine of plurality succeeded in the case of Surinam and the Antilles, where it had failed in Indonesia. It failed in that country because it came too late, at a time when Indonesian nationalists already had considerable strategic power, power which was largely absent in the Dutch West Indies.

The constitutional arrangements concerning Surinam and the Antilles ensured that the former colonies had complete internal self-government; but on certain 'Kingdom affairs' the Netherlands was to have responsibility, in consultation with the other two partners in the Kingdom. These areas are foreign affairs, external defence, citizenship and naturalization, and amendment of the constitution. This meant that the Netherlands would have to be consulted in the event of major changes concerning human rights and freedoms and the administration of justice. If the 'plenipotentiary Minister' of Surinam or the Antilles resident in the Netherlands objects to a proposal of the Dutch Parliament which affects his country, and it receives less than three-fifths of the votes in the Second Chamber, then the proposed Act must be referred to a special committee for consideration. This committee consists of the Prime Minister of the Netherlands, two Cabinet

Ministers, the Minister Plenipotentiary from the country concerned, and a special representative of the concerned government (Minister of Foreign Affairs, 1956).

Citizens of Surinam and the Antilles are, by virtue of membership of the tripartite Kingdom, automatically Dutch citizens. This means that they have automatic right of entry to the Netherlands. The granting of Netherlands citizenship is deemed to be a Kingdom affair, since it involves all three countries: a man given citizenship by Surinam would then have automatic right of entry to the Netherlands (Article of the Constitution 3.1c). But what if the Netherlands wants to put a limit to the number of West Indians emigrating to the mother country, just as Britain curbed coloured immigrants with the 1962 Commonwealth Immigrants Act? There is some ambiguity in the constitution on this point. The 1954 Charter, Article 3.1f on 'Supervision of the General Provisions governing the admission and expulsion of Netherlands Nationals' states that,

> Since all the three component parts of the Kingdom enjoy the status of Netherlands nationals, it is evident that Netherlands nationality is a Kingdom affair . . . although each of the countries is free to establish rules for the admission and expulsion of Netherlands nationals the partnership of the countries within the Kingdom makes the supervision of enforcement of general provisions on behalf of the Kingdom desirable.

In substance, if the Netherlands Government wishes to slow down coloured immigration, it is entitled to introduce a Bill into the Second Chamber proposing this. But the Government must have consulted the Plenipotentiary Ministers concerned, and if they object to the Bill it must have a three-fifths majority before it can be passed. It seems that such a Bill would cause serious strain to the delicate Kingdom constitution. It would be a strong inducement to the countries concerned to withdraw from the Kingdom, and this would be a severe blow to Netherlands pride and the self-image of that country as a just and enlightened colonial power. Each of the signatories of the Kingdom Charter has the option of withdrawal after ten years. The Charter was accepted by all concerned in 1964, ten years after its original introduction. But serious attempts by the Netherlands to slow down coloured immigration (action which is in fact very unlikely, though mooted in some left-wing quarters) might well result in the repudiation of the Charter by the former colonies in 1974.

It is interesting to compare the situation with England, for here a Conservative Government introduced control of coloured immigration, and was opposed by the Labour Opposition. In the Netherlands the political position is reversed. It is the right-wing parties who are most in favour of the constitutional links with the former colonies, since they have been traditional supporters of Dutch colonialism. They are anxious, therefore, to maintain the full Dutch citizenship of the citizens of Surinam and the Antilles, and this inevitably means uncontrolled immigration. It is the left wing, and the trade union parties, traditionally un-enamoured with colonialism and anxious about competition in the labour market, who occasionally suggest that the Kingdom links should be ended, and that Surinamers and Antilleans should not have automatic right of free entry.[7] The Catholic Centre party holds the reins of power, and governs (or influences government) in consultation with both right and left. These two opposing voices on coloured immigration will almost certainly cancel one another out, and there seems to be anxiety to keep acrimonious debate on race relations issues, which occasionally dominates the British political scene, absent from the arena of politics in the Netherlands. Race relations and coloured immigration seem to be one of those inter-*verzuiling* disputes on which the rules of political business have placed a silent embargo. In these circumstances it does not seem likely that the Dutch Government will take any action on coloured immigration in the next decade. The only circumstances which might affect the position are, as Longemann points out (1955), serious internal violence in one of the Kingdom countries leading to a government largely hostile to the Netherlands. Despite the Wilemstad riots of 1969, there does not seem to be any likely prospect of this in the immediate future. The Kingdom partners are aware that if they repudiate their association with the Netherlands, then free immigration to that country would no longer be possible.

The association with the Netherlands has considerable financial advantages for Surinam and the Antilles. The 'external' Kingdom arrangements mean that they do not have to bear the heavy cost of maintaining a foreign service. In 1961 the Netherlands Government made available $33,375,000 for the development of the Antilles. For both Antilles and Surinam the association with the

[7] There is a certain ambiguity in the left-wing position, since some sections fear that independence would lay Surinam and the Antilles open to exploitation by American capitalism.

Netherlands also has considerable commercial advantages. Longemann has suggested that the Kingdom arrangement has other functions than the purely commercial. For Surinam especially it gives a framework of nationalism and a certain loyalty to Dutch ideals, which provides the cement of a pluralistic society. For the Antilles a loose federal connection with the Netherlands has many advantages from the point of view of world trade and politics.[8]

Longemann points out that the Netherlands makes much fewer demands on the Antilles than would be the case in an association with Venezuela, which is a serious alternative for the Antilles because of the economic links with that country. The Antilles is, however, the most likely candidate to seek independence from the Netherlands in future decades. However political predictions of this nature are beset with difficulty.

## THE WEST INDIAN IMMIGRANTS IN THE NETHERLANDS

There has been a 'steady trickle' of immigration from Surinam and the Antilles to the Netherlands for many decades, but in the early 1960s this migration began to speed up. By 31 December 1966, there were approximately 16,000 such migrants in the Netherlands (Van Amersfoort, 1968), and by 1969 the number had risen to approximately 25,000.[9] Taking into account differences in population size, in British terms this would mean a population of about 100,000 West Indian immigrants in the mother country. Exact numbers are difficult to obtain since these West Indians are Dutch citizens with the right of free entry. Only since 1959 have special efforts been made to try and assess the numbers entering the country. Of the estimated 25,000, 18,000 are from Surinam and 7,000 from the Antilles. Latest estimates put the number of Surinamers at 30,000, and of Antilleans at 10,000 (Bovenkerk and van Galen, 1971). Ebbeling (1971) puts the numbers of West Indians at 45,000.

There is a dearth of information about the adaptation of these West Indian migrants, and the studies reviewed below seem to be the only ones on how West Indians fare in Dutch society. This

[8] It is in the Antilles, rather than the more pluralistic society of Surinam, that voices arguing for independence are strongest. Very radical groups of Surinamese students have been formed in Amsterdam, but these have no influence on internal politics in Surinam.

[9] Ministry of Culture, Recreation and Social Work, Community Relations Division, Personal Communication, 1969.

dearth of studies is in fact itself a function of public policy. An academic informant told the writer that there was governmental pressure on universities not to do research in this area. Research in the Netherlands is highly formalized, a doctorate being granted only after many years of advanced research. Thus the choice of a topic for research is extremely important and has to have the fullest approval and co-operation of all the authorities involved. For this reason unpopular research is unlikely to take place. What research has been conducted has been mainly under the direct guidance of the Ministry of Culture, Recreation, and Social Work, which has commissioned the studies by Bayer (1965) and Van Amersfoort (1968). It should be added that these are both excellent academic studies, and both present a rather optimistic picture of the adaptation of West Indian immigrants.[10] The one available thesis in this area, that by Soederhuizen (1965) is more pessimistic. However, this was not a doctoral thesis, but one for a social work diploma, and is not as methodologically sophisticated as the two official studies. The apparent reason for the reticence of the authorities to initiate studies in this field is that race is an area of potential controversy and social conflict; and, by the traditional rules of the *verzuiling* system, an overt silence is maintained about such matters. A similar situation exists with respect to academic studies of the class system, about which Goudsblom (1967) commented:

Today *stand* and class are unpopular subjects in the Netherlands. In contrast to *verzuiling*, social stratification is seldom made the topic of public discussion. Occasionally a case of social discrimination by landlords or housing co-operatives makes the news. These incidents invariably arouse a widespread indignation that suggests that such behaviour is not tolerated in the democratic society of the Netherlands. . . . [There is] an inevitable awareness of socioeconomic differences hampered by a reluctance to mention them outright. Even sociologists have tended to shun the subject—they have produced many valuable statistical reports bearing on various aspects of socioeconomic status, but so far no attempt has been made at a comprehensive analysis of social classes in contemporary Dutch society (p. 63).

The same can be said of study in the field of contemporary race relations.

Soederhuizen divides the immigrants into five categories:

[10] A large research project on Surinamers in the Netherlands began in September 1971, under the auspices of the Anthropology Institute of the University of Amsterdam.

(*i*) tourists, and pensioned people who may settle in the Netherlands for long or short periods; (*ii*) students attending university and polytechnic courses who are funded by their governments or by their families; (*iii*) young women aged between 18 and 23 years with some professional training, e.g. as nurses, seeking Netherlands diplomas; (*iv*) young men aged 18–40 years doing semi-skilled or skilled work, who hope to undertake part-time study for academic and technical diplomas; (*v*) a general group of men, women, and children joining those already here, as dependants.

A somewhat similar classification is made by Van Amersfoort, who points out that there has been a long tradition of migration to the mother country for study and retirement. Van Amersfoort, who is concerned with Surinamese immigration, traces a 'trek to the city' (and in particular to Paramaribo where 70 per cent of the migrants set out from) during the past half century. The 'trek to Holland' is part of a continuing movement of geographical, and upward social mobility on the part of the Negro and Hindustani populations. Van Amersfoort includes in the category of 'students' those with professional qualifications who cannot obtain specialist jobs in Paramaribo. A good proportion of those obtaining Dutch professional qualifications and degrees stay in the Netherlands.

The pattern of migration has been for a male to emigrate first, and once established in the Netherlands, to be joined by his wife and family. In the past five years, up to 1969, the rate of immigration from the West Indies has increased, and at the same time women and children are forming an increasing percentage of the immigrants. The youthful age structure of immigrants from Surinam and the Antilles in the period April 1966 to April 1967, is shown in Table 4:2.

*Table 4:2. Age Structure of Immigrants from Surinam and the Antilles*

| *Age distribution* | *Number* |
|---|---|
| 0–15 | 315 |
| 16–20 | 211 |
| 21–30 | 514 |
| 31–40 | 176 |
| 41 and older | 181 |
| Total | 1,397 |

*Source:* Van Amersfoort (1968) p. 54.

By 31 December 1966, the geographical distribution of Surinamers in the Netherlands was as shown in Table 4:3. (Antilleans tend to be concentrated in The Hague.)

*Table 4:3. Geographical Distribution of Surinamers in the Netherlands, December 1966*

| *Area* | *Number* | *Area* | *Number* |
|---|---|---|---|
| Amsterdam | 6,496 | Tilburg | 101 |
| Haarlem | 236 | Eindhoven | 75 |
| Leiden | 321 | Zeist | 114 |
| Den Haag | 1,294 | Wageningen | 137 |
| Delft | 225 | Groningen | 111 |
| Rotterdam | 2,002 | Arnhem | 121 |
| Utrecht | 1,231 | Other towns | 673 |
| Nijmegen | 150 | Total: | 13,287 |

*Source:* Van Amersfoort (1968) p. 53.

On the problems of adaptation, Van Amersfoort points out that the immigrants all speak Dutch, and are familiar with at least the broad outlines of Dutch culture. The main problems are encountered in housing, which is difficult to come by, and expensive, and in employment, where apparently the pace of work is much faster, especially for the semi- and unskilled workers, than in Surinam. This leads to the complaint on the part of some Dutchmen that Surinamers are slow: but apparently the immigrants do not take long to learn the new rhythms of work.

Common-law marriage is common in Surinam, as in other parts of the Caribbean where slavery was practised, and this fact causes some conflict with Dutch mores. Van Amersfoort suggests that discrimination may take place in the housing field, but the problem is nevertheless much less serious than in other countries.[11] During the first year of stay the immigrant may not understand the nuances of Dutch life, and rejection in social situations which are not based on race may be interpreted adversely. All Dutchmen are liable to experience the rather gruff public behaviour of their fellows, and such treatment is especially likely at the hands of officials. This point was illustrated by an

[11] 'Hoewel dus niet te ontkennen valt dat in de hele verblijfssituatie van Surinamers in Nederland discriminatie op sommige punten een role speelt, is er toch geen roden om te spreken van een rassenprobleem zoals wij dat in andered landen kennen' (Van Amersfoort, p. 51).

employee of the Social Research Division of the Ministry of Social Work. This man had lived in The Hague for twenty years, and since he was about to get married was looking for a flat. No flats were to be had in The Hague so he went to the town hall in the neighbouring urban area of Voorburg. He was told, in a gruff and authoritarian manner by a housing department official that, 'We have no houses for Hagueners here.' Such experience is not, however, universal, and an academic colleague in The Hague was given a much more cordial welcome by the housing department at Haarlem, and was in fact given a flat after some time on the waiting list.

A special study was made of the contacts which Surinamers had with the social services in Amsterdam and Rotterdam. Van Amersfoort found that of 147 Surinamers who contacted the local authority social service bureau (*Gemeentelijke Sociaal Dienst*) in Amsterdam in 1966, 61·2 per cent had been in the Netherlands one year or less, 15·6 per cent had been in the country between one and two years, 3·4 per cent had been in the country between two and three years, and 19·7 per cent had been in the country for more than three years. Figures for contacts in the first year for both Amsterdam and Rotterdam are given in Table 4:4.

*Table 4:4. Surinamers Contacting the Gemeentelijke Sociaal Dienst in 1966*

| *Duration of Stay* | *Amsterdam* | *Rotterdam* |
|---|---|---|
| One month or less | 30 | 54 |
| Two to six months | 54 | 46 |
| Seven to twelve months | 16 | 19 |
| Total | 100 | 119 |

*Source:* Van Amersfoort (1968) p. 56.

The fact that the most use of social services is made during the first year of stay, and, within that first year during the first month of stay, suggests that the immigrants are adapting to Dutch life over time, and use the social services mainly for the problems immediately associated with a new environment. Van Amersfoort also shows that it is the *ongeschoolde arbeiders*—the unskilled or semi-skilled workers with primary schooling only, who make the most demands on the services: 47 per cent of applicants came in this occupational category.

*Table 4:5. Kinds of Help sought by Surinamers from the Social Service Bureau*

| *Problem* | *Number* |
|---|---|
| Unemployment and job-finding | 119 |
| Sickness and medicine | 9 |
| Housing | 13 |
| Assistance with return to Surinam | 7 |
| Children in care | 16 |
| Other problems | 5 |
| Total | 169 |

*Source:* Van Amersfoort (1968) p. 57.

It is clear from Table 4:5 that help is sought mainly in job-finding, and that this help is sought very soon after the immigrant's arrival in the Netherlands.

The Cabinet of the Plenipotentiary Minister of Surinam in the Netherlands maintained until 1971 a special office in Amsterdam which offered advice and assistance to Surinamers, and this office is usually the immigrants' first port of call. The functions of this office, now taken over by the Welsuria Foundation are to put immigrants in touch with the appropriate social agency, and to act as a pressure group ensuring equitable treatment of Surinamers by these agencies. A detailed study of contacts which 140 Surinamers had with such agencies in Amsterdam was made by Soederhuizen (1965). The main agencies contacted were as follows: (*i*) *Gemeentelijke Sociaal Dienst*; (*ii*) *Hulp voor Onbehousden* (Assistance for the Homeless); (*iii*) *Unie voor Ongehuwde Moeders* (Society for Unmarried Mothers); (*iv*) *Federatie van Instellingen voor Kinderbescherming Amsterdam* (Federation of Institutions for Child Protection); (*v*) *Justitie* (the Justice's department); (*vi*) *Stichting Crediet en Voorschot* (an organization giving loans where the social circumstances of the applicant permit this—about 400 Surinamers a year use this agency); and (*vii*) *Gementelijke Woningdienst* (the public accommodation service).

According to Soederhuizen, Surinamers are distinguished by a number of cultural traits: their attitude to life is one of enjoyment, of mutual entertainment, and warmth to the world, with a liking for parties, dancing, and music. They are naïve about the perils of an industrial society, and have built up a picture of an ideal

Netherlands, and are often disappointed by the reality. Their attitude to marriage and the family is one based on the idea of warm and easy contact with the opposite sex, with a tolerance of common-law marriage and unmarried mothers. One particular cause of puzzlement to Surinamers, and a not infrequent cause of pain, was the Amsterdam folk humour (which we described earlier), a kind of jovial gruffness which takes delight at the physical discomfiture of an individual. But the West Indian immigrants tended to complain less frequently about this humour after they had been in Amsterdam some length of time.

Unmarried mothers with no supporting husband tend, according to Soederhuizen's study, to have a particularly difficult time from a financial point of view. He suggests that because of these sexual norms Dutch mothers are anxious about their daughters having Surinamers as boyfriends. Soederhuizen estimates that the illegitimacy rate among Surinamers is seven times that of those born in Amsterdam.

Housing is the main problem for the West Indian immigrants. The single man who is seeking only a room for himself is not eligible for the accommodation of the official housing bureau, so he must chance his luck on the open market for furnished rooms. Here there is thought to be discrimination both in the form of high rents and refusal of accommodation. Surinamers in Amsterdam have naturally sought housing in the area where tolerance is greatest, and there tends to be a relative concentration of these immigrants in the Zeedijk area of Amsterdam. This is the pleasure quarter of the city. In this quarter one may observe the interesting and curious phenomenon of the 'middle class' prostitute, respectable and comely ladies who sit in shop windows, rather like models in a Bond Street store, awaiting the custom of some respectable Dutchman. Both prostitution and pornography are governed by the rules of bourgeois civility, and are practised with dignified ritual. The high numbers of Surinamers in this quarter, relative to their numbers elsewhere in Amsterdam, has led some observers to connect these immigrants with prostitution. The writer and his wife lived in this quarter for some time, and came to know a number of the prostitutes personally. It is our impression from these informants that although there are some black *souteneurs*, Surinamers are not over-represented in this profession in proportion to their numbers in the population of Amsterdam as a whole.

Soederhuizen's conclusion is somewhat pessimistic, and he

details some case histories of unmarried mothers who have cost the local authority several thousands of guilders. He advocates a much closer control over the initial socialization and care of the new arrivals, a policy much closer to that carried out with the Indonesian immigrants. By 1969 the earlier *laissez faire* policy was in fact being replaced by one of more positive action. I shall describe this policy in detail in Chapter 5.

A study of Surinamers in Amsterdam, using ethnographic methods, was carried out by Beyer (1965 and 1966). He made contact with sixty-two male Surinamers in the 'bar culture' of Amsterdam. Of his informants seventeen were Roman Catholic, twelve were Dutch Reformed, one was Hindu, eight had no religion, nineteen belonged to Evangelistic churches, and the religion of the remaining five was unknown. Thirty-three of the subjects had come to the Netherlands with the intention of studying, and thirteen with the definite intention of improving their standard of living. More than half had family or friends already in the Netherlands. Beyer found a definite correlation between being met by friends, and the ease with which the new arrival adapted to his surroundings. In addition, immigrants with a reserve of funds settled down more readily. Twenty-one of the immigrants were met on arrival in the country and given various kinds of assistance, four by a firm, two by a college, seven by members of their family, four by friends, two by cultural organizations, and two by other contacts. The informants were unanimous in their praise of the assistance given them by social agencies, and by individual Dutch people.

The main complaint of Beyer's informants was about the 'room situation', and thirty-three informants complained about high prices, poor furnishing and decoration, and lack of freedom to invite guests or cook for oneself. One informant complained that his landlady 'snuffelt in mijn papieren' while another was troubled by 'amoureuze avances van de hospita'. The average rent informants were paying, in 1964–5 was Fl. 19 a week, including heating and lighting. This is about £2 a week by English standards, for a single room not including food. An alternative is accommodation, which some informants had, with the *Amsterdams Tehuis voor Arbeiders* (a workers' hostel) where the rent is Fl. 50 per month (about £5)—but one may not cook in one's room, or have visitors after 11 p.m. It was possible to get a much larger furnished flat for Fl. 125 a month while the rent of single rooms for a working man ranged from Fl .65 to Fl. 95 a month. Wages range from Fl. 350 per month for an unskilled worker to Fl. 480 for a skilled man. These figures suggest that rents take less than a quarter of gross wages, and this seems not unfavourable when compared with rents charged in London.[12] Wages for women (in the 1965 period) were lower than those for a man, and a woman doing unskilled factory work could expect to earn about Fl. 250 a month. If she also had a child to support, or children back in Surinam, her financial position could be very difficult, as Soederhuizen pointed out.

*Table 4:6. Patterns of Regular 'Social Mixing' of Beyer's Informants*

| | *Contact with Surinamers* | | *Contact with Dutch* | |
|---|---|---|---|---|
| | *m* | *f* | *m* | *f* |
| Married (10) | 8 | 2 | 3 | 6 |
| Unmarried (20) | 11 | 4 | 7 | 11 |

Many Netherlanders apparently ascribe sexual potency to black Surinamers, while the Surinamers have a similar stereotype of the Dutch. Dutch women are seen as perverse and sensual, more interested in sex than love or marriage, when compared with Surinamese women. For example: 'Vraag: Hoe denken de Surinamers over de Hollandse vrouwen? Antwoord: Dat ze veel beter zijn in bed. Anders dan Surinaamse meisjes . . . de Hollanders hebben dat met onze vrouwen gedaan en wij doen dat met de Hollandse vrouwen' (Beyer, 1965, p. 91).

Another informant told Beyer, 'De meisjes hier zoeken het vreemde, dat trekt, de andere kleur.' The Surinamers in fact had no trouble in finding Dutch girl friends, as the pattern of contacts above shows. Their girl friends tended to be members of the same social class, shop assistants, hairdressers, and factory workers.

With regard to discrimination, Beyer's subjects used this word (as informants in other Dutch studies have done) to cover a wide range of negative behaviour on the part of the host population, ranging from refusal of accommodation to official impoliteness. This latter behaviour, we have argued, is rather common in the Netherlands, and is applied without regard to race, colour or

[12] Cf. Milner Holland (1965) on rents paid by immigrants in London.

creed! Twenty-three of fifty-eight informants said they had experienced little or no 'discrimination'; seventeen had experienced 'some discrimination', and eighteen had experienced 'much discrimination'. The *Maatschappelijk Advies en Amsterdam Inlichtingenbureau* (social work advice and information bureau) estimated (probably rhetorically) that 80 per cent of people with single rooms to let, would not let to a coloured man—like the landlady who replied, 'Een Surinamer? O God Mevrouw, voor geen goud. Ik had er twee op mijn kamers. Op den duur zaten er twintig'[13] (1965, p. 47). But this bureau also estimated that no less than 95 per cent of landladies will not let to students, whatever their race, on the grounds of their general boisterousness, untidiness, and suspected fornication. The criterion of letting accommodation seems to be respectability rather than colour, and there is little suggestion in the literature that a respectable Surinamer—a family man with a steady job—experiences housing discrimination. A test of this hypothesis is reported in a later chapter.

One case of housing discrimination on grounds of colour rather than on grounds of the potential behaviour of the tenant has been reported, and it is of interest since it illustrates attitudes to discrimination on the part of the Dutch public, and of the press. In July 1967, an Amsterdam newspaper *Het Parool* carried a report[14] stating that a member of the Cabinet of the Plenipotentiary Minister from Surinam paid a visit to a 'Surinamese Netherlander' who reported that he had been denied accommodation because of his colour. The report carried a photograph of the man, a 35-year-old engineer with the Public Electricity Authority (G.E.B.). He was seeking fresh accommodation because his wife was expecting their second baby. His company, as is common in the Netherlands, had the option on some accommodation on behalf of its employees, and sent the engineer to view one of these properties which had become vacant. But he was told by the owner that the property was let. The company established that this was untrue. The engineer complained to the Minister Plenipotentiary, and a spokesman of this office told the newspaper, 'This is inconceivable. We shall investigate, and see what we can do.' The house-owner, interviewed

[13] 'One Surinamer? Oh God, Madam, not for any money. I took on two, and before I knew where I was there were twenty on the doorstep.'

[14] 'Man zou huis niet krijgen om huidskleur', *Het Parool* (8 July 1967), p. 5.

by the newspaper and named said, 'I had someone else in view; indeed, it is my property and I may take who I want.'

Three days later *Het Parool* reported[15] that the engineer had been offered a three-roomed flat in an Amsterdam suburb. *Het Parool* is a left of centre newspaper, secular, though somewhat similar in style and content to the London *Daily Mail.* It is interesting that this incident was reported in terms of astonishment, as if it were isolated and outrageous behaviour; it is interesting too that owners with flats available wrote to the newspaper offering to accommodate the aggrieved man. The role of the Minister Plenipotentiary as an agent for the aggrieved Surinamer is illustrated here too. What eventually happened to the landlord who refused to let we do not know. All lettings, once arranged between landlord and tenant have to be reported to the local authority to make sure they conform with regulations relating number of rooms and rent to family size and income. The legal position is not entirely clear, but it seems that besides disallowing certain lettings, the local authority can also insist that certain tenants be accepted. The penalties for transgression are not great—a relatively small fine. Probably the largest inducement to a landlord not to discriminate is the fact that if he does not comply with the local authority regulations he will be unable to let his property at all. There is no 'race relations act' comparable to British legislation, and it is assumed that in the Netherlands discrimination is a rare and a disgraceful thing. Discrimination is an area of race relations which might provide grounds for social conflict, and it seems that evidence of the existence of such discrimination is extremely disturbing and embarrassing. The *verzuiling* rule of keeping potential conflict areas out of sight seems to operate to a large extent in the case of racial discrimination. This policy could have its dangers if the incidence of discrimination were high. We shall report empirical material on this point in a later chapter which suggests that the incidence is in fact low. The use of the term 'discrimination' in a very wide context to include general unfriendliness is a useful semantic device which allows those in authority to use the term in a relatively neutral way. For example, the Minister of Culture, Recreation, and Social Work in 1968 called for increased efforts to combat 'different forms of racial discrimination' against migrant workers and students from Surinam

[15] 'Na elders te zijn afgewezen—Surinamer krijgt huis aangeboden', *Het Parool* (11 July 1967), p. 5.

and Curaçao.[16] The Minister especially mentioned the need for improvement of information and counselling services. The appeal came after questions were asked in Parliament after housing problems had been reported in relation to a newly arrived group of workers from Surinam.

A further interesting example of Dutch reaction to reports of prejudice and discrimination occurred in 1970, following a programme in the N.C.R.V. television series 'Hier en Nu' which featured the poor and overcrowded housing accommodation experienced by some West Indian immigrants. This programme provoked an unprecedented number of letters from viewers, and these were analysed by the Anthropology Institute of the University of Amsterdam. If this had been an English programme about West Indians in Britain one would have expected the bulk of the letters to have been hostile—my content analysis of letters written about coloured immigrants to the British press supports such a view (Bagley, 1971b). However, less than 3 per cent of these Dutch letters were hostile. The large majority expressed considerable sympathy with the immigrants, and many contained practical offers of jobs, accommodation, and invitations for the families featured in the film to meet them.

The shortage of housing has, according to an official of the Ministry of Culture[17] caused a number of West Indians to move from the Randstad area of western cities to other parts of the country where a flat can be obtained, as in Arnhem, for example, in a few months or less. There does not appear to be any shortage of work in these provincial districts. Some local authorities in the Randstad area, anxious that 'ghettoes' shall not form, have been giving West Indians accelerated access to public housing, so that a coloured man may get a flat in six months instead of the five years it would take a white Dutchman. The existence of this policy is unknown to the general public, and to the West Indians themselves.

Acute pressure on housing in Amsterdam has caused some West Indians to move to other parts of the Netherlands in search of housing. But it has also had the interesting effect of motivating West Indians (and some foreign workers) to seek high cost, luxury housing whose rent is not controlled and whose letting is outside the control of the local authority. In the south-east of

[16] Note in *Migration Today* (Vol. 11, 1968), pp. 67–8.
[17] Personal communication, June 1969.

Amsterdam a luxury estate has been built at Bijlmermeer. This housing is attractive, and spaciously laid out. But nearly half of the tenants are either West Indians or foreign workers, while the remainder of the tenants are, by and large, wealthy Dutch people. In order to pay the high rents (about £40 a month, which is high by Dutch, but not English standards) the immigrants have of necessity to sub-let, which means that the accommodation is much more crowded than the builders anticipated. The community is mixed, not so much racially as by social class, and this appears to have caused some resentment on the part of the upper-class white residents. Education is one area in which the middle-class parents appear resentful about the presence of the immigrants.

## INTEGRATION AND ASSIMILATION

In terms of the model proposed in Chapter 3, do West Indians tend to be *integrated* into Dutch society, or do they tend to be *assimilated*? Dutch West Indians, like British West Indians, have a strong orientation to the mother culture. The immigrants to the Netherlands from Surinam and the Antilles speak Dutch, are relatively loyal to Dutch institutions, and are anxious to conform to the major norms of society. The nuances of interaction in everyday life in the Netherlands have, however, to be learned and this process can be difficult for an individual. On arrival in the Netherlands the West Indian immigrant often looks to his fellow West Indians for support and friendship, but this is not always the case, as Beyer's study shows. West Indians in the Netherlands form loosely-integrated cultural groups or social networks but their orientation to, and connection with, the major society is strong. They seem to be well on the road to assimilation, when they will merge with the Dutch population to the point of intermarriage. There is already much evidence that intermarriage is taking place.

The recent policy of the Community Relations Division of the Ministry of Culture, Recreation, and Social Work has shown considerable changes from the earlier *laissez faire* position with regard to the West Indians. The policy applied to migrant workers from Europe is also applied to West Indians: a policy of providing very positive and active services for the newly arrived immigrant. These services take the form of residential accommodation, social work and counselling, orientation and language course, and help with housing one's family when they arrive in the country.[18] The policy is explicitly one of building up the immigrant's 'group identity' in a framework of initial seclusion from the major society. The experience of the social workers involved[19] has been that a policy of 'immediate assimilation' without first building up the immigrant's sense of identity with a group of his own countrymen can have unfortunate consequences: without such a sense of identity the immigrant is a less efficient human being. He tends to be withdrawn, sometimes aggressive, and changes jobs frequently. The present policy is one first of integration, and then of gradual assimilation. Some West Indians, Surinamers especially, have escaped this net of social policy, arguing that 'We are Dutchmen, not foreigners, and don't want all these services'. One can assume that for such individuals the process of assimilation has already begun. But a West Indian cultural consciousness in the Netherlands does exist: it takes the form of 'Surinamese consciousness' and 'Curaçaon consciousness' rather than a consciousness of a black minority. This geographical identity was illustrated by events in Curaçao—the oil refinery strike and subsequent riots in which four strikers were killed. Dutch marines were called in to keep order, and in The Hague a large number of Antilleans demonstrated against this policy. This demonstration was broken up by the police in a somewhat brutal fashion, and ten Antilleans were arrested. The Antilleans did, however, receive some subsequent support from Surinamers, since a 'Surinam Action Committee' sent telegrams of protest to the Burgomaster of The Hague, and to the Second Chamber.

## DUTCH WEST INDIANS AND THE COMMON MARKET

The entry of Britain into the E.E.C. has emphasized an interesting paradox concerning free migration between the E.E.C. countries. In an agreement negotiated in 1961, France agreed not to accord citizens of her own territories such rights, and in return the Dutch Government agreed that citizens of Surinam and Antilles should similarly have no right of free movement within the E.E.C. Böhning (1972) summarizes the position: 'France . . . does not seem to have asked for the inclusion of Algerians and/or its own citizens from the Overseas Departments in the E.E.C. free move-

[18] These services are described in detail in Chapter 5.

[19] Ministry of Culture, Recreation, and Social Work, personal communication, June 1969.

ment system for which Article 272 (2) of the Treaty requires a unanimous decision from the Council. The Netherlands pursued a similar policy.'

This policy however contains a curious paradox. The passports of Surinamers and Antilleans are identical with those of Dutch citizens. The only distinguishing feature is the stamp of the issuing authority. If the passport of a Surinamer expires while he is in the Netherlands for example, it is renewed with the stamp of, say, the Province of North Holland. When a Dutch West Indian goes to work in an E.E.C. country he should in theory apply for a work permit. But this is an invidious situation for a citizen of the Netherlands Kingdom who must be distinguished by the E.E.C. country, not by passport, but by colour of skin. In practice it has proved an impossible rule to apply, and there are at present several hundred Surinamers working in Germany, who are accepted as Dutch citizens, and have not had to apply for work permits.

Britain's legal relationship with her colonial immigrants differs from that of the Netherlands. Instead of free entry and automatic citizenship of a multinational Kingdom, entry is strictly controlled. However, all Commonwealth citizens arriving before the 1971 Immigration Act have the automatic right of citizenship after five years' residence. The Dutch have expressed concern (almost certainly unfounded) at the prospect of migration to the Netherlands of large numbers of British Asians and have pressed in the E.E.C. negotiations for some restrictive ruling on the migration rights of these British citizens.

This ambiguous stance of the Dutch—since it calls in question the *de facto* rights of their own Kingdom citizens—is probably motivated by two factors. First of all, the Dutch may feel somewhat guilty over the 1961 agreement, which was almost certainly contracted because of the Dutch fear of 'alien' groups (such as Algerians) having rights of free entry. The second, related factor is the fear of a large immigration of another 'alien' group, namely Asians from the Indian sub-continent. These Dutch fears underline a point which is emphasized in several chapters of this study—that the Dutch tend to be extremely tolerant and generous towards ethnic groups who are familiar with, and loyal to, Dutch institutions. At the same time they can be extremely suspicious of, and initially hostile towards, groups (like Italians, and Moroccans) who are not familiar with Dutch linguistic and cultural norms.

### SURINAM AND THE NETHERLANDS: THE CHANGING SITUATION

In the three years since I began the fieldwork for this study, in 1969, there are signs that relationships between Surinam and the Netherlands are changing. The Dutch experience in Curaçao in 1969, when Dutch soldiers were called in to keep order in Willemstad, was a significant event in the diminishing Dutch desire for colonial involvement. As the Netherlands has grown economically within a united Europe her vision of being a benevolent international, post-colonial power has become increasingly dim. Surinam is clearly a net economic liability, rather than an asset. The balance of benefits of the Kingdom relationship is clearly weighted in Surinam's favour.

The situation that now exists is that The Hague Government would readily accede to demands from Surinam for complete independence. Such demands, although voiced by the radical Creole party, have not been made by Mr. Lachmon's Government in which the Hindustani party has controlling power. The Government of Surinam is fully aware of the benefits of Tripartite Kingdom membership, and Mr. Lachmon was quoted in 1972 as saying that he anticipated complete independence for Surinam in ten years' time. Such independence would almost undoubtedly mean that free migration from Surinam to the Netherlands would cease.

Since 1969 the amount of immigration from Surinam to the Netherlands has increased.[20] There are a number of reasons for this. The radical Creole party in Surinam has become increasingly vociferous in its demands for independence, and it has been clear to many who have considered the prospect of migration, that once independence has been achieved this chance of migration will be lost. So there is at present something of a 'beat the ban' rush, and the recent migrants contain larger numbers of working-class Creoles. This is apparently also linked with the death of Pengel, and the decline in political confidence of the working-class Creole party in Surinam. Creoles are now obviously concerned about their possible exclusion from the system of political power in Surinam. Certainly the problem is not as serious as it was (and is) in Guyana. Lachmon, the Hindustani leader, clearly recognizes that continued membership of the Tripartite Kingdom will

[20] See *Enkele Statistiche Gegevens Betreffende de Buitenlandse en Binnenlandse Migratie* (Ministry of Culture, Stafbureau Statistiek Cahier II, 1971).

enable consolidation in many directions, not least in the economic sphere. Provided that increases in prosperity affect all groups equitably, an increase in national wealth should create a climate of political stability. It is the most radical and left wing of the Creoles, many of them educated in the Netherlands, who are demanding independence. At the present time this appears to be an idealistic demand, since immediate independence would bring severe economic problems in its train. One solution might be to nationalize the American firms—especially those in the bauxite industry. However, the possibility of the left-wing group influencing both the mainstream of Creole politicians in this direction is small. One is struck by the dilemma of the radical black intellectuals from Surinam who demand independence from the Netherlands. If such independence would mean having to choose between living permanently in Surinam or in the Netherlands, they would most probably choose the metropolitan culture of the Netherlands, where they have had their university education.

The increasing number of immigrants from Surinam, and the increase in numbers of the ordinary population (as opposed to the middle class) from that country has definitely been viewed critically by some Dutch politicians.[21] In February 1972 for example, two articles were published in the intellectual newspaper *N.R.C. Handelsblad*[22] which could only be described as hostile. This hostility, though certainly not of Powellite proportions, did suggest that Surinamers contained 'a criminal minority', and that many Surinamers were sponging on Dutch welfare facilities. It was claimed that there was a negative selection in migration, and that only those who could not easily find jobs came to the Netherlands.[23] The author of this article concluded with typical pre-Powellite phrasing, 'Our country is already much too full to be able to tolerate further immigration.' Such opinions were never expressed in newspaper columns three years before. What may be significant however is that there was very little public response by way of letters to this article, or to similar opinions expressed in

[21] See H. Van Amersfoort, 'Beperking Surinamers zweemt naar racisme', *Volkskrant* (9 September 1971).

[22] Ir R. Van Hasselt, 'Help Surinamers in hun eigen Land', *N.R.C. Handelsblad* (11 February 1972).

[23] A recent study by Zielhuis and Girdhari (1971) shows how inaccurate such a presumption is. An investigation of a large number of emigrants from Surinam to the Netherlands found that they were no more likely to be unemployed than anyone else in Surinam, and that the majority had received secondary education. The large majority already had relatives in the Netherlands.

newspapers. In the flowering of the Powell situation in 1968 a great mass of racially hostile letters was received by the press (Bagley, 1971b). The Netherlands immigration issue was also aired in the early part of 1972 in an 'open line' radio programme, in which listeners phone in questions and comments to a panel of speakers. The radio station involved indicated that about half the calls received were favourable to Surinamers, while the other half tended to be hostile. There was an interesting regional variation in these calls, and the majority of those from the rest of the Netherlands (as opposed to those from the West) were favourable to the West Indian immigrants.

There are no reasons for supposing that the situation with regard to the low level of discrimination in white-collar employment which our comparative testing revealed (*vide infra*) has changed in the past year. It still seems true that, in contrast to Britain, Surinamers are most likely to be discriminated against in the unskilled labour market. This is probably because migrant workers can be easily and cheaply hired for this work, and easily fired in times of recession simply by failure to renew their annual labour permits. Indeed, it is possible that as many as 10 per cent of these Mediterranean workers have entered the Netherlands illegally, without labour permits. During 1972 the Netherlands experienced a moderate employment recession, but at no time did unemployment reach the English proportion.

Looking ahead, it seems certain now—judging by the statements made by Mr. Lachmon—that Surinam will become an independent state in some ten years' time. By that time there will probably be about 75,000 Surinamers permanently resident in the Netherlands.

## CONCLUSIONS

Plural societies are potentially unstable to the extent that there exists an imbalance of power, and differential access to economic and educational resources on the part of any particular bloc. In the context of Surinam the possible relative deprivation of the Javanese in this respect may lead to social conflict. Economic development, provided it is not confined to one particular bloc in a plural society, is associated with increasing interaction and development of common values between members of the separate blocs. This process is most advanced in Curaçao.

The Dominion-style links between Surinam and the Antilles, and the Netherlands, are extremely useful to the two former colonial countries, and have been prestigious to the Netherlands. Such links are likely to continue for the next decade. Conservative forces in the Netherlands have in fact provided strong, and silent pressure to retain the links with the former colonies. Conservative pressures are in favour of maintaining free entry, while some left-wing pressure groups would like to see both the colonial links, and this free entry of coloured people, ended. For the same reasons, the imposition of control over immigration to the Netherlands is extremely unlikely to occur.

The inter-bloc rule in the Netherlands of keeping potentially disruptive issues out of public debate operates in the case of race relations and the possibility of immigration control. The Catholic Centre party, which mediates between right and left, is unlikely to institute immigration control. The price of introducing such control, in terms of conflict with the prized former colonial possessions, and in terms of conflict between blocs of right and left, is too high.

West Indian immigrants to the Netherlands are a group with a good knowledge of, and orientation to, Dutch culture and society. Nevertheless, learning about the nuances of Dutch life is a cause of difficulty; the two other causes of difficulty are employment (which is easily solved) and housing. The problem of housing is a chronic one and is not confined to West Indian immigrants. West Indians seeking single rooms may fare adversely in the housing market. But legal and structural factors mean that discrimination in the allocation of unfurnished flats is difficult. In the letting of single rooms discrimination on grounds of the perceived lack of respectability is more likely than discrimination on grounds of colour.

Surinamers and Antilleans are distinct cultural groups; in the Netherlands each group has a loose cultural identity which means that in the initial stages of migration Surinamers and Antilleans are integrated, in the sense of possessing a cultural identity but at the same time being tolerated by the major society. In the course of time (and probably by the second generation) we would expect, in a largely tolerant atmosphere, that West Indians will become assimilated into Dutch society, with a high degree of intermarriage with the Dutch population.

CHAPTER 5

# SOCIAL POLICY AND THE IMMIGRANTS FROM EUROPE AND THE WEST INDIES

In 1968 there were between six and seven million foreign workers in the industrialized countries of Northern Europe. Five million of these came from Italy, Spain, Greece, and Portugal, the remainder from Turkey, Morocco, Tunisia, and Algeria. In the Netherlands such workers account for 1·5 per cent of the labour force.

Dutch industry—especially the mining and steel industries—began to recruit foreign labour in 1955. The first workers came from Italy, then an agreement was made with Spain in 1961 about the admission of workers, and this was followed by agreements with various other countries, including Turkey. Since 1964 increasing numbers of migrant workers have been coming to the Netherlands of their own accord, rather than as specially recruited workers. Many of them come from Morocco (Popa-Radix, 1968). By 1968 the number of foreign workers (not including non-working dependants) was as shown in Table 5:1.

*Table 5:1. Numbers of Foreign Workers in the Netherlands, 1968*

| *Country* | *Men* | *Women* |
|---|---|---|
| Italy | 8,426 | 1,080 |
| Spain | 9,607 | 2,533 |
| Turkey | 13,243 | 400 |
| Morocco | 14,072 | 24 |
| Greece | 1,259 | 357 |
| Portugal | 1,181 | 262 |
| Other countries | 20,760 | 4,860 |
| Total | 68,548 | 9,516 |

*Source:* Popa-Radix (1968).

The demand for foreign labour has been greatest in the lowest paid jobs. Dincer (1962) in a case study of Rotterdam found that the city was short of some 2,000 municipal workers, including hospital domestic staff, and special efforts were made to recruit Italian and Spanish workers to fill these vacancies. Workers from outside the European Economic Community (i.e. all of the countries specifically mentioned in Table 5:1, except Italy) have to obtain labour permits before entry. These permits are renewable annually. The worker is required to stay in the industry for which he has been recruited for three years. After a year's residence he is allowed to bring in dependants, provided he has obtained suitable accommodation.

Social policy on how to treat the immigrant workers has developed quite slowly. None of the elaborate social welfare facilities used for the reception of the immigrants from Indonesia was used, and the arrival of these workers, in small groups, did not attract attention. According to Dincer (1962) many officials regarded their presence as temporary. True, many of the migrant workers returned home after one or two years, but many stayed, and brought in their wives and families. A similar lack of explicit social policy was also the case with the West Indian immigrants, the majority of whom were a particular category of migrant labour. Simons (1962) pointed to the uneven provision of special facilities —accommodation, recreation centres, and social work assistance— in the Netherlands. In most cases it was left to the recruiting firm to provide such facilities, or to the denominational organizations. Since the immigrants were rarely Protestant, they tended to fare badly in Protestant areas. Deakin (1968) contrasted the planned social policy on behalf of the Indonesian immigrants with the lack of such policy in respect of West Indian immigrants.

However, early in 1968 the direction of Dutch policy took a clear change.[1] By that date appreciable numbers of West Indians were in the country, and it was also realized that many European and North African immigrants were bringing in their families with the object of settling permanently in the country. The new policy was made explicit by the Minister of Culture, Recreation, and Social Work in a speech on the occasion of the official opening of the 'West Brabant Institute for Assistance to Foreign Workers' at Breda on 21 August 1968. The statement of policy referred to both European workers, and immigrants from the West Indies.

[1] Cf. the comments on the change of policy by Hogebrink (1970), and Van der Praag (1971).

The Minister, in stressing the advantages such immigration could bring, stressed in the Dutch context, a significant analogy:

> Just as a mixed marriage can enrich the lives of the people concerned, so can our culture be enriched by this daily encounter. Are we to see this as a source of conflict, or as a source of cultural wealth and as a means to improve the welfare and prosperity of us all? I should like, if I may, to quote a passage from the foreword of the June 1968 bulletin of the Netherlands Institute for Community Development: 'Community development that fails to take account of the growing cultural plurality and the accompanying need for establishing identity remains restricted to a small circle, even if this development concerns the whole of the Netherlands.'

One probable factor underlying the change in policy, which I shall outline in more detail below, seems to have been the recognition of the fact that the various groups of immigrant workers had reached sufficient numbers to begin to form pillars or blocs of society in their own right. This led too to the realization that explicit social action must be undertaken to strengthen the cultural identity of these pillars, to ensure that their members behaved in a way compatible with the smooth running of the traditional plural society of the Netherlands.

In his speech the Minister explained that when the first voluntary institution for foreign workers received a grant from the Ministry in 1960, the policy to be pursued in relation to these workers was not entirely clear. By and large no special services were provided for the migrants, and assistance to them came under the heading of 'general social work'. But a more positive policy gradually developed, and a National Institute for Assistance to Foreign Workers was set up to co-ordinate the work of the voluntary societies in regional centres. The elements of this developed policy are that firstly, the immigrant should know something about the country and the region in which he is going to live, and be aware of factors which might lead to misunderstanding, especially in the sphere of interpersonal and public behaviour. Some instruction, too, should be given in the language of their new country.

Secondly, in the Minister's words, the workers should 'develop a sense of individual responsibility'. This means that as a matter of policy their consciousness and identity as an ethnic group is fostered, and the development of autonomous workers groups (e.g. Italian associations, Spanish associations, etc.) is encouraged.

This development of group identity is seen as an extremely important part of the integration or 'fitting in' process:

> By fitting in in this particular context I mean the insertion of a group into the whole order of society while preserving the group's identity and maintaining its own way of life. For whatever reasons foreign workers have chosen to come here, either permanently or temporarily, they will feel a need to preserve their own identity. The existence of no less than seventy-five Dutch clubs and societies in Australia serves to illustrate my meaning.

This view has been underlined by Popa-Radix (Chief of the Research Division of the Ministry of Culture, Recreation, and Social Work):

> . . . it is important that the group of migrant workers should be absorbed into Dutch society while retaining their own modes of living. Otherwise there would be a danger that moral standards might deteriorate and the sense of identity be lost through lack of support from their own environment. It is therefore very important that they be able to maintain the distinctive features of their way of life. Sociology and psychology have taught us that the adaptation of migrants can best be promoted by ensuring that group ties are maintained, at any rate in the first few years. With the group as a basis, it will be easier for its members to adapt themselves in time to a new and strange society.

Dutch policy concerning migrant workers has emerged from an initial attitude of general *laissez faire* to one of very positive action. This policy involves instructing the migrant, in the context of a group of his countrymen, in the language and workings of Dutch society but at the same time retaining this group's cultural and linguistic identity. This is an explicit implementation of 'integration' as we have defined it above.[2] This policy also extends to West Indians, as will emerge from the description of the activities of some of the *Stichtingen*.

In the Netherlands a great deal of welfare activity is entrusted to the *Stichtingen*, or foundations. These are voluntary organizations, often having a denominational basis, and usually supported by state funds. The initiative in setting up foundations for foreign workers (including West Indians) has come either from interested denominational organizations (especially Catholics) or from the main industries employing these workers. Since 1964 the Ministry has guaranteed 70 per cent of the finance of these foundations, the

[2] There are radical Dutch voices who claim that Dutch policy in this respect is not in fact generous enough (Hogebrink, 1970). Suffice to say that the Dutch policy is nevertheless much more generous than English policy.

remainder having to be found from other sources, namely, the local authority, local industry, and voluntary associations. By June 1969, according to the Ministry of Culture, Recreation, and Social

*Table 5:2. Number and Distribution of Ministry-Subsidized Foundations, June 1969 (excluding Foundations for West Indians)*

| *Area* | *Number of Foundations* | *Groups whom Foundations Support* |
|---|---|---|
| *Northern* | | |
| Alkmaar | 1 | All workers (1) |
| Ijmond | 4 | Italians (1); Spaniards (1); all workers (2) |
| Zaandam | 1 | All workers (1) |
| Twente | 8 | Italians (2); Spaniards (1); Turks (1); all workers (4) |
| Haarlem | 2 | All workers (2) |
| Amsterdam | 5 | Spaniards (1); Portuguese (1); Moroccans (1); Turks (1); all workers (1) |
| *Central* | | |
| 't Gooi | 3 | Moroccans (1); all workers (2) |
| Utrecht | 7 | Italians (1); Spaniards (1); Moroccans (1); all workers (4) |
| Arnhem and Nijmegen | 4 | Italians (1); Spaniards (1); Turks (1); all workers (1) |
| Den Haag | 7 | Italians (1); Spaniards (1); Portuguese (1); Turks (1); Moroccans (1); all workers (2) |
| Rijn en Lek | 3 | Moroccans (1); all workers (2) |
| Rotterdam | 15 | Greeks (1); Italians (2); Yugoslavs (1); Spaniards (5); Portuguese (1); Moroccans (1); Turks (3); all workers (1) |
| Doordrecht | 3 | Italians (1); Spaniards (1); Turks (1) |
| *Southern* | | |
| Oss | 1 | All workers (1) |
| West Brabant | 4 | Moroccans (1); Turks (1); all workers (2) |
| Tilburg | 1 | All workers (1) |
| Eindhoven | 4 | Spaniards (1); Moroccans (1); all workers (2) |
| Limburg | 12 | Greeks (1); Italians (2); Yugoslavs (2); Spaniards (1); Moroccans (1); Turks (1); all workers (4) |

Work, the number and geographical distribution of foundations which the Ministry subsidized was as shown in Table 5:2. In addition, there are Welsuria foundations in Amsterdam and Rotterdam for Surinamers, and a foundation for Antilleans in The Hague. More foundations, especially for Surinamers and Antilleans, are planned.[3] The foundations operate from centres which act as recreation centres, and sometimes also as centres of residence for the particular group concerned. As well as centres of entertainment, offering a cultural atmosphere where the language and customs (including food) of the immigrants' own country are enjoyed, the centres are the basis of advice and training, and all have one or more full-time social workers attached to them, conversant with the language and customs of the group concerned. In addition, a priest or immam is attached to the centre, and acts as an additional agent of education and social control.

The foundations are run by twenty-six local and regional organizations (Popa-Radix, 1968). The governing bodies of the foundations were in the early years of their development often completely denominational, but the increasing religious heterogeneity of the workers has resulted in the development of governing bodies more or less representative of the communities in which the migrants find themselves. In the case of Moroccan and Turkish workers, there will almost certainly be an immam on the governing body of the foundation. The overall co-ordination of the activities of the foundations is the work of the Community Relations Division of the Ministry of Culture, Recreation, and Social Work.

The Community Relations Division is divided into four sections, dealing with, respectively (*a*) caravan dwellers; (*b*) the Ambonese; (*c*) foreign students; (*d*) immigrant workers. The development of interdenominational governing bodies for the foundation has been a ministry decision. It is interesting to note that the staff of this ministry are in fact predominantly Roman Catholic, since social welfare work was traditionally an activity for Catholics, and in earlier decades provided an entry to the Civil Service and to an area of political power. Similarly, much of the local initiative for foundations came from Catholics. Subsidies for foundations were introduced in 1964. The initial subsidy was 40 per cent of annual costs, but in 1965 this proportion was raised to 70 per cent. The Government also provides up to 40 per cent of the capital costs of

[3] In 1969, Welsuria foundations were established in The Hague, Utrecht, Groningen, and Arnhem.

the foundations. Ten per cent of the Ministry's budget for the foundations is expended on services for West Indians.[4] This budget is over and above any assistance given to immigrants by the general social work agencies.

The amount of the subsidy has risen steadily since 1964. In that year it stood at just over Fl. 1,000,000, and by the beginning of 1969 amounted to Fl. 25,000,000, with further increases estimated to reach about Fl. 28,000,000 by the beginning of 1970.[5] Taking into account the relative size of the gross national product of the two countries this would represent in British terms an *annual* expenditure on special services for immigrants of at least £15,000,000. This amount does not include capital costs (60 per cent of the total) met on a voluntary basis, and running costs (about 30 per cent of the total) met by the local authority and by industry.[6] The annual budget of the British Community Relations Commission is rather less than a million pounds.

## DE POORT: COMMUNITY RELATIONS IN THE HAGUE

'De Poort' means 'The Gateway', and is the generic name for the collection of foundations for workers of different nationalities in The Hague. The planning of the centre was begun in 1956, and was originally a Catholic venture to help the increasing number of migrant workers from Europe. De Poort is situated within walking distance of the centre of The Hague in a building which used to be a nunnery. The cost of acquiring this building, which is several storeys high and occupies the width of three or four ordinary houses, was Fl. 662,000. This money was raised by public appeal (one individual gave Fl. 100,000) and by a loan raised from the local authority at 4¼ per cent. Once acquired the building had to be extensively refitted. Subsequently adjoining buildings were acquired, and the total cost of capitalization in the early years amounted to Fl. 867,000 (i.e. about £85,000).[7]

[4] Ministry of Culture, Recreation, and Social Work, personal communication, June 1969.

[5] *Buitenlandse Werknemers* (February 1969), p. 36.

[6] Subsidies now amount to 95 per cent of running costs (Ebbeling, 1971).

[7] These details are taken from *De Poort—Verslag van de Werkzaamheden* (1 July 1965—1 April 1969), published by the three Stichtingen responsible for De Poort—*Stitchting Haags Katholiek Jongercentrum*; *Stichting Begleiding Buitenlandse Werknemers*; and *Stichting voor Antillianen*, D.H., 1969. The director of De Poort is Mr. Th. L. van Son who provided much additional information.

The three foundations involved in this development established an organizing committee consisting of local officials, business men, and priests. The special concern for the Antilleans developed in the early 1960s. By 1968 further buildings had been acquired and fitted at a cost of Fl. 732,000. In 1968 the annual running costs of the centre, whose work we shall shortly describe, was Fl. 1,901,292 (approximately £190,000). This figure does not include social workers' salaries.

The most important feature of De Poort is that it provides residential accommodation for the immigrant. This accommodation is quite free, i.e. there is *no charge* to the immigrants. Accommodation is in the form of 'casas' within the main building. These are very much like houses in an English public school, and are organized on a nationality basis, so that there are Italian, Tunisian, Portuguese, Spanish, Antillean, and Moroccan casas. The largest casa is that accommodating a hundred Moroccans, followed by that housing seventy Turks. The remaining five casas each contain about forty members. The total number accommodated is 385, in one- to four-bedded rooms. The casas are autonomous and separate from one another, and have their own kitchens where the appropriate national food is cooked, their own national bar, and common room. These casas form the basis of much group activity which is organized by special social workers, speaking the appropriate language, attached to each casa. Each casa too has its appropriate denominational and national priest.

New migrants are put in touch with De Poort by the employers who have recruited them, and in the case of the Antilleans, by the Plenipotentiary Office as well. Industries employing immigrants contribute nearly 30 per cent of the running costs of the centre; this could imply a rather paternalistic control of their immigrant workers' activities. In practice this is not the case. The immigrant worker, once accepted by De Poort as a resident can stay even if he changes his job, and his firm has no control over his activities in the centre.

By June 1969, De Poort employed six social workers, including workers speaking Italian, Turkish, Portuguese, Moroccan, Greek, and Spanish. Some of these social workers were especially recruited in the countries from which the migrant workers come. Social workers without formal training attend the Social Academy in The Hague one day a week. The total staff of the centre, including full-time administrative and domestic staff is forty. Six priests are attached to the centre too, including priests from Italy, Spain, Portugal, Surinam, and the Antilles, as well as the immam of The Hague mosque.

The casas form the basis of group work: this involves training sessions in Dutch language and way of life, and instruction in appropriate inter-personal behaviour. This is geared to personal counselling in the event of individual difficulties, and appropriate action in the case of difficulties at work. The ultimate aim is to install the immigrant in accommodation of his own, and the social workers find suitable lodgings. For families, they locate suitable flats. The social workers' (and the priests') role does not stop here. They keep a friendly eye on the immigrants in their lodgings, and investigate any complaints or requests for help from landladies. In this way the continuity of social control is maintained. Close relations are also maintained with the police and justice's department.

The atmosphere in each casa reproduces as nearly as possible the atmosphere of Spain, Italy, Greece, or whatever is the appropriate country. Here the immigrant speaks his own language, and behaves as a Spaniard, or a Greek. But at work, and when he takes his place in the wider community, he is expected to speak Dutch, and indulge in the Dutch norms of public interaction. Even when he is no longer resident, the immigrant can return to his casa at any time, and is encouraged to do so. Each casa has a national library, including local newspapers and magazines, shows national films, and organizes group excursions and sports teams. The immigrants are encouraged to obtain Dutch technical diplomas (in subjects such as electrical engineering and banking). It is the Antilleans who take the most advantage of these courses. Although there is no Surinamese casa (one is planned) Surinamers in The Hague use the centre regularly for meetings, and recreation.

De Poort also maintains a restaurant which is open to all immigrants. Here Dutch food is mainly served, but the price of a three-course meal is Fl. 2·60, at least half the price of a similar meal in the cheapest café. The casas are open to visitors from 10.00 a.m. till midnight on weekdays, and until 1 a.m. on Saturdays and Sundays. The number and type of group activities are meticulously recorded by the administration of De Poort. In 1968 there were 735 such group activities, ranging from the regular rehearsals of Gregorian chant by the Schola Cantorum of Spanish workers to Moslem religious festivals, and from dances to children's parties. These children's parties are the province of the Portuguese workers, for it is the Portuguese who are the most likely of all the immigrant groups to bring their families to the Netherlands.[8] Between 1965 and 1969 Fr. Wernink, the Dutch priest, celebrated thirty-two marriages to Dutch girls.

The work of De Poort is altruistic, but is also motivated by a desire to keep the immigrants from what the *Stichtingen* described as 'malafide pensionhouders' and the 'drift to immorality, and to the bar culture'. The *Stichtingen* admit that some immigrants do fall into bad hands, and are exploited by landladies and proprietors of boarding houses. The underlying motivation is moral and evangelical in a broad rather than a narrow sense. The purpose of De Poort is to integrate the immigrants into the 'moral community' of Dutchmen. But at the same time, and to its very great credit, the cultural identity of the immigrant is respected. There are interesting parallels between this policy and the Dutch colonial policy of 'culture tolerance' which we described earlier.

In their report for 1969 the *Stichtingen* set out their aims for the future. These are impressive, and include:

A larger attention to inland migration; a Foundation for Surinamers; the study of 'wild migration'; more selective recruitment by employers; solution of 'oppressive housing' problems; finding more housing for uniting immigrants with their families; rooting out the non bona-fide pensions; a better service to industry, and co-operation from industry; better co-operation with trade unions on the social and economic welfare of immigrants; better co-operation with ambassadors and consuls; better information about how the Dutch perceive foreign workers.

The overall purpose of the *Stichtingen* is that the immigrants '. . . beter gaan zien en beseffen, dat zij, na hun plicht to hebben gedaan, ook rechten kunnen doen geleden'. In other words, that the immigrant shall have the legitimate expectation that if he behaves according to Dutch norms, he may expect justice.

The record of The Hague *Stichtingen* is extremely impressive, and parallels activity in Rotterdam and Amsterdam, and several other parts of the country. One is struck by the efficiency and smooth running of these community relations activities, and the businesslike way in which the Dutch organizers achieve their aims. This success probably reflects three factors: the Dutch trait of

[8] A recent unpublished study by the Ministry of Culture indicates that many Turks are now bringing their families to the Netherlands.

achieving goals by means of industry and the minimum of interpersonal conflict; generous financial endowment from the Government, industry, and private individuals; and a climate of good will at both an official and an industrial level, and on the part of a large section of the Dutch population. There is little doubt that the future proposals of the De Poort will be achieved.

De Poort serves The Hague and adjacent urban areas of Rijswijk and Voorburg, and also serves Delft and Leiden, cities which merge almost imperceptibly into The Hague conurbation. The total number of male immigrants employed in this area is about 7,000. This estimate, which relates to 1969 was made by De Poort using figures supplied by local industry. The large majority of immigrants do not have their families with them, but taking into account wives and children of immigrants, and students and professionals, the total number of recent immigrants is about 12,000.[9] For an immigrant population of 12,000 a year, community services have been provided which cost at least £200,000 a year to run, in buildings whose capital cost was a little under £150,000.[10]

It is difficult to find an appropriate area in England to compare this expenditure with: but in the London Borough of Wandsworth the number of recent immigrants, including the Irish and West Indians and Indians and Pakistanis, and other foreign categories, plus African students is nearly 20,000. In this Borough which has nearly twice as many recent immigrants as The Hague the *total* expenditure on community relations since the war does not exceed £100,000. The annual income of the Wandsworth Council for Community Relations is about £30,000 a year. If one adds the capital cost of De Poort to its annual running costs, and then includes expenditure on Indonesian immigrants in The Hague, the expenditure on immigrants since the war is probably in excess of ten million pounds, even on the most conservative estimate. The post-war figure for Wandsworth of £100,000 (which is a somewhat generous estimate) must be added to an unknown amount allocated locally in the recent urban renewal programme. This programme benefits those living in decaying urban areas, and since the majority of people in these areas are English this cannot be said to be direct expenditure on immigrant welfare. If

[9] This figure excludes the Diplomatic Community of The Hague.

[10] These running costs include the repayment of a loan covering part of the initial capitalization. But the large majority of expenditure is on current running costs.

one estimates such expenditure in Wandsworth at a quarter of a million pounds (and this is probably too generous an estimate) the total expenditure on immigrants in Wandsworth since 1945 has been less than £500,000, while the expenditure in The Hague on a similar number of immigrants has been £10 millions or more. In interpreting this figure we should take into account differences in national income per head between the two countries. In 1965 (Ernst, 1967) the income per head of the Netherlands was 81 per cent that of Britain (i.e. some $250 a head less than in Britain).[11] These financial comparisons do not take into account devaluation, and I have converted Dutch florins into English pounds at the pre-devaluation rate. An adjustment for devaluation would, of course, show Dutch expenditure in more favourable light.

### THE PROCESS OF INTEGRATION

I have suggested that considerable effort and expenditure has been put into efforts aimed at the integration of immigrant workers. This is a relatively recent policy, and even in 1970 had not yet come to its full fruition. In the year of writing there is considerable increase in the activity of the foundations, and of the amount of money allocated to them. How effective has this work been, and how did immigrants fare before the provision of such facilities? There were in fact serious clashes between Italian and native workers in the province of Twente in the autumn of 1959. Italian workers were attacked by Dutch youths who claimed (correctly, it seems) that the Italians were gaining the affection of Dutch girls. What was particularly objected to was the ease and manner of seduction, carried out in a typically Italian, and a most untypically Dutch, manner. Dutch courtship tends, like other Dutch relationships, to be somewhat stiff, restrained, and formal. Formality and restraint were notably lacking in the Italian approach. As a result of this, some bars, cafés, and dance halls put up posters saying 'No Italians Allowed'.

In the clashes between Dutch and Italians, police action was somewhat brutal and appeared to be biased against the Italians. In protest against this, a number of Italian workers went on strike.

[11] The economy of the Netherlands is, however, growing at a faster rate than that of Britain. By 1967 the G.N.P. per head in the Netherlands was $173 less than that of Britain (Wilson, 1971). By 1972 the G.N.P. per head of the Netherlands had overtaken that of Britain.

A subsequent study of the riots by Simons (1962) compared the integration of Italian workers in Twente, and in the province of Limburg. Simons suggested that in Protestant Twente, there were few facilities for integration and recreation of the Catholic Italians; but in Catholic Limburg, social and cultural facilities, as well as religious social control, were readily provided. In Limburg, the Italian workers were integrated and there was very little friction. Meerloo (1961) pointed out that café owners who barred Italians had the often difficult job of deciding whether individuals were Spanish or Italian; there was no objection to Spaniards, but they often experienced blanket discrimination meant for Italians. Meerloo cites instances of Italians entering cafés saying 'No Italians' and sitting peacefully at tables. Police were called, and the Italians forcefully ejected.

The study by Motta (1964) illustrates factors which made integration difficult for Italians and much less difficult for Spaniards. Motta interviewed twenty-five officials in Amsterdam, Utrecht, and Rotterdam, all of whom had regular contact with Italian and Spanish workers. Among these officials there was an almost unanimous stereotype of the Italian worker. The Italian worker, it was said, did not work hard, was often absent, had no interest in learning Dutch, was unreliable, frequently flirted, seduced 'our girls', and spent money as fast as he got it. But the informants produced quite another stereotype of the Spanish worker. He was said to be serious, hardworking, not stopping even to smoke a cigarette, purposeful, honest, reliable, faithful to his wife, moderate in courtship, punctual, respectful, and thrifty. These are all traits of the ideal Dutchman. Motta's hypothesis is that the first experience of the foreign worker in a new culture is an alienating one; but as the Italians got negative feedback because of their non-conformity to Dutch mores, their alienation would increase, while the Spaniards' alienation would decrease because they earned 'positive feedback' for their conformity to Dutch notions of civic behaviour. In Eisenstadt's terminology this hypothesis is that 'Italians have failed to internalize the meaning of migration, or alternatively, have failed to comprehend the meaningfulness of the roles they are supposed to play in the Netherlands'. In the investigation of this hypothesis, Motta (a Brazilian speaking both Italian and Spanish) interviewed a sample of fifty workers in Rotterdam factories.

In response to the question 'why did you migrate?' significantly more Italians gave 'meaningless' reasons (e.g. 'I don't know', 'to travel', 'I didn't like my father'). Again, in comparison with the Spaniards a large proportion of Italians had vague and imprecise plans for the future. The predominant reason the Italians gave for coming to the Netherlands was that treatment there was better than in Germany; for the Spaniards the predominant reason was that the Netherlands was a country where hard work would be rewarded. Asked whether they were satisfied with life at home, the Spaniards complained of poverty, which was their prime motive in migrating; while the main reason for the Italians was boredom and oppressive social control in Italy. There was a higher job turnover in the Netherlands among Italians than among Spaniards. Significantly more Spaniards complained that they had too little work to do in the Netherlands and would like to earn more money if they could. Significantly more Spaniards were saving from their wages. Many more Italians reported trouble in working with the Dutch; they had fewer Dutch friends; and significantly more Italians reported that their health was worse in the Netherlands. Both groups shared a unanimous dislike of Dutch food. Not only did the Spaniards have more Dutch friends than the Italians, but they also had more Spanish friends than the Italians had Italian friends. Of the single Spanish workers, markedly more dated Dutch girls than the single Italians. The Italian view of the Dutch was that they were 'ungrateful, despise us, envy us', while the Spaniards saw the Dutch as 'good, helpful, serious'. One practice which Motta discovered was for a Spaniard to take a Dutch workmate and his family home to Spain for a holiday, a service for which payment was made. Both Spaniards and Italians drew unfavourable comparisons between their treatment in West Germany and that in the Netherlands.

Motta concludes that his hypothesis was sustained: in comparison with the Spaniards, the Italians suffer from 'meaninglessness', having 'failed to internalize goals for the sake of which their migration is supposed to have taken place'. Meaninglessness, and the lack of it, was related to interaction with the Dutch. The Spaniards were not acculturated, but nevertheless were able to co-operate and live alongside the Dutch in an atmosphere of mutual respect. The position of the Spaniards is one of successful integration; that of the Italians, one of unsuccessful integration.

There is some evidence that with the passage of time the Dutch perception of migrant workers becomes more equable, hostility being transferred to the most recently arrived nationality group.[12] At the same time, the longer any group is resident, the more likely its members are to learn what behaviour is expected of a citizen in his daily affairs. Through a combination of coincidence and a desire to succeed, the Spanish worker—deferential, religious, hard-working in his native Spain as well as in the Netherlands—rapidly gained acceptance in Dutch eyes. But over time, because of the social control process, the Italian worker will also learn to adopt the outward signs of civic obedience which Dutch culture requires. At the same time, the internal culture of the group need not be affected.

In 1972 it was the Turkish and North African groups who appeared to have the greatest difficulty in their relationships with the Dutch population, while the Italians were by and large an accepted group (Bovenkerk, 1971). I shall discuss this point in more detail in a later chapter when data on attitudes to Surinamers and Moroccans in a sample of the Dutch population will be presented.

Migrant workers bringing their families pose the problem of education, and this aspect of integration has been discussed by Van der Velden (1968) in a review of 'the social reception and assistance of migrant workers and their families in the Ijmond region'. Migrant workers for the Royal Netherlands Blast Furnaces and Steelworks began to be recruited in 1956 in Italy, and later in other countries. The steelworks ('Hoogovens') took on the responsibility for the care and accommodation of these workers. Under E.E.C. arrangements, migrant workers from the common market have been able to bring their families with them since 1960. In the Netherlands workers from outside the E.E.C. area are also allowed to bring their families into the country once they have been established for a year. However, a family may not join a worker from outside the E.E.C. area until he has successfully obtained accommodation for his family, and it is here that social work assistance is necessary.

In Ijmond this assistance is provided by Hoogovens and also by the *Perigrinus-Stichting Ijmond*, a foundation started through Catholic initiative. The centre run by this *Stichting* is called 'Nuestra Casa Nostra'—a combination of the Italian 'Casa Nostra' and Spanish 'Nuestra Casa' both of which mean 'our home'. The

[12] From unpublished research carried out by the Ministry of Culture, Recreation, and Social Work.

work of Nuestra Casa Nostra is similar to that of De Poort in The Hague. It is similarly organized and financed, and by 1967 had been used by more than 100,000 foreign workers since the late 1950s. The Hoogovens have the option on a large number of houses in the Ijmond region on behalf of their employees, and these are allocated to the foreign workers after a year's qualifying employment, in the same way that they are allocated to Dutch employees. There is one exception however, in that a policy of dispersion of the migrant workers is consciously followed. By the time a man is joined by his family it is assumed that the 'training process' in Dutch norms of language and behaviour will be sufficiently advanced for the beginning of assimilation; integration, it is assumed, has already taken place. Like the foundations in The Hague and Rotterdam, the work of the *Perigrinus Stichting* in Ijmond has considerably increased since the early sixties. Given the evidence put forward by Simons (1962) we would expect that the services provided by the *Stichtingen* would reduce the 'alienation' of Italian workers by orienting them both to a realistic appraisal of their migration, and to an understanding of Dutch standards of behaviour and view of the work.

When a foreign employee of the Hoogovens applies for a house an employee of the housing department of the company makes a visit to the family *in the worker's native country*. This official tells the family about the kinds of housing they may expect and discusses with the wife the various problems and financial matters involved. He works out the cost of travel for the wife and her children, and freight charges for the family's possessions. If the family does not have enough capital for this venture a loan will be made by the company. Reports are prepared for the employment department of the Hoogovens, and a duplicate sent to the *Perigrinus Stichting*. When the house is actually allocated the migrant worker goes to see the appropriate social worker at Nuestra Casa Nostra to discuss schooling for his children, and matters such as house decoration and the possibility of employment for his wife.

Up to 1964 children of foreign workers were sent to Dutch schools appropriate for their age, but no special provisions for language teaching or orientation to Dutch culture were made. But after 1964 a much more positive policy was followed. In Ijmond the *Perigrinus Stichting* negotiated with the Government in that year to establish special reception classes. This activity was concentrated on St. Franciscus school at Heemskerk. This class was specially designed to give the children a working knowledge of Dutch and of Dutch society, and of the life of their new age peers. Instruction is individualized and transfer to the normal classes is effected as soon as possible. In 1968 the local education authority installed a thirty-booth language laboratory at St. Franciscus to help this work. The instruction is pupil-centred, and the classes small. Absorption into normal classes is on a 'setting' basis: that is, the child joins groups of differing ability according to his own ability in various subjects (e.g. he may be in an A stream for geography, a B stream for mathematics, and a C stream for art). Children living outside the Heemskerk area where these special 'language and integration classes' are provided are given special transport to St. Franciscus. This transport is provided by volunteers.

The principle of 'integration'—adjusting the immigrant to the culture of the Netherlands without eroding his own culture or cultural identity—is incorporated in this educational programme. The children are taught about the language, history, geography, and culture of their *own* country, and the Dutch teachers are anxious to avoid creating any kind of intellectual breach between parents and children. Dutch teenagers who have left school for employment still have to attend a further education centre on two half-days a week. Immigrant teenagers have this time off work too, and this opportunity is used to provide similar orientation courses in language and culture of both the Netherlands, and their home country. These teenagers can also attend the regular classes in Dutch in the *Perigrinus Stichting* in the evenings and on Saturday mornings.

In his conclusion Van Der Velden draws an analogy between 'a well-ordered community, a well-ordered trade, traffic, economy etc. etc,' and the obvious necessity for a well-ordered migration policy: 'This problem calls for a special ordering in all its sections. It is particularly important for those who are responsible in some way or other to use all possible efforts to eliminate the chaos which so often prevails in the situation of the migrant workers.' This, I would submit, is a rather Dutch approach: the necessity for order and regularity is stressed at an overt level. Underlying this, I suspect, is an important social system need: unregulated sub-cultures must not be allowed to form in Dutch society, a society whose cohesion and smooth running is based on the *regulation* of sub-cultures, and of orderly and precise relations between these sub-cultures (the pillars of society). The social policy which regulates this potential 'disorderliness' in Dutch society is firm, moralistic in outlook, generously provided, and kindly in enactment. One cannot help comparing the Dutch treatment of immigrants to their treatment of children: firm, somewhat authoritarian with a fairly rigidly defined structure, but consistent, and very kindly. This, as argued in my account of Dutch society, is an extremely powerful form of socialization.

A detailed study of Spanish workers in Rotterdam has been carried out by Geyer (1967) in work financed by the *Stichting Arbeidsvoorziening Scheepsbouw-en Metaalindustrie*. Geyer and his colleagues studied a hundred Spanish workers in Rotterdam during 1965–6 and also carried out interviews with fifty Dutch workers to provide comparative data. Geyer found that 66 per cent of the Spanish workers had friends in the Netherlands before migration, and 51 per cent had discussed their proposed migration with someone who had been to the Netherlands. For the majority, the decision to come to the Netherlands was based on personal contact with someone whose experience of Dutch life and working conditions had been favourable. Fifty-one of the Spanish workers considered that relations between the sexes were markedly different than in Spain, and of these the majority disapproved of the freedom which Dutch women had. Over three-quarters of respondents had plans to stay in the Netherlands for at least some years. Many said that if they could find housing they would bring their families to the Netherlands, and those with their families already in the Netherlands wanted to stay indefinitely.

Geyer found that 35 per cent of his subjects had regular contact with foundations offering help for Spanish workers; of the remaining sixty-five workers, nearly two-thirds had some contact with foundations. Geyer concludes that there is room for considerable development in these services, and the recommendations of his report, made in 1967, are having their effect in the expansion of activities for foreign workers in Rotterdam and elsewhere. The author found that the Spanish workers reported higher levels of satisfaction with their work than the Dutch controls, and more Spanish workers wanted to work overtime than Dutch workers. This finding is in line with Motta's earlier one (1964). Eighty-two per cent rated their contact with Dutchmen as positive; 64 per cent had Dutch friends, and of these 62 per cent had visited their Dutch friend's house, and 64 per cent were on drinking terms with their friend. The longer a Spanish worker had been in the Netherlands, the more Dutch friends he had. Only 7 per cent of the Spaniards reported an overall negative impression of their Dutch workmates. This study, like those of Surinamese workers, suggests that integration increases over time.

An interesting study of the attitudes of the press to foreign workers has been made by Van Emmerik-Levelt and Teulings (1967). The authors studied the contents of a sample of fifty national newspapers representing both the employers' and the trade union point of view, published in the year 1965. In addition a similar analysis was made of fifty-two copies of a sample of provincial newspapers published in the same year. Reports concerning immigrant workers were classified, and housing problems (36 per cent) were found to be the most numerous, followed by recruitment and reception problems (30 per cent), work problems (25 per cent), crime and public disturbances (23 per cent), the issue of whether immigrants should be permanent or temporary (19 per cent), and the difficulties involved in bringing families to stay in the Netherlands (16 per cent). Many of the articles classified referred to more than one area, which accounts for the overlapping percentages.

The authors found that the use of stereotypes—both negative and positive—was common. Only in the area of crime and relations of immigrants with Dutch girls did negative stereotypes predominate. The regional press was most likely to use such stereotypes, while the 'employers' press' viewed immigrants most favourably. The source of the news affected the use of stereotypes. Where the newspaper used its own reporters, the writing was much less informed, and more sensational—for example, implying that a single deviant case was representative of the majority. But where the source of the news was an official body rather than a reporter, the reports were less stereotyped. In other words, the Dutch newspapers accepted in good faith official versions of immigrant behaviour and problems, and the official versions tended to view immigrants in a favourable and sympathetic light.

With regard to crime amongst immigrant workers, Geyer (1967) in his study of Spanish workers, reported that the crime rate amongst them was no higher than amongst workers generally. One national newspaper published in Amsterdam, *De Telegraaf* is noted for its rather sensational reports of crime amongst immigrants, including Surinamers. *De Telegraaf* is the one 'yellow' newspaper in the Netherlands. This newspaper is itself deviant in being outside the bloc system. Lijphart comments: 'An independent paper like *De Telegraaf* is more adventurous and does not feel bound to guard all political secrets. But its access to such classified information is severely limited, and it tends to be more noisy than knowledgeable' (p. 133). Official figures suggest that the crime rate[13] in immigrants from Italy is 16·14 per 1,000, from Spain 9·8 per 1,000, from Turkey 9·2 per 1,000, and from Morocco 11·37 per 1,000.[14] These are not particularly high figures. The age distribution of the offenders shows that they are in their late twenties and thirties. Germans in the Netherlands have a much higher crime rate than other immigrant groups, and their age distribution shows that the majority of these offenders, unlike the other groups we have mentioned, are teenagers or in their early twenties. These young Germans come to the Netherlands for a short time to enjoy themselves, and escape the bonds of social control; but migrant workers to the Netherlands are generally older than these German youths. Since crime is predominantly a youthful act, the working immigrants tend to have relatively low crime rates. The figures for marriage of immigrants in the Netherlands[15] for 1967 show that 293 of the 314 Italians marrying in the Netherlands married Dutch girls; 156 of the 204 Spaniards marrying in the Netherlands married Dutch girls; 28 of the 29 Portuguese did so; 117 of the 131 Greeks; all of the 97 Turks; and 62 of the 63 Moroccans.

## CONCLUSIONS

Immigrants to the Netherlands from Southern Europe and North Africa and Turkey are coming to the country in increasing numbers. Many of them stay for long periods, and many will bring their families to the Netherlands and settle permanently. Their growing numbers, and the realization that these immigrant groups were forming incipient blocs of society in their own right

[13] *Buitenlandse Werknemers* (No. 4, April 1969), p. 71.

[14] The crime rate in Surinamers has been estimated at 9·0 per 1,000. See also 'De delinquent van Surinaamse afkomst in Nederland', *Maatchapelimjk werk*, 1969, *293*, 321–325; and Bovenkerk and van Galen (1971) who point out that the immigrant crime rate is generally below that of the native population. But see also Buikhuisen (1971) on the rising crime rate in young Moluccans.

[15] *Buitenlandse Werknemers* (No. 1, January 1969), p. 10.

led the Dutch to reconsider their previous rather *laissez faire* policy on immigrants (including West Indian immigrants).

The late 1960s have seen the vigorous expansion of foundations aimed to assist these workers. These foundations have aimed to provide the immigrant with a command of Dutch language and an understanding of the Dutch way of life, and the nuances of inter-personal behaviour. At the same time conscious efforts have been made to ensure that the immigrant's original cultural identity is not lost. The development of the activities of the foundations suggests that the increasing numbers of immigrants to the Netherlands was perceived as a potential threat to the existing smooth relations between the various blocs of society. Vigorous efforts have been made to ensure that the immigrants form blocs on the Dutch pattern, retaining their cultural identity, and customary norms of private behaviour, but at the same time conforming to the Dutch code of civility and inter-bloc relations.

The Dutch provision for foundation activities has been very generous—extraordinarily generous by British standards; the foundation's activities—which I have illustrated by case histories of The Hague and Ijmond—are vigorous, businesslike, and efficient. They are carried out in a climate of official support, and a general atmosphere of public tolerance.

Public tolerance of activities on behalf of immigrants, and of immigrants themselves, relates to the need to make the immigrant groups part of the bloc system in an orderly way, and to the extent that immigrants conform to Dutch norms of public and inter-bloc behaviour. A comparison of Spanish and Italian workers suggests that in the early years of their migration the Italians, for various reasons, often deviated from Dutch norms. This behaviour was not tolerated by the Dutch public. This lack of toleration has been a form of social control influencing conformity to Dutch norms. Other things being equal, the increased activity of the foundations should tend to decrease deviance in immigrant groups.

The longer an immigrant group had been settled in the Netherlands, the greater the degree of integration of that group there appears to be. Integration is a process by which the immigrant group retains its original cultural identity, but at the same time conforms to Dutch public behaviour. Over time one would expect these immigrant groups to be absorbed into Dutch society (assimilated into existing blocs). This assimilation is subject to their similarity to existing religious groups, and we would expect

Moslems to form a distinctive and more permanent Moslem pillar of society. The more recent the arrival of a group in the Netherlands, the more difficult will it be for members of that group to understand Dutch public norms, and therefore the greater the hostility (social control) on the part of the Dutch population.

Events in the Schildersbuurt area of The Hague, which are outlined in detail in Chapter 6, illustrate the way in which groups, such as Indonesians, Turks, and Moroccans, who are perceived to be non-conforming can be the subject of some very harsh social control behaviour. It is possible too that the instigators of this 'social control' behaviour may themselves be breaking Dutch norms of orderliness and tolerance.

CHAPTER 6

# DEVIANCE, SOCIAL CONTROL, AND RACISM IN DUTCH SOCIETY

I have argued that Dutch society is marked by kindly authoritarianism, deference to one's elders and those in positions of authority, with particular respect for the moral dogmas of Christianity. The force of these institutionalized ethical principles is one motivating individual behaviour in the direction of tolerance of disparate minorities, ethnic and religious. But I have argued, too, that tolerance is extended only to the extent that the minorities conform to the Dutch *verzuiling* rules, and the parallel rules of restrained and deferential inter-personal behaviour.

Deviance may thus, by this argument, take two main forms. First, minorities will be deviant to the extent that they do not behave in accord with the social system principles of inter-bloc behaviour. Secondly, there may exist deviants who, although nominally members of established pillars of society, do not accord tolerance to members of minority groups. We would suppose that such individuals have resisted, or have been imperfectly exposed to, the normal processes of bloc socialization. Before examining these kinds of deviance I shall discuss briefly the puzzling case of South Africa, and also the tenets of Calvinism which may have a bearing on this case. The Netherlands is ostensibly a tolerant country, tolerant of minorities and interracial mixing and marriage. South Africa, a society strongly influenced by Dutch settlement and institutions, is a manifestly racist society. How can this paradox be explained?

The answer seems to be that Dutch emigrants to South Africa were deviant from Dutch society in that they were individuals most likely to resist social change of a liberal nature—for example the development of inter-bloc tolerance in the nineteenth century. Patterson (1957) comments of the early Huguenot settlers in South Africa: 'These newcomers were characterized by their knowledge of viticulture, by their industriousness and high capacity and organization, by a stern Calvinist fanaticism, and by a rejection of Europe and all her ways. The two latter traits at least were to become part of the Boer ethos' (p. 2). This 'Calvinist fanaticism', which has been a central part of Boer philosophy, relied very strongly on the support of the Dutch emigrants to South Africa and their descendants who formed the backbone of the Dutch Reformed Church. Assisted immigration to South Africa ceased in 1710. As a result of this, Patterson suggests, 'the Afrikaners have from then until the present day had to rely on natural increase and individual immigration for the augmentation of their numbers'. The Dutch East India Company, which used South Africa as a provision centre, preferred to use slave labour rather than to import 'unruly' European labour. As a result no intermediate, white, lower middle class developed (as, for example, in Curaçao), so that there existed only an elite ruling class of whites controlling a mass of slaves.

The Calvinist ruling class did not make efforts to convert slaves to Christianity, and by the end of the eighteenth century 'white man' and 'Christian' had become synonymous. The Roman Catholic missionaries who worked in the West Indian colonies were largely absent in South Africa, and white farmers made strong efforts to prevent any activities to convert Hottentots to Christianity (Patterson, 1957, p. 9). Catholic and Anglican missionaries were imbued with ideas of spiritual and therefore actual equality between men, and were very strongly resented by the Boers whose own extreme Calvinism had an excessive concern with propriety and sexual morality, and equated any kind of black–white marriage or union as extreme sinfulness. The ideal woman was 'a white woman, chaste and aloof amongst a coloured sea' (Patterson, 1957, p. 242). From an early date the various states legislated against sexual relations between whites and non-whites, and these laws were codified in the 1927 Immorality Act.[1]

The 'Dutch Reformed Church' dominates much of South African life, and provides ideological support for apartheid. This church is *not* the same as the Dutch Reformed Church of the Netherlands, which is a reformed and liberal institution. Ideologically and liturgically the D.R.C. of South Africa is closer to the more conservative Re-Reformed church of the Netherlands,

[1] See Bagley (1969b) for an account of the 'alienation' of human rights in contemporary South Africa.

but its ideology and theological views are nevertheless considerably more conservative than even those of the Dutch Re-Reformed Church. Roman Catholic missionaries have made progress in more recent times, and there are now about half a million Catholics in South Africa, the large majority of them black. The Calvinists severely distrust the universalism of the Catholic faith, and there have been systematic campaigns against the Catholic church. In 1950 the D.R.C. called for a ban on Roman Catholic immigrants from the Netherlands. Subsidies to Roman Catholic schools have been systematically denied.

The D.R.C. of South Africa has shown an excessive concern with sexual morality to the extent, for example, of condemning modern dancing as 'heathen, dangerous and promiscuous', and suggesting that 'modern dress' in women (in the early 1950s) constituted a sexual enticement to blacks. There appear to be strong sexual undertones to the policy of 'apartness' which, we would suggest, have their origin in the conservative theology of Calvinism.

South African society developed in the way it did because, from the first, it was a refuge of the extreme zealots of Calvinism. South Africa was not commercially colonized, as were the Dutch East Indies, but remained the private province of private emigrants—extreme Calvinists—from Europe. The relationship of Afrikaners with the British in South Africa makes the situation a more complex one to analyse, but the relationship, in which Afrikaners traditionally felt a sense of inferiority because of the presence of the British, has probably emphasized Afrikaner rigidity. The Dutch emigrants to South Africa have been deviants from Dutch life, the extreme Protestants for whom any kind of compromise with other religious groups, including reformed Calvinists and Roman Catholics, was unacceptable. It is possible that this emigration of extremists from the Netherlands has indirectly contributed to the stability of Dutch society. Members of the mainstream of Dutch society migrated not to South Africa, but to Indonesia, and here relationships with the native population were much more liberal. Interracial marriage, as we have seen, was common and socially approved.

Echoes of this extreme Calvinist attitude to race relations, which view contact between black and white as an incitement to sexual relations and therefore to sin, can still be found in the Netherlands: de Boer-Lasschuyt (1959) interviewing Dutch officials after disturbances in The Hague (which are described below) between immigrants from Indonesia and Dutch youths, was told by a police official that, 'There are, and will come in the future, enough difficulties with these Eastern people. And especially these Indo-Europeans, born in sin, with their bad background will have a difficult, nearly impossible task to adapt themselves to Dutch morals' (pp. 4–5). De Boer-Lasschuyt suggests that this attitude illustrates the Calvinist concept of the mixed blooded Indo-Europeans as 'children of sin' descended from illegitimate relationships. A similar kind of attitude was discerned by Motta (1964) who interviewed a Calvinist trade-union leader who argued that Italian workers (who also happened to be Catholics) 'are a danger to Dutch families, and a danger to themselves, because, living away from their families, the occasions of sin [an oblique reference to sexual relationships with Dutch girls] will finish by leading them to Hell'.

## PREJUDICE IN THE NETHERLANDS

Dutchmen tend to define prejudice somewhat differently than Englishmen. For a Dutchman, as I have previously observed (1968a), the term 'prejudice' covers behaviour such as failing to invite your coloured workmate home to dinner; in Britain 'prejudice' seems to cover only the grosser forms of hostility and ungraciousness. When they talk or write about prejudice, Dutchmen tend to be self-doubting and self-questioning. 'What has my conduct in this matter been?' and 'Have my actions been of the best?' are the implicit questions underlying such discussions. These questions reflect the theological and moral undertones that inform much debate in the Netherlands about public issues. An example of this self-questioning attitude is the academic study by Reijnders (1969) of the treatment by Dutchmen of Jews in the period 1600 to 1942. Reijnders suggests that Dutch treatment of the Jews has been less than liberal, and has been unworthy of a Christian nation. Now, in theological terms this treatment has been less than perfect; but nevertheless this treatment has been less harsh than in any other European country.[2] A study of Persser's account (1965) of the fate of the Dutch Jewish community in the years 1940–5 confirms this view.

[2] Including, we would add, Britain. See Scharf's account (1966) of anti-semitism in Britain.

A number of public opinion surveys carried out in the Netherlands have provided important data on attitudes to minorities. A question relating to race relations was included in a survey of 'Love and Marriage in the Netherlands' carried out by Attwood Statistics of Rotterdam in 1965. This was a nation-wide random sample of 1,600 adults aged 17–70 years.[3] Among the questions asked in this survey was one which inquired: 'If you had a daughter who intended to marry a man with different religious beliefs, would you object . . .?' This was followed by a question on racial intermarriage. Now, there is a weakness in the second question in that it has been contaminated by the first, i.e. there is the strong possibility that respondents have in mind a man of a different race who is also of a different religion, so their responses to this question will be less liberal than to a question specifying a coloured man of the same religion. The results, nevertheless, are of interest, and we give them in Table 6:1. In this table the percentages

[3] *Polls* (Vol. I, No. 4, Summer 1966). I am grateful to the Directors of Attwood Statistics, Rotterdam, for providing additional data from this survey.

*Table 6:1. Dutch Attitudes to Interreligious and Interethnic Marriage*

| | *No Objection Whatever* % | | *Accept, but Reluctantly* % | | *Would be Opposed* % | |
|---|---|---|---|---|---|---|
| | *Religion* | *Race* | *Religion* | *Race* | *Religion* | *Race* |
| All | 32 | (31) | 49 | (43) | 14 | (21) |
| *Religion* | | | | | | |
| R.C. | 24 | (31) | 52 | (41) | 21 | (22) |
| Dutch Reformed | 29 | (27) | 54 | (44) | 13 | (24) |
| Re-Reformed | 11 | (24) | 53 | (51) | 23 | (17) |
| Other religion | 28 | (34) | 55 | (42) | 10 | (13) |
| No religion | 56 | (38) | 38 | (41) | 4 | (10) |
| *Age* | | | | | | |
| 17–25 | 42 | (43) | 45 | (37) | 10 | (13) |
| 26–35 | 37 | (40) | 49 | (36) | 12 | (19) |
| 36–50 | 26 | (22) | 53 | (49) | 15 | (23) |
| 51–70 | 26 | (21) | 50 | (47) | 19 | (26) |
| *Area* | | | | | | |
| Three main cities | 48 | (33) | 42 | (47) | 6 | (16) |
| Other urban areas | 32 | (36) | 51 | (40) | 12 | (18) |
| Rural areas | 21 | (23) | 51 | (44) | 23 | (27) |

*in brackets* refer to responses to the questions on a man of a different race, while the figure which precedes it refers to the response on a marriage partner of different religion.

The results shown in Table 6:1 are interesting in that they suggest that there is still considerable resistance to inter-bloc marriages, and that this resistance is strongest in rural areas, among older people, and among the Re-Reformed. It is particularly interesting to note too that Re-Reformed church members are the most liberal of the religious groups on the issue of interracial marriage. It is noticeable that the Re-Reformed are the only group in which respondents are *more* liberal on interracial marriage than they are on inter-faith marriage.

A further random sample of the Netherlands population in 1967[4] inquired whether respondents thought that the churches should express opinions in favour of or against apartheid. The results are shown in Table 6:2.

*Table 6:2. Dutch Attitudes to the Churches and Apartheid*

| | *'Churches should be in favour'* % | *'Church should oppose'* % | *(Remaining respondents favoured neutrality, or did not know)* |
|---|---|---|---|
| Roman Catholic | 3 | 60 | |
| Dutch Reformed | 4 | 71 | |
| Re-Reformed | 7 | 69 | |
| Other religion (Protestant sects) | 7 | 58 | |

These results are particularly interesting in that they suggest that there may be a small sub-group of Re-Reformed Calvinists (and of other minor Calvinist sects) who favour apartheid; but nevertheless, a large proportion of Re-Reformed church members feel that their church should speak out against South Africa's apartheid policy.

A survey by Attwood Statistics of 'Churches and Religion in the Netherlands'[5] asked the question, 'Supposing you got neighbours of a different race, would you have no objections whatever, would you accept it but not like it, or would you protest?'

[4] *Polls* (Vol. III, No. 2, Autumn 1967).

[5] This was a random survey of 1,590 men and women aged 17–70 years, and was carried out in March 1965. *Polls* (Vol. III, No. 2, Autumn 1967).

*Table 6:3. Dutch Attitudes towards having Neighbours of Different Race (Polls)*

| | *Men* | *Women* |
|---|---|---|
| No objection at all | 85 | 86 |
| Would not like it | 13 | 11 |
| Would protest | 1 | 1 |
| Depends | 1 | 1 |

We do not have comparable data for the British population, but an American survey (reported in the same volume of *Polls*) suggests that 37 per cent of Americans would have no objection to a Negro living next door.

A further survey of 'politics in the Netherlands' by Attwood Statistics provides data on attitudes to Provos (an anarchist group of young people centred in Amsterdam, believing, among other things, in sharing possessions).[6] Table 6:4 gives statements presented about Provos.

*Table 6:4. Dutch Attitudes to Provos*

| *Provos are . . .* | *Agreeing —men %* | *Agreeing —women %* |
|---|---|---|
| Too lazy to work | 69 | 73 |
| Come up with some new ideas | 43 | 45 |
| Are rowdies | 84 | 87 |
| Want to improve society | 28 | 33 |
| Should really be clapped under lock and key | 38 | 37 |

These findings suggest that although the Dutch people surveyed can be quite liberal on questions of race, they can nevertheless express some very conservative ideas over the treatment of deviant minorities. In this context we would reiterate our earlier proposition that immigrants are accepted and tolerated in Dutch society to the extent that they can be absorbed into the *verzuiling* system; any group will be treated harshly to the extent that they

[6] This survey, like the other Attwood surveys, was carried out for the Amsterdam magazine publisher, *De Geillusteerde Pers*. The survey was of 1,594 adults aged 17–70 years, interviewed in August 1966. *Polls* (Vol. III, No. 4, Summer 1968).

reject the traditional *verzuiling* rules, or do not understand them.

The Attwood survey of 'Churches and Religions in the Netherlands' provides some interesting data on the difference in outlook and values between members of different churches (see Table 6:5). The survey showed, first of all, that 85 per cent of Catholics attended church regularly (at least once a fortnight) compared with 39 per cent of Dutch Reformed, 88 per cent of Re-Reformed, and 60 per cent of other churches (mostly minor Protestant sects).

*Table* 6:5. *Variations in Religious Values* (*Attwood Survey*)

(1) 'Do you believe in the existence of Hell, or not?'

*Per cent answering 'Yes'—*

| *R.C.* | *Re-Reformed* | *Dutch Reformed* | *No Denomination* |
|---|---|---|---|
| 66 | 90 | 54 | 11 |

(2) 'Do you believe in the existence of Heaven, or not?'

*Per cent answering 'Yes'—*

| *R.C.* | *Re-Reformed* | *Dutch Reformed* | *No Denomination* |
|---|---|---|---|
| 90 | 100 | 82 | 22 |

(3) 'Do you believe that what happens in the world happens according to a certain plan, do you think it happens by chance?'

*Per cent accepting 'a certain plan'—*

| *R.C.* | *Re-Reformed* | *Dutch Reformed* | *No Denomination* |
|---|---|---|---|
| 37 | 57 | 89 | 24 |

(4) 'Do you believe that there is a God who concerns himself with everyone personally?'

*Per cent answering 'Yes'—*

| *R.C.* | *Re-Reformed* | *Dutch Reformed* | *No Denomination* |
|---|---|---|---|
| 59 | 93 | 66 | 18 |

Table 6:6 shows some items from the survey on 'Love and Marriage in the Netherlands' mentioned above.

One further point of interest emerges from this review of survey data from the Netherlands. This concerns the perception of social problems by 462 individuals surveyed by the National Institute of Public Opinion Research in August 1966.[7] Respondents were asked, 'What do you feel should be the government's first task to carry out?' The item singled out by the largest number of respondents was housing (34 per cent), followed by taxation

[7] *Polls* (Vol. II, No. 3, Spring 1967).

*Table 6:6. Dutch Attitudes to Sexual mores*

(1) 'A girl should remain a virgin until she marries.'

*Per cent answering 'Yes'*

| *R.C.* | *Re-Reformed* | *Dutch Reformed* | *No Denomination* |
|---|---|---|---|
| 68 | 83 | 68 | 53 |

(2) 'Do you think it normal for young people to kiss in public, e.g. in the street, or do you think it improper?'

*Per cent considering it improper—*

| *R.C.* | *Re-Reformed* | *Dutch Reformed* | *No Denomination* |
|---|---|---|---|
| 65 | 87 | 67 | 59 |

(17 per cent). Immigration was not reported as a cause of concern by any of the respondents. A survey in Britain carried out in March 1965, provides some comparison with these findings.[8] The comparison cannot be an exact one, however, since the British subjects were given a prepared list of subjects to choose from, whilst the Dutch subjects had no such list. Of the British subjects 66 per cent nominated housing as a serious social problem, and 55 per cent nominated immigration of coloured people. We would interpret these findings to mean that there is a quite considerable concern with housing in both Britain and the Netherlands, but only in Britain is coloured immigration perceived to be a problem.

Gadourek and his colleagues (1962) have submitted data from an earlier public opinion survey in the Netherlands (concerning 1,297 individuals in eighty-five different communities) to a systematic analysis and sociological interpretation. They inquired first about the subject's religious denomination, and occupational group, and then measured the intensity of an individual's involvement in his religious organization (or, in the case of a secularist, the appropriate sectarian or political group). Each subject commented on the values of his organization; the amount of study he had done on its teaching; the degree to which he had discussed it with others; and how much he would regret his children joining a different church or organization.

It will be noticed that the highest involvement occurred in the Re-Reformed who, we have seen in the survey data above, are the most conservative groups (both socially and theologically) in the

[8] *Polls* (Vol. III, No. 2, Autumn 1967).

*Table 6:7. Intensity of an Individual's Involvement in Religious Organizations*

| *Group* | *Per cent in Survey* | *Mean Involvement Score* |
|---|---|---|
| Roman Catholic | 41·0 | 2·9 |
| Protestant (Dutch Reformed and Re-Reformed) | 33·0 | 2·9 |
| Small sects | 1·1 | 3·2 |
| Socialists | 8·8 | 2·6 |
| Liberals | 1·9 | 1·5 |
| Humanists | 2·8 | 2·5 |
| *All subjects* | | 2·6 |
| Re-Reformed | Not Stated | 4·5 |
| Unskilled labourers | ,, ,, | 2·0 |
| Technical workers | ,, ,, | 3·0 |
| Farmers | ,, ,, | 3·0 |
| Professionals | ,, ,, | 3·3 |
| Social workers, nurses | ,, ,, | 4·3 |
| Teachers and priests | ,, ,, | 4·6 |

Netherlands. The high score of social workers and nurses reflects the fact that such services are organized on sectarian lines, and these vocations are taken by individuals highly involved with the life of their church or organization.

Interesting ecological variations were observed. The 'cultural involvement' scores in individuals in Utrecht and The Hague were 3·0 and 2·64 respectively, higher than the countrywide average of 2·6; while in Amsterdam and Rotterdam, the scores, at 2·3 and 2·5, were lower than the national average. In large cities (population more than 200,000) Gadourek and his colleagues found that there was a significant under-representation of scorers in the middle of the scale; migrants too, tended to have scores of 0 or 1, or 5 or 6. Similar distribution of scores was found too, in individuals who had married a partner of a different religion, in individuals whose traditional reference group had broken down, and individuals who manifested 'meaninglessness' or 'inner tensions'. These interesting findings suggest the possibility that internal migrants in the Netherlands, and others who for various reasons have lost contact with their traditional kinds of social organizations, tend either to lose all kinds of cultural involvement, or to throw themselves with particular vigour into new religious and cultural groups.

A further study by Gadourek (1969) throws some light on deviance in the Netherlands. This is a study of political radicalism in a hundred Dutch communities. 'Radicalism' is defined as support for the party of the extreme right—the Farmers' party—of the extreme left—the communist and pacifist parties. The hundred communities studied excluded large cities; the largest community studied was the city of Haarlem, population 162,000. Various social indicators were examined, including population change, income change, secularization, and industrialization. A multivariate analysis of these ecological data led Gadourek to conclude that the extreme right-wing Farmers' party drew most of its support from Dutch Reformed communities, from the less secularized communities, and from communities with a small percentage of industrialized workers. A connection was found too between a trend towards secularization over time, and support for the communist and pacifist parties. Surprisingly however, no connection between industrialization and urbanization and radicalism of the left was found, nor between such radicalism and increasing levels of education, or increase in population size.

The Farmers' party, founded in 1958, obtained 2·1 per cent of the votes in the 1963 election, and under the proportional representation system gained three seats in Parliament. In the 1966 elections the Farmers' party polled 6·7 per cent of votes, and 9 per cent of votes in the city of Amsterdam, suggesting that support for this party is not confined to farmers themselves. Nooij studied a sample of 290 farmers[9] to see whether responses to various attitude scales distinguished between supporters of the Farmers' party and others.

Rather surprisingly Nooij found that responses to the California F-(fascism) scale were only weakly related to support for the Farmers' party. There was however a much higher relationship between anomie scores (representing insecurity and normlessness) and support for this party. Nooij concludes that 'it is not authoritarianism but anomie which is the central explanatory factor that brings about sympathies with the Farmers' Party'.[10] These data also provide some support for our earlier propositions that extreme right-wing groups in the Netherlands have not been racialist (i.e. anti-black, or anti-semitic).

[9] This study was carried out at the Agricultural University of Wageningen.

[10] In the 1971 election the Farmers' party lost virtually all its electoral support.

Dutch versions of the F-scale have also been used with Dutch populations by Weima (1964 and 1965). Weima was particularly interested in religious observance and attitudes to other groups, such as Catholics, in Re-Reformed church members. He found, in a sample of 244 Calvinists that there was a very marked correlation (in the region of 0·8) between authoritarianism (as measured by the F-scale) and hostility to Catholics (e.g. agreeing with statements such as, 'The Roman Catholic Church is a menace to religious liberty.') However, Weima found (using Wilson's 'extrinsic religious involvement scale') that these prejudiced Calvinists (prejudiced both against Catholics and against ethnic minorities) were individuals who conformed to outward aspects of religious behaviour and for whom religion was merely a means to gaining social respectability. Such individuals had little cognizance of the 'inner' meaning of their religion: 'The authoritarian personality' concludes Weima, 'is characterized by a defective integration of religious values.' A further study in Utrecht of Catholics (n = 168) confirmed the relationship between authoritarianism and hostility to other religious groups in a deviant sub-group of Catholics.

### THE SCHILDERSBUURT INCIDENTS

'Schildersbuurt' means 'painters' quarter', and is a district of The Hague lying between the main Delft–Leiden railway line and the centre of The Hague. It is called the 'painters' quarter' not because it is the home of artists, but because many of the streets are named after famous artists. It is an area of densely populated working-class apartments, built around the turn of the century. Over 100,000 souls live in this quarter, in an area of less than a square mile.

The Schildersbuurt is of interest in the study of race relations because it was the scene of one of the few disturbances which followed the large-scale immigration from Indonesia. In June 1958 there were street fights between groups of white and coloured youths. Daily newspapers devoted a good deal of attention to these disturbances, and some of them carried headlines such as 'Racial hatred caused by jealousy', 'Youth war over Hague girls' (de Boer-Lasschuyt, 1959). In her analysis of this situation de Boer-Lasschuyt cited an official of the Children's Police, who declared:

Better not to emphasize these fights between these Indonesian and Dutch rascals; these boys are all little scoundrels! They love a fight!

The feelings of 'racial hatred' were completely overstressed and overemphasized by the press. There are no racial hostilities in our Christian society. The basis for the fights was jealousy: the dark Indo-European boys are attractive to a certain kind of Dutch girl; these boys are good-looking, they are well dressed in their modern narrow trousers, they are good dancers and their behaviour is polite, pleasant and graceful. They are much more popular with these girls than their clumsy and plump Dutch brothers. Sexual jealousy is aroused!

De Boer-Lasschuyt suggested that deviants from the 'Dutch creed' of non-discrimination and protecting the rights of minorities are likely to be young men in the age range 16 to 26 years, and she cites some evidence to show that such men—or a minority of them, at least—may go through a transitional period of deviance when they may be liable to reject the codes of conduct laid down by their elders. Alternatively, or in parallel with this tendency, we must consider the possibility that the action of the Dutch youths was motivated (as was the action of Dutch youths in Twenthe in the Italian riots) through a sense of outrage because the immigrant youths were not obeying traditional rules of courtship, which involve restraint and civility.

The possibility of group enforcement of mores as a means of social control is particularly interesting in the light of an incident which occurred in May 1969, while I was carrying out fieldwork in The Hague. The K.R.O. television station sent a camera team to an apartment in Jan de Baenstraat to interview a couple who both appeared to be mentally unstable, and who were living in squalid surroundings and apparently illtreating their children. The neighbours were enraged at the unfortunate couple who had let the neighbourhood down by their behaviour. A large and threatening group gathered round the apartment using abusive and threatening language. The K.R.O. cameramen again arrived on the scene and filmed these good citizens in the performance of their civic duty![11] Two things are interesting about this incident. Firstly, anger was directed not at the T.V. company,[12] but at the

[11] For a fuller account of this incident see *Boulevard* (Den Haag, No. 37, 25 May 1969), pp. 8–9.

[12] On 29 April 1969, a major T.V. network broadcast a programme in which they tried to provoke an incident depicting racial discrimination. A motorist, in fact a confederate of the cameramen, collided with a taxi driven by a Turkish immigrant (also a confederate). The motorist (whose fault the accident was) then abused the taxi driver. It was expected that passers by might join in this tirade. In fact, the bystanders sided with the Turk, and reproached the motorist for making an unnecessary fuss! He was of course deviant in straying from the norms of bourgeois civility.

family; the action and the presence of the cameramen on both occasions was accepted as the legitimate activity of an established authority. Secondly, the action of the community was explicit, vocal, and violent, and extremely intolerant of deviant behaviour.

A few weeks after this incident, in nearby Van Ravensteinstraat an incident occurred which is of direct relevance for the consideration of race relations in the Netherlands. On the night of 15 June, just as the bars were closing, a gathering of citizens advanced on a hostel housing thirty Moroccan workers. They damaged a Mercedes car belonging to one of the immigrants, broke the windows of the hostel, and forced their way in. The Moroccans were then beaten up. They fled, pursued by a gang of stout citizens. By this time the police arrived—shortly after midnight—and the gang dispersed. But the Moroccans were taken into custody. Three of them were found to be without the proper papers. Without further ado they were driven in a police car to the German border and dumped. This role of the police is interesting, for it suggests that some levels of officialdom share the dislike of Moroccans displayed by sections of the working-class population.

One is struck by the similarity of these incidents to the 'mob-law' events in Britain which took place at about the same time[13]—the action of the populace of St. Ives against hippies, and of a section of the Leeds population against coloured people, in which Pakistani property was attacked and damaged.

The causes of the sacking of the Moroccan hostel are obscure, but the perceptions or misperceptions of a number of local residents interviewed at the time suggested possible reasons—that the Moroccans flirted too readily with local girls, that some of them stood naked at their bedroom windows beckoning to women in the street, and that the hostel had seventy immigrants packed into it (in fact there were thirty). The ostentatious ownership of a Mercedes was also said to be improper for a working man.[14]

Whatever the immediate causes of the behaviour of the Schildersbuurt residents on this occasion, the behaviour seems to be part of a general pattern of social control. The Moroccans were perceived as deviant, and the community took direct action. This rather brutal socialization experience may have the result of causing the Moroccans to be, at least, more discreet in the future.

[13] *Guardian* (12 July 1969 and 29 July 1969).
[14] *De Volkskrant* (17 June 1969).

It is an interesting point that the Moroccans in this hostel had not had very much contact with the facilities offered by De Poort.

In July 1971 further incidents occurred in the Schildersbuurt, this time involving street rioting and attacks on Turkish workers.[15] Disturbances lasted intermittently for two days, and were finally broken up by police using water canons. Bovenkerk (1971) in an analysis of factors underlying this incident, suggests three possible causes: (*i*) competition with working-class people for jobs and especially for scarce housing resources; (*ii*) exploitation of Turks in the housing market, especially the charging of high rents for inferior accommodation; (*iii*) a minority of whites projecting feelings of aggression onto minorities.

It is quite obvious from the preceding paragraphs that there is hostility and discrimination towards minority groups in the Netherlands. To what extent has Dutch law been cognizant of this problem?

A number of European countries were signatories to a 1965 International Convention on the Elimination of All Forms of Racial Discrimination. The various signatories undertook to act against discrimination, and this obligation has been interpreted in various ways. The British, with the Act of 1968, have produced what now seems to be a rather ineffectual law, with civil penalties only, and a number of acute procedural difficulties, such as the inability to subpoena witnesses (Hetherington, 1971). The Dutch provision outlawing racial discrimination was enacted on 18 February 1971. This law made various forms of discrimination illegal, including the practice of discrimination by employers. The law has penal provisions—that is, unlike the British law it is part of the criminal rather than the civil code. One Dutch jurist (Swart, 1970) has protested that the law is too strict, and curtails the liberties of the individual in conducting his own affairs. I have not been able to discover reports of any cases prosecuted under the act during 1971.

## CONCLUSIONS

The conclusions from this discussion of various aspects of deviance and social control in the Netherlands are as follows:

[15] *De Volkskrant* (16 July 1971). A similar kind of area, with a relatively heavy concentration of Turks and Moroccans (about 38 per cent in a neighbourhood of 6,000 people), exists in the Oudwest area of Rotterdam. There appear to be some communal tensions in this area also.

1. It is possible that the difference in the quality of race relations in the Netherlands and in South Africa can be accounted for by the fact that the Dutch influence in South Africa has not represented the mainstream of Dutch culture. Dutch migration to South Africa has been individual migration, unlike the officially and commercially sponsored migration to the East Indies. These migrants to South Africa were in fact deviant in Dutch society, being extreme Calvinists who would not accept social change in the Netherlands which involved the liberalization of the extreme Calvinist outlook, and acceptance of other religious groups in society. The migration of such deviants has probably strengthened the elements of compromise and integration of diverse religious groups in Dutch society. It is probable that the philosophy of apartheid (apartness) has its roots in Calvinist sexual puritanism, and fear of sexual relationships between black and white.

2. There appears to be a small group of extreme Calvinists in the Netherlands who are sympathetic to the ideologies of the Dutch Reformed Church of South Africa, and its support for apartheid. There is some evidence that these are individuals who have failed to internalize the 'inner meaning' of the religion to which they adhere.

3. Public opinion data suggest that there is prejudice in the Netherlands. It seems, though, that those holding prejudiced opinions may be a small minority of the population.

4. Despite the existence of a small group of apparently prejudiced Re-Reformed Church members (in sympathy with apartheid), there are public opinion data suggesting that taken as a whole members of this church are as liberal as members of other churches.

5. Public opinion data show that the Re-Reformed are particularly conservative on some social and theological issues. The Re-Reformed attend church more often, are much more inclined to believe in hell, in predestination, and in the idea of a personal God. They are also particularly conservative on questions of sexual morality. The Re-Reformed also show the greatest amount of 'social integration'.

6. Public opinion data suggest that immigration is not a cause for concern to the Dutch electorate (unlike the British electorate). However, both Dutch and British respondents show concern over the problem of housing.

7. Between 5 and 10 per cent of voters in both rural and urban

areas have supported the extreme right-wing Farmers' party. There is evidence however from a study in a rural area that supporters of this party do not display anti-semitic or anti-colour prejudice to any extent.

8. Deviance in the form of apparent lack of respect for the norms of civility and public behaviour (e.g. on the part of Provos, and of recent immigrants) is not tolerated. The toleration of the Dutch for minorities extends, apparently, only so far as these minorities respect the traditional rules of inter-bloc behaviour. In cases of perceived or imagined deviance, social control can take a direct and sometimes brutal form. The authorities seem to connive at this social control behaviour.

These conclusions suggest the following hypotheses, which I attempt to test in later chapters.

(*a*) The overall level of tolerance in the Netherlands will be greater than in a comparable English sample.

(*b*) Immigrants who are oriented to Dutch culture, and who largely conform to inter-bloc behaviour, will be accepted and tolerated.

(*c*) Immigrants who do not conform to the rules of civility and inter-bloc behaviour will be much less tolerated.

(*d*) Levels of hostility to immigrants (prejudice) will be reflected in behaviour towards immigrants (discrimination). My proposition is that there will—(*i*) be little discrimination against 'conformist' West Indians; (*ii*) more discrimination against 'non-conformist' Dutchmen; (*iii*) more discrimination against 'non-conformist' non-Dutchmen.

(*e*) Individuals who declare a religious allegiance, but are not, by some behavioural criteria, integrated with the life of that church, will tend to be less tolerant of ethnic minorities.

CHAPTER 7

# RACIAL PREJUDICE IN BRITISH AND NETHERLANDS SAMPLES

In preceding chapters I have argued that there appears to be a much greater acceptance of coloured immigrants in the Netherlands than in Britain. In this chapter I present a test of the corollary hypothesis that there will be much more racial prejudice in Britain than in the Netherlands, using data from a large British survey which I have already described (Bagley, 1970b). The questionnaire was translated into Dutch, and administered to a quota sample of the Dutch population by professional Dutch interviewers. The sample consisted of the following groups:

1. Fifty professional men (or their wives) representative of the age spectrum 21–65 years. The professional categories of this group were similar to the British market research categories AB. This sample of fifty contained twenty-five men and twenty-five women.
2. Fifty white-collar workers (or their wives) being white-collar supervisory or clerical workers, similar to the British market research category C1. The age and sex samplings were similar to those in the professional category.
3. Fifty skilled workers (or their wives), equivalent to the British market research category C2. Again, this sample contained twenty-five men and twenty-five women, and was representative of the age spectrum 21–65 years.
4. Fifty unskilled manual workers (or their wives) equivalent to the British market research categories DE. The age and sex distribution was similar to that in the preceding category.
5. Seventy-nine 'young professionals' aged 21–30 years, attending full or part-time course of professional education in Amsterdam. Just under half of this sample were women.

Categories 1 to 4 were all resident in The Hague. The Hague

sample was chosen by the method of random sampling within areas of known socio-economic composition. However, not all subjects randomly chosen were interviewed, the criteria of whether or not to interview being the numbers needed to fill the age, sex, and occupational categories prescribed by the quotas. Table 7:1 shows the age and religious distribution of the Dutch sample. The sample

*Table 7:1. Age and Religious Distribution of the Dutch Sample*

| *Age* | | *Religion* | | *Sex* |
|---|---|---|---|---|
| 21–30 | 50 | Roman Catholic | 89 | 100 of The Hague quota |
| 31–40 | 42 | Dutch Reformed | 67 | sample male; 100 |
| 41–50 | 45 | Re-Reformed | 49 | female. 44 of 78 |
| 51–60 | 40 | Other Protestant | 11 | Amsterdam 'young |
| 61–65 | 23 | 'Humanist' | 15 | professionals' were |
| | | No religion | 48 | female. |
| Total | 200 | | | |
| | | Total | 279 | |
| Plus 79 'young professionals' aged 21–30 | | | | |

of 200 is not therefore a random sample of the population, but does, according to the criteria of quota sampling, give some indication of the views of the occupational groups interviewed. (The refusal rate in the Dutch quota sample was less than 5 per cent.) What is important about the sample is that it is compared with an age, occupational, and sex matched British sample. The Amsterdam sample makes no pretence at being representative, and subjects were interviewed through the co-operation of their course tutors. This is a social psychological rather than a sociological study, and its strength lies not in the numbers or sampling procedure involved, but in the fact that exactly matched individuals in the two cultures were compared. A similar kind of study, comparing Sweden and England has been carried out by Ingham (1971).

The Dutch subjects were given the Wilson–Patterson scale of conservative values; seven items measuring prejudice (items used in the British study); and questions about the tolerance of religious and racial intermarriage, and religious affiliation and behaviour. The English version of the questionnaire used the term 'coloured people'. Now, use of this term with a Dutch sample might well have elicited attitudes to immigrants from Indonesia whom, we have argued, are a well-accepted and a well-settled group. Surinamers are a group whose large-scale immigration is a more recent phenomenon, which has been surrounded with greater controversy than that of 'brown Dutchmen', from Indonesia. Accordingly, although some questions have been asked about 'kleurlingen' (coloured people), subjects were advised at the outset that this phrase referred to Surinamers.[1]

The English sample from which control subjects were drawn were interviewed in a random sample, carried out early in 1967, of the inhabitants of Lambeth, Ealing, Nottingham, Wolverhampton, and Bradford. All of these areas (like The Hague and Amsterdam) have an above average proportion of coloured people in their populations. The parent sample of 2,490 individuals has been described in detail in Bagley (1970b). Exact matches, in terms of age, sex, and occupational class were obtained for each individual in the Dutch sample with respondents from the larger English sample.[2] The controls for the 'Young Professionals' were all under thirty, in professional jobs, with education beyond the age of 16 years.

Responses were compared in the two samples to a six-item prejudice scale, and to a question about discrimination in housing. The questions asked in the English and the Dutch surveys were as follows:

1. Do you consider that the majority of coloured people in Britain are superior to you, inferior, or equal?
(*Beschouwt U kleurlingen in Nederland over het algemeen als Uw meerdere, Uw mindere, of Uw gelijke?*)
2. Suppose there are two workers, one coloured and one white, who do exactly the same work. If one, and one only, had to be declared redundant, should it be the coloured or the white worker?
(*Veronderstel er zijn twee werknemers, een Surinamer en een blanke, die precies hetzelfde werk doen. Als er nu, bijvoorbeeld vanwege reorganisatie in het bedrijf, slechts een van hen beiden ontslagen moet*

[1] 'Deze vragenlijst gaat over wat we telkens noemen: Kleurlingen, of "Gekleurde Immigranten". Daar bedoelen we steeds mee mensen uit Suriname.' Van Amersfoort (1968) points out that to the Dutch public 'Surinamer' means 'Creole' (i.e. individuals of African origin).

[2] The Hague sample of 200 were not matched for educational level with their English controls; in fact the English subjects had overall a slightly higher level of education, a factor slightly influencing the British subjects in the direction of tolerance.

*worden, vindt U dan het de Surinamer of vindt U dat het de blanke dient te zijn?*)
Subjects were taken to be prejudiced if they said that the coloured worker should be sacked, rather than suggesting that the dismissal should 'van andere faktoren afhangen' (depend on other factors).
3. Suppose there are two workers, one coloured and one white, who do exactly the same work. If one, and one only, had to be promoted, should it be the coloured or the white worker?
(*Veronderstel dat er twee werknemers zijn: een Surinamer en een blanke, die precies hetzelfde werk doen. Als er nu slechts een in aan merking kan komen voor promotie, vindt U dan dat dit de Surinamer of vindt U dit de blanke dient te zijn?*)
Prejudiced subjects chose 'de blanke werknemer dient promotie te maken' while unprejudiced subjects decided that 'de promotie dient van andere faktoren af te hangen'.
4. Do you think coloured people should be let into Britain or settle on the same basis as other people from abroad, or should there be special regulations for coloured people?
(*Vindt U dat er geen gelijke regeling moet zijn voor het zich vestigen in Nederland door kleurlingen, als door andere buitlanders? Of vindt U dat er een speciale regeling moet zijn voor kleurlingen?*)
Prejudiced subjects were those who wanted entry regulations for coloured people over and above those necessary for people from abroad.
5. There are various things that coloured people who have come to Britain could do to improve their position. What do you think they should do?

In the British questionnaire this was an open-ended question. Respondents suggesting one or more of the following possibilities were judged to be prejudiced: (*a*) They should go back to their country. (*b*) They should not be so cheeky or aggressive. (*c*) They should be cleaner. (*d*) They should be segregated. (*e*) They should stop overcrowding and/or improve their living conditions. (*f*) They should give up alien religions or cultural practices, and abide by our laws and customs. (*g*) A general expression of dislike such as 'They shouldn't be here' or 'They take advantage of social services'.

In the Dutch questionnaire this was not an open-ended question; instead the subjects were given a list of responses including translations of (*a*) to (*g*) to choose from; they could, if they wished, choose more than one reason. It must be borne in mind that giving the Dutch subjects a prepared list to choose from may have put the idea of a prejudiced response into their minds, and so made them appear more prejudiced than if they had been tested in the same way as the British subjects who had no such prepared list.

6. Do you feel more or less sympathetic towards coloured immigrants than about white people who live in similar conditions? (*Met wie hebt U het liefst te maken: met kleurlingen, of met blanke mensen die in dezelfde omstandigheden leven?*)

7. In addition to these six items the following question was asked, but not included in the six-item scale. It was not included in the original scale for technical reasons (Bagley 1970b).

Do you think the authorities should let or refuse to let a council house or flat to a family born in the West Indies? (*Vindt U dat de gemeente woningwet-woningen moet verhuren aan Surinamers?*)

*Table 7:2. Prejudice in a Sample of Fifty Professional Workers (Class AB) in Britain and the Netherlands*

| | *Netherlands* % | *Britain* % |
|---|---|---|
| Consider coloured people inferior | 10 | 50 |
| Advocate discriminatory regulations for entry | 18 | 50 |
| Lack of sympathy for coloured people | 28 | 30 |
| Derogatory statements about coloured people | 16 | 28 |
| Sack coloured worker | 6 | 30 |
| Advocate discrimination in housing | 4 | 42 |
| Promote white worker | 2 | 34 |
| Opposed to marriage of relative with Surinamer on grounds other than religion* | 30 | — |
| *Score on 6-item prejudice scale* | | |
| 0–1 | 78 | 44 |
| 2–3 | 16 | 36 |
| 4–6 | 6 | 20 |
| Significance of difference: p less than ·01 | | |
| Numbers on which percentages are based | 50 | 50 |

* No data for British subjects on this question available.

Altogether, seven comparisons between Netherlands and British samples were carried out. The first comparison, of fifty professionals and their wives (twenty-five men and twenty-five women, evenly distributed in the age range 21 to 65 years) with fifty professionals of exactly similar age and sex distribution is shown in Table 7:2. The differences between the two samples are large and significant. Only on the item of 'lack of sympathy' are the responses similar. On the six-item scale, 78 per cent of the Dutch subjects are virtually free of prejudice, compared with 44 per cent of the British subjects.

*Table 7:3. Prejudice in a Sample of Fifty White-Collar Workers (Class C1) in Britain and the Netherlands*

| | *Netherlands* % | *Britain* % |
|---|---|---|
| Consider coloured people inferior | 6 | 56 |
| Advocate discriminatory regulations for entry | 12 | 46 |
| Lack of sympathy for coloured people | 18 | 20 |
| Derogatory statements about coloured people | 20 | 36 |
| Sack coloured worker | 4 | 32 |
| Advocate discrimination in housing | 2 | 46 |
| Promote white worker | 14 | 24 |
| Opposed to marriage of relative with Surinamer on grounds other than religion | 26 | — |
| *Score on 6-item prejudice scale* | | |
| 0–1 | 78 | 36 |
| 2–3 | 20 | 46 |
| 4–6 | 2 | 18 |
| Significance of difference: p less than ·01 | | |
| Numbers on which percentages are based | 50 | 50 |

The same kind of pattern is repeated in the comparison of the fifty clerical and middle-range administrative workers (Class C1) and their wives; fifty skilled manual workers (Class C1) and their wives; and the fifty unskilled and semi-skilled workers (Class DE) and their wives, with a similar number of exactly matched British subjects. (See Tables 7:3–5.) The differences on the prejudice scale when the clerical workers are compared is especially marked, 78 per cent of the Dutch subjects having a score of 0 or 1, compared with 36 per cent of the British subjects. There is nearly three times as much prejudice in the British sample of unskilled workers than in the Netherlands sample. Table 7:6 which gives the results

*Table 7:4. Prejudice in a Sample of Fifty Skilled Workers (Class C2) in Britain and the Netherlands*

| | *Netherlands* % | *Britain* % |
|---|---|---|
| Consider coloured people inferior | 8 | 48 |
| Advocate discriminatory regulations for entry | 14 | 46 |
| Lack of sympathy for coloured people | 14 | 26 |
| Derogatory statements about coloured people | 24 | 42 |
| Sack coloured worker | 6 | 40 |
| Advocate discrimination in housing | 12 | 54 |
| Promote white worker | 4 | 30 |
| Opposed to marriage of relative with Surinamer on grounds other than religion | 34 | — |
| *Score on 6-item prejudice scale* | | |
| 0–1 | 80 | 42 |
| 2–3 | 18 | 60 |
| 4–6 | 2 | 28 |
| Significance of difference: p less than ·01 | | |
| Numbers on which percentages are based | 50 | 50 |

for the two matched groups of 'young professionals' suggests that it is these individuals in the British sample who display least prejudice, 56 per cent of them being virtually free of prejudice. However, no less than 97 per cent of the Dutch sample have scores of 0 or 1 on this scale. These results suggest that there is considerably less prejudice against West Indians in the Netherlands than there is against coloured people in Britain in a comparable sample. It should be noted that where the British questions did specify ethnic group (as in the question on letting a council house) comparable results suggested that attitudes to West Indians, as compared with attitudes to Indians and Pakistanis, were identical (Bagley, 1970).

*Table 7:5. Prejudice in a Sample of Fifty Semi- and Unskilled Workers (Class DE) in Britain and the Netherlands*

| | *Netherlands* % | *Britain* % |
|---|---|---|
| Consider coloured people inferior | 10 | 46 |
| Advocate discriminatory regulations for entry | 26 | 54 |
| Lack of sympathy for coloured people | 24 | 36 |
| Derogatory statements about coloured people | 18 | 56 |
| Sack coloured worker | 14 | 48 |
| Advocate discrimination in housing | 30 | 62 |
| Promote white worker | 18 | 40 |
| Opposed to marriage of relative with Surinamer on grounds other than religion | 26 | — |
| *Score on 6-item prejudice scale* | | |
| 0–1 | 74 | 26 |
| 2–3 | 14 | 52 |
| 4–6 | 12 | 22 |
| Significance of difference: p less than ·01 | | |
| Numbers on which percentages are based | 50 | 50 |

The combined prejudice scores of the 279 Dutch subjects compared with the 279 British control subjects are shown in Table 7:7, together with the prejudice scores of all 2,490 subjects in the parent sample from which the British controls were drawn. Eighty-three per cent of the Dutch sample had a prejudice score of 0 or 1 compared with 42 per cent of the British controls; but the British controls are in fact significantly less prejudiced than the parent sample. Four per cent of the Dutch sample were extremely hostile to coloured people (score 4–6 on the prejudice scale) compared with 19 per cent of the British controls, and 28 per cent of the British parent sample. The difference between the British control and parent samples is accounted for by the fact that the inclusion of the seventy-nine 'young professionals' biased the control sample somewhat in the direction of youth and education, both factors associated with tolerance. What is important however is that the Dutch samples and English controls were exactly matched, so that one can say that the incidence of prejudice appears to be much lower in the Netherlands.[3]

*Table 7:6. Prejudice in a Sample of Seventy-nine 'Young Professionals' in Britain and the Netherlands*

| | *Netherlands* % | *Britain* % |
|---|---|---|
| Consider coloured people inferior | 3 | 50 |
| Advocate discriminatory regulations for entry | 0 | 40 |
| Lack of sympathy for coloured people | 5 | 13 |
| Derogatory statements about coloured people | 5 | 33 |
| Sack coloured worker | 1 | 16 |
| Advocate discrimination in housing | 0 | 25 |
| Promote white worker | 11 | 16 |
| Opposed to marriage of relative with Surinamer on grounds other than religion | 1 | — |
| *Score on 6-item prejudice scale* | | |
| 0–1 | 97 | 56 |
| 2–3 | 3 | 33 |
| 4–6 | 0 | 11 |
| Significance of difference: p less than ·01 | | |
| Numbers on which percentages are based | 79 | 79 |

*Table 7:7. Prejudice in 279 Dutch Subjects and 279 British Controls, and the British Parent Sample*

| *Prejudice Score* | *279 Dutch Subjects* % | *279 English Subjects* % | *2,490 English Subjects* % |
|---|---|---|---|
| 0–1 | 83 | 42 | 34 |
| 2–3 | 13 | 39 | 38 |
| 4–6 | 4 | 19 | 28 |

[3] Cf. Sampson (1970) on a cross-national survey of 17,000 residents in England, Ireland, France, Norway, Sweden, Italy, the Netherlands, and other countries: 'We (the English) do not emerge as particularly tolerant; we are less likely to *approve* of someone marrying into a different country, religion or especially race.'

### ATTITUDES TO MOROCCANS AND ITALIANS

In Chapter 6 I described incidents which took place in the working-class quarter of The Hague—de Schildersbuurt—in which a group of Moroccans were attacked because of their apparent non-conformity to Dutch norms. This incident occurred shortly after the survey of attitudes to Surinamers in a sector of the Dutch population had been concluded. The majority of the working-class subjects in the quota sample lived in the Schildersbuurt, and I was struck by the fact that attitudes to Surinamers in these subjects were, by and large, liberal. It seemed plausible that if I gave the attitude questionnaire to a working-class sample in the Schildersbuurt inquiring about attitudes to Moroccans, rather than attitudes to Surinamers, a much greater incidence of prejudice would be revealed. In terms of my earlier propositions, I hypothesized that Surinamers were accepted because they spoke Dutch, and conformed to Dutch norms of public behaviour. Moroccans on the other hand, handicapped by difficulty in learning Dutch and by their relatively short exposure to Dutch norms and interaction with Dutch people, were the subject of hostility, this hostility being part of a social control process.

In order to find out whether the level of prejudice against Moroccans was appreciably higher than that against Surinamers, I carried out a further fifty interviews with working-class (C2 and DE) residents of the Schildersbuurt. The sample was evenly divided between men and women, and over the age range 21 to 65 years. The attitudes of this sample were compared with those to Surinamers in a control group of fifty subjects, similar in sex and occupational grouping and age structure.

In the discussion of the adaptation of migrant workers in the Netherlands (Chapter 5) I pointed out that Italian workers arriving in the Netherlands in the late 1950s and early 60s were the subject of both discrimination and prejudice. But I argued too that attitudes to this group should become more favourable with time as Italians grew accustomed to living in Dutch culture, and as the activities of the *Stichting* expanded. In The Hague, *Stichting* activities on behalf of Italians are much better developed than those for Moroccans, a migrant group of recent arrival in the Netherlands. I hypothesized that attitudes to Italians would be more favourable than attitudes to Moroccans, but not as favourable as attitudes to Surinamers. In order to test this hypothesis I administered the questionnaire to a further fifty working-class subjects, similar in age and sex structure to the fifty Shildersbuurt subjects. The questionnaire was identical to that outlined above, except that 'Italians' was substituted in the questionnaire to the Schildersbuurt subjects. The majority of the sample questioned about attitudes to Italians came from the Schildersbuurt area; the rest came from other districts of The Hague. The attitudes to Surinamers, Moroccans, and Italians in these three matched samples have been compared with attitudes to coloured people in fifty British subjects, exactly matched for age, sex, and occupation, and drawn from the larger British survey described earlier.

The results of this four-way comparison are presented in

*Table 7:8. A Comparison of Attitudes to Coloured Immigrants in Britain, and to Surinamese, Moroccan, and Italian Immigrants in the Netherlands*

| | *British* % (*B*) | *Netherlands —to Surinamers* % (*S*) | *Netherlands —to Moroccans* % (*M*) | *Netherlands —to Italians* % (*I*) |
|---|---|---|---|---|
| Consider group inferior | 48 | 2 | 20 | 12 |
| Advocate discriminatory regulations for admission | 50 | 18 | 26 | 18 |
| Lack of sympathy for group | 30 | 12 | 58 | 40 |
| Derogatory statements about coloured people | 50 | 30 | 38 | 36 |
| Sack immigrant worker | 44 | 6 | 50 | 12 |
| Advocate discrimination in housing | 32 | 22 | 24 | 20 |
| Promote native worker | 36 | 4 | 28 | 16 |
| Opposed to marriage with group member on grounds other than religion | — | 34 | 58 | 30 |
| *Score on 6-item prejudice scale* | | | | |
| 0–1 | 44 | 80 | 54 | 64 |
| 2–3 | 32 | 18 | 32 | 30 |
| 4–6 | 24 | 2 | 14 | 6 |
| Numbers on which percentages are based | 50 | 50 | 50 | 50 |

*Significance of differences*: Six item prejudice score: B cf. S, p less than ·01; S cf. M, p less than ·05. No other differences are significant at the 5 per cent level.

Table 7:8. As predicted, attitudes to Moroccans are much more hostile than those to Surinamers, while attitudes to Italians fall in the intermediate range. Moreover, attitudes to Moroccans in the Dutch sample on all items but one were more favourable than the attitudes of the British subjects to coloured people. The one item in which attitudes to Moroccans are less favourable is that referring to sympathy for the immigrant group in difficult conditions. An inspection of Tables 7:2 to 7:6 also indicates that it is on 'lack of sympathy for Surinamers' that the attitudes of the Dutch sample most nearly converge with the British attitudes. We would interpret this finding in the light of our previous arguments about Dutch culture: that 'sympathy' for people in difficulty—for example, kindness to strangers—is not a characteristic of Dutch society. Justice and fair play are built into the Dutch system of public behaviour, and this notion of justice extends to immigrants who conform to Dutch norms. *Sympathy* is not a prominent part of this system.

This suggestion is supported by the national survey of the Netherlands by Lijphart (1968) which was cited earlier. In this survey a question was asked about the most admired qualities in an individual. The Dutch sample, when compared with responses in similar surveys in Britain, Germany, Italy, and the United States, were the *least* likely to choose an individual who was 'generous, considerate of others'. Twelve per cent of the Dutch respondents chose such an individual, compared with 49 per cent of British respondents. Dutch culture, I conclude, lays great emphasis on rights, duties, and obligations, and little emphasis on inter-personal friendliness. Such inter-personal behaviour, as argued in Chapter 1, is in fact dysfunctional for bloc solidarity. According to my present analysis the British may be superficially friendly but they do not extend this friendliness to the point of actually treating coloured people as equals. More evidence on this point is presented in the chapter on racial discrimination in the two cultures, Chapter 8.

## THE STRUCTURE AND CORRELATES OF PREJUDICE AND SOCIAL ATTITUDES

A complex analysis of the data has been carried out by means of principal components analyses. The results of these analyses are included in an Appendix, for the statistically-minded reader. The data analysed included the 6-item prejudice scale, demographic data, responses to the Wilson–Patterson 50-item scale measuring conservative values, and data about religious affiliation and church attendance.

The method of analysis used calculates the correlation between a large number of variables, and by means of a complex operation based on matrix algebra, clusters the variables which vary together with high frequency into groups, or components. The significant correlations of the 6-item prejudice scale with *individual* items are: being older; being working class; being Roman Catholic; and being a church member, but attending infrequently. The following variables were negatively correlated: being Humanist; and belonging to the Re-Reformed Church.

The Re-Reformed were the most frequent church attenders, and were most likely to give to church funds, and to have a function in church life. Such religious involvement was inversely related to prejudice. Older and working-class Catholics showed the least religious involvement, and the most prejudice among the subjects studied.

The following components emerged: firstly, an 'Age versus youth' component, with high statistical loadings on being middle class, older, and a Re-Reformed church member, with commitment to values opposing the autonomy and pleasurable activities of youth; secondly, a 'Protestant–conformist' component, involving both Dutch Reformed and Re-Reformed church members; thirdly a 'Racialist' component, including all the variables used to measure prejudice; fourthly a component measuring 'Class values', having a high loading on middle-class status, and involving the view that coloured people are inferior—but without prejudice on other items measuring racialism. This probably reflects a kindly but paternalistic attitude to race relations among a number of middle-class subjects. The fifth component was termed 'Female-puritanical' and involved the objection of women subjects to sexual freedom—these were unconnected with any racial attitudes. Component six was termed 'Imperialist' and involved favourable attitudes to overseas empire, patriotism, and variables such as military drill; but the component was unconnected with racialist items, except an apparent acceptance of apartheid.

The overall conclusions from this analysis are that there is strong evidence for concluding that racialism is the province of a small group of deviants who are deviant not only from the dominant values in the Netherlands (tolerance towards coloured immigrants who conform to Dutch mores), but who are deviant also from the value system and social control networks of the religious denominations to which they nominally belong. In particular, working-class Catholics tend to display this kind of deviance.

## PREJUDICE IN THE NETHERLANDS: SOME FURTHER EVIDENCE

Since this study of prejudice in a small sample of the urban population of the Netherlands, and the situation testing of discrimination (reported in the following chapter), unpublished data on racial attitudes in random samples of the Dutch population have come to hand.[4]

The 1969 survey, together with evidence given by Bovenkerk and Van Galen give data on the extent to which random samples of Dutch people consider that racial discrimination exists in the Netherlands. The results are shown in Table 7:9.

*Table 7:9. Views on Racial Discrimination in the Netherlands*

| | *1967* | *1969* | *1970* |
|---|---|---|---|
| Considers that there is some racial discrimination | 33 | 48 | 51 |
| Considers that there is no racial discrimination | 66 | 50 | 47 |
| Don't know, no reply | 1 | 2 | 2 |

Do these findings mean that racial prejudice (and discrimination) are in fact increasing in the Netherlands? Or do they mean that the population is becoming more sensitive to an already existing situation? There is some interesting evidence that the latter is the case. In a stratified random sample carried out in 1968 (reported below) individuals who said that there was racial discrimination in the Netherlands were *more* accepting of ethnic minorities (as measured by a Bogardus social distance scale) than people who thought that there was no discrimination. Sensitivity to discrimination is associated, therefore, with tolerance. And this

[4] 'Rassendiscriminatie in Nederland', Nederlands Instituut voor de Publieke Opininie en het Marktonderzoek (Amsterdam, Bericht nr. 1921, June 1969); 'Rassenvooroordeel in Nederland' Nederlands Centrum voor Marketing Analyses (June 1968, mimeo); and Bovenkerk and Van Galen (1971).

sensitivity is increasing over time. These findings do not necessarily mean that prejudice is in fact decreasing, but they also offer no support for the conclusion that it is increasing.

The study of racial prejudice (which is an attitude, as opposed to discrimination, which is an action) was carried out in the spring of 1968. The sample consisted of 416 respondents aged 18 years and over, obtained through a stratified random sample of urban and rural areas of the Netherlands. Nineteen per cent of the sample came from the three large cities of Amsterdam, Rotterdam, and The Hague, while 37 per cent came from towns and villages with less than 20,000 inhabitants.

Subjects completed a Bogardus social distance scale. The most intimate acceptance—accepting the individual as a member of one's family, especially as a son-in-law or brother-in-law—was scored 1 through various categories of acceptance to complete rejection ('I would keep them out altogether'), which was scored 7. The optimum level of acceptance was elicited for each of eight groups—a Frenchman, a German, an Italian, a Turkish guest-worker, an Indonesian Dutchman (Indische Nederlander), an Ambonese, a Surinamer, and a young man with long hair. On this scale the most accepted were the Frenchman and the Indonesian Dutchman while the least accepted were the young man with long hair, and the Turkish guest-worker.

In order to provide further evidence on comparative levels of prejudice in Dutch and English samples we translated the Dutch social distance scale into English, and administered it to a stratified random sample of 206 residents in an urban area in southern England. Four wards were sampled on the basis of their known socio-economic characteristics, so as to obtain a representative cross-section of the area. The register of electors was used as a sampling frame. Various checks indicated that the sample was a representative one. The two major differences between Dutch and English samples is that the English sample contained no rural respondents, and was carried out some three years after the Dutch one. In 1971, young men with long hair appear to be more acceptable in England (and perhaps in the Netherlands) than they were in 1968. A further important point is that the religion of the individuals was not mentioned, so that some Dutch respondents may have rejected individuals on the basis of supposed religion. If this variable of religion had been controlled in the Dutch sample the acceptance of the various groups might have been greater.

*Table 7:10. Levels of Acceptance of Ethnic Groups in Dutch and English Samples*

| | *French* % | *Indonesian/ Anglo-Indian* % | *Surinamer/ West Indian* % | *Ambonese/ Pakistani* % | *Long Hair* % | *Turk/Turkish Cypriot* % |
|---|---|---|---|---|---|---|
| 1. I would keep them out altogether | 1 (1) | 3 (5) | 4 (7) | 4 (8) | 12 (0) | 11 (7) |
| 2. I would allow in as visitors only | 5 (4) | 2 (7) | 5 (12) | 8 (10) | 4 (2) | 19 (10) |
| 3. I would allow them to become a citizen* | 3 (3) | 5 (5) | 4 (8) | 8 (7) | 13 (2) | 5 (7) |
| 4. I would accept as a colleague at work | 4 (5) | 6 (14) | 11 (19) | 11 (26) | 4 (1) | 13 (15) |
| 5. I would accept as a neighbour | 5 (3) | 6 (6) | 7 (7) | 8 (10) | 10 (6) | 8 (10) |
| 6. I would accept in my home | 12 (7) | 17 (18) | 17 (10) | 15 (17) | 7 (4) | 12 (19) |
| 7. I would accept as son-in-law or brother-in-law | 67 (75) | 58 (41) | 48 (34) | 42 (20) | 41 (82) | 28 (30) |
| Totals (including 'don't know') | 100 | 100 | 100 | 100 | 100 | 100 |

*Note*: Figures in brackets are responses of English sample. Dutch N—416; English N—209.

* The full translation of this question is: 'Zou ik best aanvaarden als *burgers* van mijn land met dezelfde rechten en plichten als ik zelf heb,' i.e. with a particular emphasis on the rights and duties of the citizen.

Table 7:10 classifies responses on the basis of the most accepting attitude of respondents. Thus a man who would accept a West Indian in his home, but would not accept a West Indian as a son-in-law is classified in the appropriate column opposite category 6.[5] There are interesting and significant variations in the results when the Dutch and English responses are examined. Acceptance of the Frenchman is very similar in both cultures, but for the three 'coloured' groups the Dutch show markedly more acceptance. The acceptance of six groups has been compared in the two cultures, and questions about more or less equivalent ethnic status groups were asked in the English sample. Dutch respondents are significantly more accepting of Indonesian Dutch than the English are of Anglo-Indians; the Dutch are significantly more accepting of Surinamers than the English are of West Indians; and they are significantly more accepting of Ambonese than the English are of Pakistanis. Levels of acceptance of a

[5] As is implied, these results conform fairly well to Guttman criteria of scaleability. Cf. the English results from a social distance scale of Wells (1970).

*Table 7:11. Mean Acceptance Scores of Various Ethnic Groups in Dutch and English Samples*

| *Ethnic Category* | *Dutch sample N 416* | *English sample N 206* | *Significance of Difference* |
|---|---|---|---|
| Frenchman | 6·2 | 6·4 | N.S. |
| Indonesian Dutchman/Anglo-Indian | 6·0 | 5·2 | P less than ·01 |
| German | 5·8 | — | — |
| Surinamer/West Indian | 5·6 | 4·9 | P less than ·01 |
| Italian | 5·4 | — | — |
| Ambonesian/Pakistani | 5·3 | 4·6 | P less than ·01 |
| Young man with long hair | 5·0 | 6·5 | P less than ·01 |
| Turkish guest-worker/Turkish Cypriot | 4·4 | 5·0 | P less than ·01 |

*Note*: A high score indicates greater acceptance.

Turkish guest-worker, and of a Turkish Cypriot are similar in both cultures, but the English are markedly more accepting of the young man with long hair.

In Table 7:11 'acceptance scores' of the groups in the two cultures are shown. These scores summarize the social distance scale and mean, for example, that the average highest point of acceptance of the English sample for a Frenchman lies midpoint between the sixth and seventh levels, while the average highest point of acceptance for a Pakistani is midway between the fourth and fifth levels (accepting as a colleague at work, and accepting as a neighbour). It is clear from this table that there is significantly more acceptance of coloured groups in the Netherlands sample than in the English one. Although I have presented specific comparisons for significance testing, for example in comparing responses to an Indonesian Dutchman with responses to an Anglo-Indian, *any* comparison indicates that there is more prejudice against coloured people in the English sample. For example, the Dutch respondents are *more* accepting of the West Indian than the English respondents are of the Anglo-Indian. What is of particular interest is the hostility with which the Dutch regard both the young man with long hair, and the Turkish guest-worker. The lack of acceptance of the Turk is of course similar to the lack of acceptance of the Moroccan in The Hague sample. The rejection of the young man with long hair underlines the points made about the importance of respectability and conformity in Dutch culture. The position of the Italian on the social distance scale also confirms my results. The low position of the Ambonese is interesting, and doubtless relates to the recent militant separatist policy of the Ambonese in the Netherlands. This survey was carried out before the political events of 1970 (see Chapter 3) when Ambonese nationalists killed a policeman in The Hague. There has in fact been a revival of Ambonese nationalism since 1966 (Mariën, 1971).

## CONCLUSIONS

I have examined the incidence of racial prejudice in two exactly matched Dutch and British samples of 279 individuals. Responses of these two groups of subjects to a similar questionnaire have been compared. The results indicate that there is considerably less hostility to Surinamers in the Netherlands than to coloured people in Britain.

However, when responses to Moroccans in a Dutch sample are considered, it was found that there was considerably more hostility to this group than to Surinamers. Nevertheless, there was less hostility to Moroccans than there was hostility to coloured people in a comparable British sample. I interpreted this finding as indicating that hostility to immigrants in Dutch culture is related, not to skin colour, but to lack of conformity to Dutch norms. An examination of attitudes to Italian immigrants to the Netherlands in a comparable sample supported this view.

However, despite this general acceptance of immigrants in Dutch culture, on an item inquiring about sympathy to immigrants in difficult conditions the Dutch emerged as a rather unsympathetic group (nearly as unsympathetic as the English were to coloured immigrants) despite their acceptance of coloured immigrants as equals. A negligible proportion of Dutch subjects considered that coloured people were inferior to them, compared with nearly half of all British respondents. Equality of treatment for appropriate behaviour is a strongly institutionalized social system mechanism in the Netherlands. But sympathy and warmth in public inter-action are notably lacking. Both these aspects of Dutch culture are related to the problem of co-ordinating relationships between distinct pillars of blocs of society, ensuring equality of treatment for members of different blocs, and at the same time ensuring that inter-action between members of different blocs remains at a minimum.

An examination of the correlates and clusters of prejudice and other variables indicated that the prejudiced individuals—who tend to be older, working-class Catholics, who attend church rather infrequently—are deviant from the values of tolerance incorporated in Dutch public life, and also from the values system and social control networks of the religious denominations to which they nominally belong.

A further comparative study of prejudice using the Bogardus social distance scale indicated that in the Netherlands the most accepted individuals were a Frenchman and an Indonesian Dutchman, and the least accepted a young man with long hair, and a Turkish guest-worker. The Dutch sample were significantly more accepting than the English sample of the coloured individuals—in the Dutch questionnaire an Indonesian, a Surinamer, and an Ambonese, and in the English questionnaire an Anglo-Indian, a West Indian, and a Pakistani. Questions about religion were not asked in the Dutch survey, so there is a distinct possibility that the Dutch survey over-estimates the amount of social rejection of various individuals on grounds of ethnic origin; that is the British sample may be even more prejudiced compared with the Dutch sample, than these results actually show.

CHAPTER 8

# RACIAL DISCRIMINATION IN THE NETHERLANDS—AN EMPIRICAL TEST

Prejudice is an attitude; discrimination is an action. Now, there is a good deal of social psychological evidence to show that prejudiced people will not necessarily discriminate (e.g. the person advocating that the coloured person shouldn't be allocated a house may, when the decision is his, nevertheless let the house to a coloured man). The study by La Piere (1934) on precisely this issue suggests that the *situation* may determine whether prejudice is translated into discriminatory behaviour. The existence, for example, of significant social controls may discourage prejudiced individuals from discriminating.

Further studies, for example Lohman and Reitzes (1954), and Defleur and Westie (1958), have suggested that factors such as the roles individuals play in different organizations and their differing ideologies concerning race relations may account for a gap between attitudes and action. Various attempts have been made to account for the discrepancy (for example, Fendrich [1967], and Tarter [1969]. Werks (1969) has argued that the distinction between attitude and behaviour is not very valid; that responding to a questionnaire is in itself a behaviour. This can be true in certain important circumstances—where, for instance, referenda are held which affect policy, as they sometimes are in the State of California. In Britain, advocates of such policies as reducing the rights of coloured immigrants and repatriation often argue that the will of the country ought to be made known on this issue by means of a referendum. In the silence and anonymity of a polling booth it is quite likely that reactionary voices would prevail. Given that in Britain the majority of people are prejudiced on at least some issues while only some 14 per cent are apparently completely free of prejudice (Bagley, 1970b) such a referendum in Britain would have far-reaching effects if it were linked, as in California, to policy.

Werks makes the further proposition from his analysis of questionnaire responses, that the grounds for a white American accepting a U.S. Negro are most specific (and therefore most predictable) in the case of letting a room, employment, and access to public accommodation; and most diffuse (and therefore least predictable from questionnaire responses) in the case of friendship, dating, and marriage. The implications of this analysis is that in these latter areas questions concerning prejudice will have to be rather detailed if they are to predict behaviour with any accuracy. There is a statistical aspect to this question. In social science, correlations of between 0·5 and 0·7 between two indicators, or between an indicator and a dependent variable, are considered to be very respectable, considering the measurement problems inherent in social science methods. But a high correlation of 0·7 can only predict 49 per cent of the variance held in common by the two indicators. In other words, although the association is much greater than might have occurred by chance, a prediction based on such an association will, in a large population, be correct in only about half of the cases.

My conclusion is that prejudice and discrimination are related, and that measured prejudice is an imperfect though nevertheless useful indicator of discrimination. The statement by Jahoda, Deutsch, and Cook made in 1951 usefully sums up this position:

> As a rule, prejudice and discrimination are reciprocally related: prejudice breeds discrimination and discriminatory practices breeds prejudice, since they act as a medium of indoctrination. Independently of the motives behind a particular prejudice, when this has been translated into acts of discrimination, future generations will acquire it mainly through the influence of prevailing customs. Prejudice is mainly sustained by social usages and sanctions (Jahoda et al., 1951, p. 365).

The best evidence on the prevalence of racial discrimination in Britain comes from the report prepared by Political and Economic Planning (1967) and published in an expanded form by Daniel (1968). This important survey first of all interviewed a sample of 1,700 immigrants to find out what their experiences in seeking employment and accommodation had been. A sample of employers, managers, and trade unionists was also interviewed. Both these exercises suggested that there might be widespread discrimination against coloured people.

What is of particular relevance for this study is the individual testing of discrimination carried out by P.E.P. It is possible to show with some degree of certainty that discrimination has taken place by 'situation testing'. This consists of sending a coloured man to apply for a job or vacant room. If he is told that no vacancy exists, an Englishman with similar qualifications, age, professional standing, style of dress, and so forth applies for the vacancy shortly after the rejection of the coloured man. If the Englishman is offered the vacancy the reasonable inference can be drawn that discrimination has occurred against the coloured man. Whether the discrimination was on grounds of colour, or on grounds of foreignness or lack of good English can be tested by sending along a white foreigner to apply for the vacancy before sending along the white Englishman.

In the P.E.P. study a Hungarian was used as the foreign tester, and the results indicated that the widespread discrimination experienced by the coloured tester was on grounds of colour alone. For example, forty employment situations were tested. In ten of these it was found that there was no job available for anyone; in the thirty cases where employment was possible the coloured applicant was refused on twenty-seven occasions, the foreign applicant on thirteen occasions, and the English applicant on no occasion (Daniel, 1968, pp. 76–7). Personal and telephone inquiries to landlords and housing bureaux suggested that high levels of discrimination also existed in this field. For instance of sixty personal applications to landlords, in only fifteen cases were all three applicants given similar information; in thirty-eight cases the West Indian was told that the accommodation was taken while the other two applicants were told it was vacant; in four cases the West Indian was asked a higher rent than the other applicant; in two cases both the West Indian and the Hungarian were told that the accommodation was taken, but it was offered to the Englishman; and in one case both West Indian and Hungarian were asked a higher rent than the Englishman.

The comparison of levels of prejudice in a Netherlands sample, compared with a British sample similar in age, sex, and occupational composition has indicated that there is much less prejudice in the Netherlands than in Britain. Since I have hypothesized that prejudice is a reasonably good, though not a perfect predictor of discrimination, one would also expect that the level of prejudice in one sample of a population would be able to predict at least with rough accuracy the level of discrimination in another sample of the same population. I hypothesize, in other words that as with prejudice, the incidence of discrimination in a Dutch sample will be much lower.

In the situation testing I was fortunate in obtaining three testers who had very similar qualifications and experience, one being a Dutchman, one a black Surinamer, and one a Yugoslav. All had studied economics and industrial management in the Netherlands and had obtained their *Doctorandus* qualification (approximately equivalent to an English M.A.). Both the Surinamer's and the Yugoslav's high school education had been in their own country. All were in their middle twenties, and all had had industrial and commercial experience. The Dutchman, of course, spoke excellent Dutch. The Surinamer also spoke good Dutch, but with a West Indian accent.[1] The Yugoslav's command of Dutch was adequate for purposes of communication in an industrial setting, but he nevertheless had a clearly detectable accent.

The first test was in the field of job-seeking, and represents a replication of one of the P.E.P. tests. There is a difficulty in exactly replicating the P.E.P. test of forty job applications, because the P.E.P. report does not specify the type and level of employment sought. All of the forty jobs which my testers applied for were white-collar clerical jobs. The P.E.P. study indicated that it was in white-collar jobs that coloured immigrants experienced most discrimination. Since all the testers were applying for white-collar jobs, and since some of the English test situations may have involved blue-collar jobs, I may in fact be underestimating the differences in discrimination between the two cultures, i.e. there may be even less discrimination in the Netherlands than the comparison with the P.E.P. figures indicates.

For the purposes of the Dutch applications (all of which were carried out in Amsterdam and nearby urban areas) the qualifications and experience of each applicant were tailored to suit the kind of job sought. Details of the jobs were obtained from newspaper advertisements, employment bureaux, and by telephone inquiries to large organizations by a Dutchman co-ordinating the testing.[2] All posts were in the field of accounting, in which all

[1] The inflexions which a West Indian Surinamer gives to Dutch are rather similar to the inflexions a West Indian from a former British colony gives to English.

[2] I am extremely grateful to my academic colleagues in the Netherlands who acted as testers, and co-ordinated the tests and acted in various advisory and administrative capacities.

applicants had actual experience. The results of the comparison are given in Table 8:1. These suggest that there was markedly and significantly more discrimination in the English situations than in the Dutch. In cases where a job was available, 90 per cent of the British coloured testers were discriminated against, compared with 18 per cent of occasions on which the Dutch coloured tester applied for a job. It is interesting to note that the Yugoslav was rejected in the employment situation on 32 per cent of occasions, compared with the British rejection of the Hungarian tester on 43 per cent of occasions. These results are in line with those from our attitude survey, which suggested a greater acceptance of coloured Dutchmen than of white foreigners. In the British situation the pattern of acceptance is reversed, but nevertheless there seems to be more acceptance of the foreigner in the Dutch situation tests than in the British ones.

*Table 8:1. Employment Discrimination in Britain and the Netherlands in Forty Situation Tests*

| | *Dutch* | *Yugoslav* | *Coloured Dutchman* | *English* | *Hungarian* | *Coloured Englishman* |
|---|---|---|---|---|---|---|
| (*a*) Offered job or told vacancy existed and advised to apply | 16 | 7 | 13 | 15 | 10 | 1 |
| (*b*) Told 'no vacancy at present', but details taken for future reference; or asked to call back; or told vacancy would occur shortly | 6 | 4 | 5 | 15 | 7 | 2 |
| (*c*) Told 'no vacancy' | 18 | 26 | 22 | 10 | 23 | 37 |
| Totals | 40 | 40 | 40 | 40 | 40 | 40 |

| | *Dutch Situation* | *English Situation* |
|---|---|---|
| Number of cases where no job available for anyone | 18 | 10 |
| Number of cases where employment possible | 22 | 30 |
| Per cent of occasions when native tester discriminated against | – | – |
| Per cent of occasions when foreign tester discriminated against | 32% | 43% |
| Per cent of cases when coloured tester discriminated against | 18% | 90% |

An interesting perspective on the nature of discrimination in Britain has been provided by a correspondence concerning discrimination against highly qualified black professionals seeking employment through a London employment agency specializing in qualified accountants. This professional category is particularly relevant for this present study, since it was in this field that our situation testers were qualified, and applied for a range of jobs, including fully professional posts carrying high salaries.

The director of the London agency specializing in accountants wrote a letter to the London *Evening Standard* on 17 February 1970, reporting the following case:

A young, highly-intelligent and exceptionally well-qualified man from one of our former colonies applied to me recently for help in finding a job. After taking an Honours Law Degree in London he obtained three further degrees—Associate of the Institute of Banking, Associate of the Chartered Institute of Secretaries and Associate of the Institute of Cost and Works Accountants. Were he not coloured, by now he would have been offered the pick of several dozen jobs paying £3000 a year and more; however, as he is coloured I have been unable to fix up even one interview for him. This occurs at a time when there is a vast shortage of young qualified accountants—in my experience about 20 jobs for every man.

This letter prompted some rejoinders to the director of the employment agency, which were printed in the *Guardian* (21 February 1970) in an article discussing racial discrimination. The first of these letters was postmarked Islington, London, N.W., and declared: 'Sir, Your letter in today's Standard fairly made my heart bleed. Think of it the poor wog bastards couldn't get a job. Maybe he didn't have the sense to piss off back to his former colony after all he was probably one of the sods that screamed for independence and told the British to get out.' Another letter said,

It is the working class white worker who objects to these coloured people not the bosses. The white workers have to live with and near these coloured immigrants who stink and eat food which gives off foul smells when being cooked. They also live in dirt and filth . . . [the letter here contains an obscenity] and their bed-clothes and curtains are often as black as they are. *White workers* don't want the niggers here and the *white workers* are in control or will be very soon! (Italics and construction as in original).

This good gentleman is presumably a socialist. Another reader wrote to the *Evening Standard*:

Dear Sir, In reference to your letter in the Evening Standard, well its just too bad a particular situation embarrasses you, its a great pity your not living amongst these coloureds then probably you would be *embarrassed* more. If the person you stated is so highly intelligent I'm surprised he came here in the first place, besides our own white people should come first for such jobs and such good money £3000 a year. They should accept these conditions in any words when in Rome do as Rome does. These coloureds aren't doing too bad here in this over-crowded small Island; you never read of any going back to the West Indies or wherever they belong in fact they fare better here than the White man does here, its a pity you can't mind your own business and shut up. PS Its the likes of you writing such letters that cause Racial trouble, belt up and stop writing such rubbish. (Italics and construction as in original).[3]

According to the *Guardian* these letters were part of a large post received by the director of the employment agency, and all but two were in terms rather similar to those quoted above. The director told the *Guardian*:

I've had dozens of applicants in and two-thirds are unqualified—but they are easily placed as accountants in jobs originally advertised for qualified men. Some are still studying, others have given up. But 20 per cent of the applicants have been coloured. . . . Some have two qualifications, and this particular one has four, which is exceptional by any standards. So far I have not placed one.[4]

In the Dutch situation tests ten of the testers applied for jobs as fully qualified professional accountants. In three of these no job was available for any of the testers, and in the remaining seven tests discrimination occurred against the black Dutchman on only one occasion.

### HOUSING DISCRIMINATION

In the Netherlands there appears to be considerably less discrimination in employment than in Britain. How do black Englishmen and Dutchmen fare in the housing market? In order to provide some information on this point I replicated the P.E.P. tests of housing discrimination. The same three testers were used

[3] Cf. Hoogvelt's study (1969) of writers of letters to the English press which express hostility to immigrants.

[4] Van Amersfoort (1972) has suggested that a professionally qualified Dutch West Indian finds it very easy to find employment, while greater difficulty is encountered by black unskilled workers. This situation is the *reverse* of that revealed in Britain by the P.E.P. study.

as in the employment testing, and the same areas—Amsterdam and surrounding districts—were chosen.

Lists of furnished rooms were obtained from housing agencies by the Dutch tester. First the Surinamese tester went along to inspect the room. If he was offered it, he said that he would think the matter over, and telephoned or called within half an hour to say that he did not want the room. Half an hour later the Yugoslav tester called and the same procedure was followed. This call was followed by that of the white Dutch tester using the same techniques. The testing was continued until sixty cases were obtained in which there was evidence that the room was vacant (i.e. it was offered to at least one of the testers).

In order to replicate as far as possible the conditions of the P.E.P. test the applicants were each given two professional roles which they each used alternately in the tests. The Surinamer was a junior doctor or tram conductor; the Yugoslav was an accountant or van driver; the white Dutchman was a school teacher or a bricklayer. These professions were used with each alternate test, but were co-ordinated so that each tester presented the same kind of profession (blue-collar or white-collar) in each test with the same landlord or landlady. Each tester introduced himself with the words: 'Good morning, sir (or madam—Mijnheer or Mevrouw). I am a . . . (giving appropriate occupation) and I have recently come to work in Amsterdam. I am looking for accommodation . . . .' The description of the P.E.P. tests given in the original report do not make it clear what the family circumstances of the testers were supposed to be; in my tests all applicants said that they were married, but had no children.

The results of the testing are given in Table 8:2. It is clear that there is considerably less discrimination against the West Indian tester in the Netherlands than against the West Indian tester in Britain. In the British tests discrimination occurred against the black Englishman in forty-five out of sixty cases; in the Netherlands discrimination occurred against the black Dutchman in eighteen out of sixty cases. This difference is statistically highly significant. However, discrimination against the foreign tester occurred in twenty out of sixty cases, compared with only three out of sixty cases in the British test situation. This finding suggests, like my earlier ones, that although there is not a great deal of discrimination against a black Dutchman, there is a good deal more discrimination against a white foreigner.

*Table 8:2. Housing Discrimination in Britain and the Netherlands in Sixty Situation Tests*

| | *Netherlands* | *Britain* |
|---|---|---|
| Occasions when discrimination occurred against West Indian | 18 | 45 |
| West Indian and native applicants given similar information | 42 | 15 |
| *Total number of testable situations* | *60* | *60* |
| Occasions when foreigner discriminated against | 20 | 3 |
| Foreign and native applicants given similar information | 40 | 57 |
| *Total number of testable situations* | *60* | *60* |
| *Types of discrimination* | | |
| West Indian told rooms taken; both other applicants told vacant | 5 | 38 |
| West Indian asked for higher rent than both other applicants | 1 | 4 |
| West Indian and foreigner told rooms taken; native told vacant | 5 | 2 |
| West Indian and foreigner asked for higher rent than native | 7 | 1 |
| Foreigner told rooms taken; both other applicants told vacant | 6 | 0 |
| Foreigner asked for higher rent than other applicants | 2 | 0 |

## DISCRIMINATION, COLOUR, AND RESPECTABILITY

I have argued that conformity to Dutch norms, especially those of bourgeois civility and restraint and deference in social relations are much more important factors in social acceptance than skin colour or ethnic category. I tested such a proposition with thirty more situation tests. Three testers, a black Dutchman (a Surinamer), a Dutch 'hippy', and a respectable Dutchman, applied for accommodation. Both the Surinamer and the respectable Dutchman wore suits and ties, and presented themselves in their professional roles. The hippy tester, a white man in his early twenties, politely presented himself as a postgraduate student at the University of Amsterdam. He had newly-washed, shoulder-length hair, jeans, an

*Table 8:3. Discrimination in Accommodation Against a Respectable Black Dutchman, a Non-Respectable Dutchman, and a Respectable Dutchman*

| | *No. of Cases* |
|---|---|
| Discrimination against 'hippy', other testers given similar information | 11 |
| Discrimination against both 'hippy' and black Dutchman | 6 |
| Discrimination against black Dutchman, other testers given similar information | 2 |
| Discrimination against respectable Dutchman | 0 |
| Total number of testable situations | 30 |

open necked shirt, and a leather waistcoat. Table 8:3 gives the results of the thirty situation tests. The results bear out the hypothesis: the respectable black Dutchman was rejected in eight out of thirty tests, but the unrespectable white Dutchman was rejected on no less than seventeen of the thirty occasions. The large majority of the discrimination took the form of denial of accommodation rather than asking for higher rent (in sixteen of the seventeen cases of discrimination against the hippy, and in one of the six cases of discrimination against both the Surinamer and the hippy). It should be mentioned that these tests were carried out in Amsterdam not long after radical students had occupied and barricaded themselves in the University of Amsterdam, followed by the arrest and trial of hundreds of students.

*Table 8:4. Summary of the Amount of Discrimination in Accommodation*

| | *Discrimination against Black Dutchman* | *Discrimination against White foreigner* | *Discrimination against Non-Respectable Dutchman* |
|---|---|---|---|
| First test (60 cases) | 30% | 33% | — |
| Second test (30 cases) | 20% | — | 57% |

The results summarized in Table 8:4 are compatible with the following interpretation: although there is some discrimination in the Netherlands which seems to be largely on grounds of colour, nevertheless there is probably at least as much discrimination against white foreigners. There also appears to be appreciably more discrimination against a non-respectable Dutchman, suggesting that conformity to Dutch norms is a factor of great importance. The level of housing discrimination against West Indians in Britain—in 72 per cent of testable situations—is much higher than the level of discrimination in any of the Dutch situations. But the level of discrimination against the foreigner in the English situation (in 7 per cent of testable cases) is much less than the level of discrimination against the foreigner in the Dutch situation (in 33 per cent of testable cases). Discrimination in Britain is based on the colour of skin; discrimination in the Netherlands is based on non-conformity, or on lack of familiarity with Dutch codes of civility, deference, and inter-personal behaviour.

### DISCRIMINATION AS A PREDICTOR OF PREJUDICE

I pointed out at the beginning of this chapter that prejudice (an attitude) is an imperfect predictor of discrimination (an action); and, conversely, individuals who discriminated could not always be shown to be prejudiced. Nevertheless, I argued that the two would correlate at a statistically significant level. I have investigated this hypothesis by follow-up interviews with the sixty landlords and landladies in the situation tests in the Netherlands. All but four of the landlords and landladies agreed to be interviewed. Two refusals came in individuals who had discriminated, so that data are available on sixteen individuals who discriminated and on forty individuals who did not discriminate. The scores of these individuals on the 6-item scale of prejudice and on the question regarding the advocacy of discrimination in council housing are given in Table 8:5. These results suggest that the P-scale, which does not contain any questions regarding the private letting of houses to coloured people, is nevertheless a good predictor of individuals who discriminate. The question on the letting of council houses is, as might be expected, a somewhat better predictor. Sixty-nine per cent of individuals prejudiced on this item also discriminate, while only 23 per cent of the non-discriminating landlords were so prejudiced.

*Table* 8:5. *Prejudice in Landlords and Landladies who Discriminated, and did not Discriminate*

| | *Subjects who discriminated* | *Subjects who did not discriminate* | *Significance of difference* |
|---|---|---|---|
| Per cent of subjects with Score of 1 or more on the 6-item P scale | 62% | 25% | P ·01 |
| Per cent of subjects who advocated housing discrimination | 69% | 23% | P ·01 |
| Number of subjects | 16 | 40 | |

CONCLUSIONS

(1) Prejudice is a reasonably good predictor of discrimination, according to the results obtained with Dutch landlords and landladies who discriminate, and who do not discriminate. Since the level of prejudice in the Netherlands is much lower than in Britain I hypothesized that the level of discrimination would be much lower too.

(2) A replication of the P.E.P. situation tests was carried out to test this hypothesis. Forty tests of employment and sixty tests of housing confirmed that there is significantly and markedly less discrimination against a coloured tester in the Netherlands than in Britain. However, there is a not inconsiderable amount of prejudice against the foreign tester in the Netherlands situations.

(3) A non-conforming Dutch tester is markedly more often rejected in applying for housing than a respectable black Dutchman.

(4) These results are compatible with the interpretation that the crucial factor in acceptance or rejection in Dutch situations is not colour, but overt conformity to Dutch linguistic and social norms.

CHAPTER 9

# PREJUDICE, PLURAL SOCIETIES, AND SOCIAL CONFLICT

## THE THREE LEVELS OF PREJUDICE

In a previous report (Bagley, 1970b) which analysed data on prejudice in a large English sample, it was stressed that prejudice could be studied at three levels: at a cultural level, at the level of social system or social structure, and at a personality level. This Parsonian hierarchy has been used by Allport (1954) who suggests that, 'Prejudice is manifestly a value-orientation. It can be, and should be, studied at the level of *personality system*, at the level of *social system*, and at the level of *cultural system*.' While this hierarchy has been criticized by sociologists, it nevertheless has some explanatory power, and articulates with other explanatory models (Michelson, 1970).

Prejudice can thus be analysed in three ways—on a psychological basis, studying hypothetical correlates of prejudice such as an individual's relationship with his family in early life; and his strongly embedded style of emotional response, such as authoritarianism. This approach is exemplified by the classic study of Adorno and his co-workers on authoritarianism (1950).

The second approach studies the relationships between people performing roles within social institutions. This approach is exemplified by Rex and Moore's study (1967) of race relations in Birmingham. Psychology, the authors suggest, could explain some of the prejudice encountered, but:

> . . . it is also the case that a great deal of it was sufficiently explained, once we knew something of Birmingham's social structure and conflicts, and the constellation of interest and roles which was built into Birmingham society. At the very least it must be said that the universal factors and those having their roots in the individual personality could only be known if the factors arising from the social, economic and cultural system were first sorted out.

The third approach, the 'cultural', is concerned with the values of the society which implicitly inform behaviour at all levels of interaction. In Britain, such values are most likely to be those derived from the historical fact of being a colonial power and the kinds of colonial policy employed. These are the values which tended to assume that colonial exploitation was justified, and that the white man was superior to the coloured, on both biological and cultural grounds. These values assumed too that the native was a creature whose social and cultural ambitions could be ruled by the operation of law whose purpose was to ensure efficient economic exploitation. Though the underlying or implicit purpose of Dutch and British colonialism was probably the same—social or legal control to further economic exploitation—the practice of Dutch colonial policy has lacked the inherently racist aspects of British policy.

In the Netherlands the most important cultural feature is the division of society into religious blocs, which reflects the important influence which religious ideology has on social organization and behaviour at all levels. This religious ideology has also (as argued in Chapter 2) been an important factor influencing Dutch colonial policy in the direction of tolerance.

At the personality level one can assume that in the Netherlands the incidence of abnormal personalities predisposing individuals to prejudice is not markedly different from the incidence in Britain. There are few grounds for supposing that this factor should differ between the two countries. The demographic structure of the population in the age range 21 to 65, and the occupational roles they play, are also very similar in the two cultures.[1]

In the study of prejudice in English subjects I drew the conclusion that:

[1] A similar proposition has been made by Pettigrew (1958) in accounting for differing levels of prejudice in the Northern United States, Southern United States and South Africa. He argued, on the basis of an analysis of F-scale responses that the incidence of individuals prejudiced because of personality abnormalities was the same in all three areas. But, '. . . conformity to South African or Southern mores is associated with racial intolerance, while deviance from these mores is associated with tolerance. . . . In areas with historically imbedded traditions of racial intolerance, externalizing personality factors underlying prejudice remain important, but sociocultural factors are unusually crucial and account for the heightened racial hostility.' The study by Colman and Lambley (1970) of authoritarianism and racial attitudes in South Africa supports this view: '. . . the results of this study support a theoretical interpretation of tolerated prejudice, which views such attitudes as serving a utilitarian rather than an ego-defensive function for many of its (non-authoritarian) members.'

It remains a depressing fact however that a considerable amount of the variance remains unaccounted for. Even amongst the least prejudiced group—young respondents who are non-manual and have further educated, 21·6 per cent were prejudiced on three or more items. In other words, a considerable amount of prejudice cannot be accounted for by the structural and demographic factors we have examined (Bagley, 1970b).

I hypothesized that much of the variance in prejudice might be accounted for at the cultural level: that the dominant cultural values, derived from the fact and style of colonial rule, influenced behaviour, and attitudes in the field of race relations at all age, educational, and occupational levels.

The comparison of data from the English sample with a Dutch sample provides an opportunity of testing this hypothesis. I have pooled the data on the quota sample of 200 Dutch subjects with the data on prejudice in 200 age, sex, and occupation matched controls drawn from the large English sample. In combining the two samples I am making the assumption that the occupational and sex distribution in the population aged 21–65 in the two countries is similar. Level of education was not controlled in comparing the Dutch and English subjects, and in fact the 200 English subjects had a slightly higher level of education[2] than their Dutch controls. Since level of education is a factor associated with tolerance this factor has tended to reduce the difference between the two samples, i.e. if education had be taken into account the Dutch subjects would probably have been even less prejudiced.

I have used the technique of multiple regression analysis with the combined sample of 400 subjects[3] to try and predict as much as possible of the variance in the amount of prejudice in the combined samples. In the multiple regression technique the correlations of the predictor variables with the dependent variable (in this case the 6-item P scale) are calculated, as well as the correlations of the predictor variables amongst themselves. Then, in a series of steps the correlation of first one and then several predictor

[2] Level of education was rated as follows: 1 = education beyond age 18; 2 = education beyond statutory minimum; 3 = statutory minimum only. 'Statutory minimum' indicates education to age 14 only, in a greater number of Dutch than English subjects, since the school leaving age was not raised to 15 in the Netherlands until some years after Britain had introduced such a rule.

[3] The inclusion of the seventy-nine 'young professionals' would have made the sample demographically unrepresentative.

variables with the dependent variable is calculated taking into account their correlation with the other predictor variables. The variables at each step in the 'regression set' form an equation which predicts a greater amount of the dependent variable (prejudice) than any variable considered by itself. At each step progressively more predictor variables are taken into account until no significant increase in the multiple correlation can be obtained.

*Table* 9:1. *The Multiple Correlations of Age, Sex, Occupation, Education, and Cultural Values with Prejudice in 400 Dutch and English Subjects*

| | *Correlations with Prejudice* | | | | |
|---|---|---|---|---|---|
| *Variable* | *Step 1* | *Step 2* | *Step 3* | *Step 4* | *Step 5* |
| Age (low to high) | ·28 | ·33 | ·34 | ·32 | ·31 |
| Sex (male/female) | ·11 | ·13 | ·13 | ·13 | ·13 |
| Occupation (high to low) | ·20 | ·23 | ·23 | ·12 | ·12 |
| Education (more to less) | ·23 | ·20 | ·20 | ·20 | ·19 |
| Cultural Values (Dutch/British) | ·53 | ·55 | ·56 | ·57 | ·57 |
| Multiple correlation | ·280 | ·599 | ·608 | ·646 | ·652 |

The results of these calculations[4] are shown in Table 9:1. All of the variables considered—age, sex, occupation, education, and culture—make a significant contribution to the explanation of the amount of prejudice. Cultural values necessarily have a zero correlation with age, sex, and occupation; but education has a slightly positive correlation with cultural values (i.e. the British subjects are somewhat more educated). As a result of this in the later stages of the analysis the correlation of cultural values with prejudice (the highest in the equation) is increased when its negative association with education (scored more to less) is taken into account. In the first step the correlation of prejudice with British cultural values is ·53; in the final step this correlation rises to ·57. The final regression equation has a correlation of ·652 with the 6-item P scale. In other words, we have accounted for 42 per

[4] The calculations were carried out using a standard programme of the University of Sussex I.C.L. 1900 computer. For an explanation of the statistical techniques involved in multiple regression analysis see Hope (1968).

cent of the variance in the amount of prejudice, a much higher figure than if cultural values (Dutch/British) had not been taken into account.

It should be borne in mind that in making this comparison we have not taken the important structural variable of housing into account. Rex and Moore's study of Sparkbrook (1967) stressed that 'the constellation of interest and roles' in the social structure of Birmingham (which were strongly influenced by competition and insecurity in the field of housing) could influence attitudes to coloured immigrants. Despite the importance of this factor we feel that it cannot account for the low level of prejudice in the Netherlands; on the contrary, it makes this lack of prejudice all the more important.

As argued in Chapter 1, the housing problem in the Netherlands is much more serious than in Britain. The Netherlands is the most crowded industrial country in the world and the pressure of population on available housing resources is acute. Compared with the Netherlands, Britain's housing problems viewed in overall perspective, are mild. There is of course a difference between the two countries in their policy of allocating housing, and we have seen that the Dutch are much more liberal in both the public and the private sphere in allocating accommodation to coloured immigrants. This fact reflects the liberal policies of the Netherlands on race, and does *not* mean that the Netherlands has fewer housing problems than Britain. What we can conclude is that if the structural variable of housing had been controlled the differences between the Dutch and the British samples would have increased, i.e. our estimate of a high amount of prejudice in the British sample and a low amount in the Dutch sample is a conservative one.[5]

ASSIMILATION, INTEGRATION, AND ALIENATION: A MODEL

We have stressed two ideal kinds of relationship between immigrants and members of the host community. The first type (integration) is that in which the immigrants (e.g. Javanese, Ambonese) maintain a coherent cultural identity, reinforced by linguistic and ritual bonds. At the same time this group is law-abiding and contributes to the economy and welfare of the country

[5] The psychological correlates of prejudice in national or random samples remain to be investigated, an exercise we hope to carry out in a future study.

as a whole; in return, the larger society recognizes and supports the distinct cultural identity of this group. This policy has been fostered by recent developments in community relations in the Netherlands and applied especially to migrant workers from Europe and North Africa.

The second ideal kind of relationship is that of assimilation in which the immigration group has largely similar folkways, rituals, ideologies, norms, customs, and values to those of the major society, and seeks to be absorbed into that society, both geographically, occupationally, and by intermarriage. At the same time the conformity of these immigrants (e.g. from Indonesia, and Surinam and the Antilles) is recognized by the host society, and they are treated in all respects as Dutch citizens.

Before a group reaches a state of integration or assimilation there may be a learning period, a period of adjustment when the immigrant is unsure of, or unaware of, the behaviour expected of him in the new culture. Ex's study of the adaptation of immigrants from Indonesia illustrates this very well. Other evidence we have gathered together (e.g. on group hostility to Italians, Indonesians, and Moroccans) suggests that non-conforming immigrants are the subject of social control. There is evidence too (e.g. on the acceptance of Italians over time) that this social control activity is successful, in that immigrants learn appropriate inter-personal and normative behaviour, which is in turn rewarded by equality of treatment, regardless of skin colour or ethnic group.

Immigrants to the Netherlands from Indonesia, and from Surinam and the Antilles are strongly oriented to the 'motherland'. They are loyal to her institutions, they speak her language, they share her national sentiments. Immigrants to Britain from the West Indies and India and Pakistan have journeyed to the mother country. They are loyal to Britain, devoted to her institutions, often well-qualified and economically ambitious. West Indians especially are ideal candidates for assimilation into British culture, while linguistic and religious factors suggest that some Indians and Pakistanis (like some Jews in Britain) would prefer a relationship with the host society which is one of integration, in which their cultural homogeneity is tolerated.

The evidence in the chapters on prejudice and discrimination suggests that conformity, in terms of either assimilation or integration has met with little positive response, in terms of acceptance or equality of treatment, on the part of the majority of the British population. In the British model, conformity is rewarded by rejection, and the evidence suggests that this rejection is because of skin colour, not because of foreign origin. The rejection of an individual or a group is an alienating situation. A schematic representation of this model is presented in Table 9:2. I have reviewed and presented

*Table 9:2. The Outcome of Various Kinds of Interaction between Immigrants and Hosts*

| | *Individuals* | | | *Groups* | | |
|---|---|---|---|---|---|---|
| | *1* | *2* | *3* | *1* | *2* | *3* |
| *Situation* | | | | | | |
| Society's mores known and conformed to. | Y | N | Y | Y | N | Y |
| Society's mores not conformed to, resulting in sanctions and social control. | N | Y | N | N | Y | N |
| Both conformity and non-conformity result in rejection and discrimination by hosts. | Y | N | N | Y | N | N |
| *Outcome* | | | | | | |
| Personality disorganization, or alienation. | Y | ? | N | Y | ? | N |
| Inter-group conflict. | N | N | N | Y | ? | N |
| Integration possible in short run, *cet. par.* | N | N | Y | N | N | Y |
| Integration possible in long run, *cet. par.* | N | Y | Y | N | Y | Y |
| Assimilation possible in short-run, *cet. par.* | N | N | ? | N | N | ? |
| Assimilation possible in long-run, *cet. par.* | N | ? | Y | N | ? | Y |

*Note*: Table should be read vertically.
*Legend*: Y = Yes; N = No. *cet. par.* = *ceteris paribus.*
*1* E.g., West Indian, Indian, and Pakistani immigrants in Britain.
*2* E.g., Moroccan immigrants in the Netherlands.
*3* E.g., Surinamese immigrants in the Netherlands.

evidence on the effect of this rejection of individuals, and of groups elsewhere (Bagley 1968b, 1969d and e, 1970d). The outcome of alienation for an individual is likely to be personality disorganization (in extreme cases, mental illness); the outcome for groups is disenchantment with the existing organization of society in so far as the oppression of blacks is institutionalized. The likely outcome in this case of group alienation is vigorous civil rights activism, as black people try and wrest some power from the whites in order to obtain just treatment.[6]

Our model can be summed up as follows:

For immigrants to Britain: (1) Non-conformity→social control→conformity→rejection.
(2) Conformity→rejection.

For immigrants to the Netherlands: (1) Non-conformity→social control→conformity→acceptance.
(2) Conformity→acceptance.

Acceptance leads to either assimilation or integration; in the long run integration tends to lead to assimilation. Rejection for an individual is an alienative process leading to personality disorganization in individuals. But when there is a group consciousness of rejection, the likely outcome is social conflict. We would predict that the future pattern of race relations in Britain will be one of overt or explicit conflict as black people struggle to obtain justice, while the future pattern of race relations in the Netherlands will be one of harmony, so long as ethnic groups within society accept the premises of integration, and bloc rules of accommodation. The separatist aims of Moluccans in the Netherlands imply that relations between Moluccans and Dutchmen will involve friction from time to time.

## PERSPECTIVES ON THE PLURAL SOCIETY: SOCIAL CONFLICT AND SOCIAL INTEGRATION

Plural societies are those which contain two or more cultural groups who are more or less separate from one another in terms of ideology, norms, folkways, and institutions. Such groups may also be linguistically, ethnically, and geographically distinct from one another. In Chapter 1 it was argued that the Netherlands is such a plural society, and has also discovered a workable formula for ensuring social peace, democracy, and minority rights.

[6] Cf. Rex (1970): 'The question is whether their children [i.e. second generation coloured immigrants in Britain] would be allowed the possibility of assimilation or incorporation and, if not, what would happen. At this point a lot would depend upon numbers and upon relative power. The development of a permanent posture of militant self-defence is the most likely outcome if numbers are small. Otherwise alternatives similar to those in the United States would open up' (p. 114).

The notion of the plural society has attracted increasing attention from sociologists since its original formulation in the work of Furnivall on Burma and Indonesia. Its importance has been especially stressed in the study of nations whose ethnic diversity is a result of colonial policy. Despres (1967), writing about pluralism in British Guiana suggests: 'As a case, British Guiana is not unique. It belongs to a class of newly emerging nations that many writers have described as socially and culturally pluralistic. Like most of these nations it has a colonial history. It also is economically underdeveloped' (p. 1). Later in his book Despres elaborates his framework to include 'the comparative study of developing nations'. Here 'the structural dimensions of system integration in the plural society present a persistent problem of tension management between culturally differentiated groups at all levels of the social order' (p. 287).

Other writers have stressed the importance of the pluralist concept in analysing multi-ethnic societies. Van den Berghe (1967), writing in particular about South Africa, Mexico, and the United States suggests that: 'The concept of pluralism . . . is of great value in analysing multi-racial societies and in relating race to other dimensions of social cleavage and conflict' (p. 148).[7] Oxaal (1969), another student of pluralism in post-colonial societies, has pointed out the merits of comparative analysis in this field: 'These two countries (Trinidad and Guyana) provide an almost unique basis for comparative study because while they represent non-identical sociological twins they have none the less had quite different passages to interdependence. The pluralistic but peaceful development of Trinidad during the past decade stands in sharp contrast to the pluralistic but violent passage Guyana underwent' (p. 156).[8] I would add that the comparison of Surinam and Guyana

[7] Van den Berghe's chapter, 'Social and Cultural Pluralism' is a valuable discussion of this topic, especially in relating pluralism to the problem of power and conflict. See too studies and critiques by M. G. Smith (1960), Haug (1967), Magubane (1969). See also Bruyn's analysis (1965) of pluralism and race relations in the Netherlands.

[8] It appears, unfortunately, that we cannot include Trinidad in the group of post-colonial countries which have escaped inter-bloc conflict. Indians have been wary of supporting the emergent 'black power' movement. This apparently, has led to 'attacks on Indian shops and businesses. Maraj, the leader of the 300,000 Hindus here, has rejected Black Power overtures of brotherhood and accused them of causing only chaos and trouble' (*Guardian*, London, 13 March 1970). A further exacerbating cause of this 'deterioration in race relations in what was once probably the least race-conscious country in the

is an equally valuable exercise, not least for their geographical contiguity and economic similarity: Surinam is a closer twin to Guyana than is Trinidad, and it too has had a peaceful passage to independence. Nevertheless, Surinam as a plural society marked by peaceful social change has largely escaped the attention of English and American scholars.

There are degrees of plural society: that is, the degree to which blocs of the plural society are separate from one another is variable. Societies can range in van den Berghe's terms, from 'maximum cultural pluralism' (e.g. South Africa) to 'minimum cultural pluralism' (e.g. U.S.A., where black and white interact in the same cultural framework, but where especially in the South the social separation of the two groups reaches caste proportions). According to van den Berghe, 'maximum cultural pluralism' has the following features: many ethnic groups, none in clear majority; much regional concentration of groups; membership of groups unambiguous; ascribed group membership plus endogamy; autonomous culture and institutions; historically unrelated institutions; low overall consensus; consensus on narrow range of issues; distinct and incompatible values; passing impossible.

Many societies have 'moderate plurality' in that they meet some, but not all of these criteria. The Netherlands for example meets most of these criteria, although the various blocs of society cannot be said to be ethnically distinct, and passing is possible. There is too a high overall consensus, albeit on a narrow range of values. It is an interesting and curious fact, as Lijphart pointed out, that the Netherlands has been largely ignored by students of the plural society. The Netherlands is nevertheless vitally important in the consideration of such societies, since it is an example of a country which maintains a high degree of plurality in conjunction with democracy and social peace. It may be possible for us to examine the progress of a plural society such as Guyana through nationalism to social conflict, and suggest what social system artefacts might

---

world' may possibly have been the combination of economic deprivation with the inability of Trinidadians to emigrate to the mother country (John Palmer, *Guardian*, 23 and 24 April 1970). Palmer writes that, 'Last year a mere 34 Trinidadians were admitted into Britain with labour vouchers—less than a fifth of the figure for 1968. At the same time the United States authorities have cut back on their immigration quotas for the West Indies.' It seems probable too that Despres's analysis of the development of nationalism and social conflict in Guyana (*vide infra*) could fruitfully be applied to Trinidad. For a full account of the conflict in Trinidad see Nicholls (1971).

have prevented this conflict, in the light of our knowledge of Netherlands society.

Guyana is a traditional plural society. The two major ethnic groups, East Indians (48·2 per cent of the population) and Africans (33·5 per cent) were transported from their homelands as a result of colonial enterprise. Despres (1967) distinguishes between 'local' and 'broker' institutions in societies such as Guyana. Local institutions (e.g. language, family, religion) serve to structure activities and express cultural values within the context of local communities; broker institutions (e.g. trade unions, political parties) function to link activities to the wider spheres of societal activity. The cause of social conflict in Guyana, Despres argues, was an over-rapid social change in the growth of nationalism, which upset the delicately balanced situation in power relations which had been developed by the broker institutions.

In the early fifties, the developing nationalist movement was encapsulated in the People's Progressive Party, which at that time was a multiracial institution. As a party seeking electoral support, the P.P.P. stressed interdependence and national goals (full and immediate independence) rather than particularistic interests. The nationalist unity was not maintained, and by 1960 nationalist forces had redrawn around two sectional groups, each clearly allied to one of the two major ethnic groups. The 1960 elections gave Jagan's East Indian P.P.P. a clear numerical majority (twenty seats) over Burnham and Carter's African P.N.C. (eleven seats). In the years which followed violence broke out between Africans and East Indians, and continued until the granting of independence in 1966, under the surveillance of British troops.

Integration in Guyanese society was (as Despres shows) based upon a system of social relations between cultural units of unequal power, based on the differential adaptation of Africans and East Indians to the institutions of British colonialism. The delicate balance of social relations was maintained by the degree to which institutions of the two major blocs were autonomous. Nationalism, in seeking to merge ethnic institutions in a national framework, threw into stark relief the imbalance of status and power between these institutions. As Despres says,

> Under present circumstances, the functional autonomy of these units is maintained by the differential status they occupy in the power structure of society. This power structure in turn, is reinforced by the political order of Guianese society that the forces of nationalism seek to change.

Thus in seeking to implement changes in the political order, the forces of nationalism must inevitably pose a threat to the functional autonomy of cultural sections and create problems of tension management between the groups that these sections represent (p. 279).

The changes brought about by nationalism (according to Despres's analysis) occurred so rapidly that compensatory mechanisms could not be put in motion, and the tensions generated between cultural sections in their struggle for power and leadership in the nationalist movement reached an explosive level.

What compensatory mechanisms could have prevented the explosive conflicts severing social conflict in Guyana? The Netherlands underwent a similar kind of change—the uniting of sectional groups in a nationalist framework—in the early part of the century. This social change was achieved without overt conflict of any kind, and laid the foundations of an extremely stable society. The nationalistic framework of the Netherlands, far from obscuring sectarian differences, emphasized them, and guaranteed the autonomy of diverse ideological groups. It is worthwhile repeating the rules of political behaviour which the Netherlands has evolved (Lijphart, 1968, Chapter 7). These are:

(1) politics is a business, a serious means to a serious end;
(2) there shall be agreement to disagree; the fundamental convictions of other blocs shall be tolerated, if not respected;
(3) diplomacy is carried out at an elite level with compromise as the goal;
(4) proportionality—a simple procedural device for solving a host of troublesome problems—is the rule in the allocation of both resources and power to all the blocs and sectors of society;
(5) the rule of depoliticization involves the neutralization of potentially disruptive disputes by interpreting them as legal, constitutional or technical issues;
(6) relationships between the blocs shall take the form of diplomatic negotiations between different countries, and shall be undertaken, like such negotiations, largely in secret.

It is quite possible that stable relations can be maintained between groups having different traditions and ideologies by using only some of these rules, or variations of them. Probably the three most important rules are the second (agreement to disagree), the fourth (proportionality), and the last (diplomatic negotiations). The rule of proportionality means that in elections minorities are represented in government and other organizations having power in exact numerical relationship to their numbers in the community. A system of electing only one candidate in each geographical area means that it is possible for a party to poll a third of the votes in many constituencies, and not gain a single seat in the house of assembly. This kind of electoral machinery in Britain, for example, ensures serious under-representation of Liberals in Parliament, and of Catholics in the Six Counties.[9]

It is this kind of electoral machinery, of the simple majority, which British colonial rule bequeathed to Guyana, and it is this structural mechanism, we contend, which has had not a little responsibility for the social conflict in that country.[10] Few of the scholars writing about political and ethnic conflict appear to have commented on this point,[11] but there seems to be a fairly close relationship between the ascent to power of a particular ethnic political group, and social conflict resulting from the dominance of that group because of the operation of electoral machinery. It is clear, on the evidence given by Despres (1967, Chap. 1) that when one party, such as the P.P.P. gained power, other parties such as the P.N.C. representing substantial ethnic groups, were excluded from power and decision-making, and probably from a voice in how resources should be apportioned between ethnic groups. Despres tells us, 'The P.P.P. polled 46·7 per cent of the total votes cast for all three political parties. The P.N.C. polled 44·7 per cent. These percentages are almost identical to the ratio of Indians and Africans in the population when the Coloured are counted with the Africans. In terms of these data, it would seem that very few voters crossed racial lines in the 1961 elections' (p. 8). But on the basis of this election Jagan's P.P.P. won twenty seats, and total political power; the P.N.C. representing African interests, was excluded from power with only eleven seats, but virtually the same number of votes cast as the Indian party. This competition for leadership was a significant factor in the inter-ethnic violence following the 1961 election.

In neighbouring Surinam, where ethnic groups and their

[9] The House of Lords, in June 1971, rejected a bill to give proportional representation to the Six Counties. Electoral reforms promised by the Ulster Government in October 1971 did not include proportional representation.

[10] Conversely, Surinam's system of proportional representation has been a stabilizing factor in that country.

[11] The notable exception is R. T. Smith (1971) who points to the ironic fact that the imposition of a system of proportional representation in Guyana in 1964 was an American inspired device for removing Jagan from power.

political parties are quite evenly balanced, a situation such as this could hardly have arisen. The electoral machinery of a locally based proportional representation would have ensured that in Guyana all three parties in the election would have gained representation in proportion to the votes cast. This would have meant a coalition government, with agreement on important matters of policy taken by an elite at 'diplomatic' and secret cabinet meetings.

In planning a constitution for a country like Guyana, a constitution should have been formulated in which the cultural autonomy and equality of different ethnic groups was specifically recognized; such a constitution should have recognized too that the leaders of these ethnic groups should be drawn into all consultations in direct proportion to their numbers in the population; that apportionment of resources should be directly related to the size of the groups involved; and that the electoral machinery should take the form of proportional representation. None of the constitutions of the former colonies of Britain have followed this pattern, and one can only comment that the legacy of the English constitutional pattern—in Guyana, Trinidad, Nigeria and elsewhere—has been, or may be in the future, one of social conflict. The machiavellian system of proportional representation imposed in Guyana in 1964 (Smith, 1971) was not designed to offer an equitable share of power to different ethnic groups, though it may have had this effect.

In Surinam the working of the machinery of proportional representation is illustrated by the fact that in the 1969 elections Mr. J. Lachmon's East Indian party won 49 per cent of the seats, which is a close approximation of his actual electoral support in the population. Mr. Lachmon is reported as saying:

> My party won the largest number of seats in last year's election—19 out of 39—and I could have been Prime Minister. But I was afraid that if I did, there would be trouble with the Creoles. So I put in as Prime Minister Dr. Jules Sedney, leader of the Progressive National Party, the second largest of the Creole parties, and I became Speaker and President of the House.[12]

Mr. Lachmon went on to say:

> It's a narrow path we walk here in Surinam. Some groups try to cause trouble, but they have no support. . . . When the population is racially divided, peace depends on how the big groups behave. Every part of the

[12] *Guardian* (London, 30 April 1970).

community has to take a lot for the sake of peace. My people understand this, and I think the Creoles understand it too. I've tried to get away from racial politics.

This is an explicit statement of the politics of accommodation, and an excellent example of how the principle of proportionality works in practice. The relationships between Mr. Lachmon and Dr. Sedney and other party leaders will almost inevitably take the form of diplomatic negotiations carried out in secret. The House of Assembly is presented with decisions on which it comments, and votes according to the wishes of the party leaders. Politics, as in the Netherlands, is dull and unexciting.

The conclusion from this discussion is that the workings of the principles of accommodation, proportionality, elite rule, and diplomatic negotiations are almost certainly an important factor in ensuring democracy, social justice, and social peace in Surinam, in comparison with demographically, geographically and economically similar countries whose constitution is different.[13]

## PLURALISM, CONFLICT, AND NORMATIVE INTEGRATION

The future of plural societies is important for sociology generally because the explicit recognition that they are plural draws attention to the fact that social systems do exist in which conflict is more obvious than consensus. The model of the plural society, when its workings are more fully understood, is one which is just as essential to the sociologist as is, say, Parsons' model of an integrated social system. The process of social and political change currently going on in Britain's multi-racial colonies provides us with the sort of empirical material against which such a model can be tested and refined (Rex, 1960).

There is, as Despres points out (1967, p. 17) some disagreement between Parsonian and pluralist viewpoints. In the view of some Parsonian critics, the plural society model seems to overlook the fact that there must be a minimum core of shared values if the integration of a society is to be maintained. Critics of the 'normative integration' model of society have examined pluralist theory with interest, and have pointed to the obvious inadequacies of the normative consensus model in explaining conflict in societies such as Guyana.

In my view the problem of relating theories of pluralism and

[13] But note Nettl's reservations about the efficacy of proportional representation for mobilizing political power (Nettl, 1968, Chapters 8–9).

those of the Parsonian model of normative consensus in society is one which can be easily solved. Societies, by virtue of being societies, possess a high degree of normative integration. But it is a mistake to equate societies with national boundaries. Such boundaries, especially in colonial countries, are often arbitrary and have no connections with the realities of social interaction. A plural society is not a society as such, but a collection of two or more integrated societies bound together by rather arbitrary national boundaries, and perhaps by trading interests, or by economic competition or economic exploitation of one group by another. Lijphart's analogy of the blocs of society with countries, and inter-bloc relations as analogous to diplomatic negotiations, is enlightening in this context. Europe is in some sense a plural society made up of different blocs (e.g. France, Germany) ideologically and culturally distinct, but bound together by various interests and interactions (e.g. in the marketplace of the E.E.C.) Relationships between the blocs are carried out (like the relationships between Netherlands blocs) at a diplomatic level. Both France and Germany can be said, in a Parsonian sense, to be fairly integrated societies, but the countries forming the E.E.C. do not form a society in a collective or integrated sense.

Parsons, in *The Social System* (1952), defines a society as a social system having 'long term persistence from within its own resources'. A social system is defined by Parsons as having (i) individuals, who are (ii) interacting with others, on the basis of a minimal degree of, and according to (iii) a shared system of beliefs, standards, and means of communication. I have argued (Bagley, 1969c) that the family can meet all these requirements of a society and can, in order to be 'long term stable from within its own resources' legitimize sexual relationships which other 'societies' have tabooed (e.g. by means of the incest taboo). The point of this comparison is to emphasize that within the arbitrary boundaries of a country, sub-cultures—often very small—can and do exist. It is much more likely that the Parsonian theory of normative consensus will apply to sections of a political nation rather than to that nation as a whole.

Rex (1960) makes the interesting suggestion that pluralism might be a useful concept with which to examine class relations in countries such as Britain. The relationships between economic classes in a country and between blocs in that country are interesting and problematical. A country like West Germany or England is not a plural society in the sense of being made up of blocs with distinct ideologies and traditions like the Netherlands. But they are countries in which a wealthy minority of capitalists and rentiers enjoy prosperity at the benefit of a large industrial proletariat. Moreover, the economic interests of these two sections of the country are largely at variance with one another.

How are classes, in the Marxian sense, distinguished from blocs of society, in the pluralist sense? The crucial differences seem to be in the sphere of *institutional separatism*. In England the working classes do not have control of separate institutions of communication and education. These vital agencies of socialization are in the hands of the bourgeois, ruling class. The ruling class have abrogated the institutions of culture and have provided for the proletariat a debased form of culture, a pale, seductive, and deformed creature whose function is that of an opiate.[14]

De Kadt (1965) has perceptively indicated ways in which the consciousness of their oppression is kept from the proletariat: the ruling class control not only the material existence, but also the cognitive existence of the proletariat. They asked for bread, and they were given the *Daily Mirror*. There can be no revolution, nor conflict, without the consciousness of revolution and conflict.

My argument is that separate strata or blocs of society have no coherence, no feeling of separate existence unless they have control of the important agencies of socialization, education, and communication. In England the proletariat has no such control, and the working classes cannot be said to form a separate bloc of society. They are a deferential and subordinate adjunct of the ruling class.[15]

Blocs of the plural society, like Catholics, Protestants, and socialist blocs in the Netherlands, are defined by the extent that they are institutionally autonomous, and control their own schools, newspapers, magazines, radio stations, and universities, and prescribe specific modes of inter-personal behaviour. In some countries, perhaps in France and Italy, where Catholics and communists have degrees of institutional separateness and autonomy, class relations have a plural character.

[14] See Raymond Williams's *The Long Revolution* (1961) for an elaboration of this point.

[15] See MacKenzie and Silver (1968) for an account of deferential attitudes in the English working class. Cf. Rex (1970): '. . . ruling class control of ideological instruments does mean that some of those whom they rule accept their values. This is the phenomenon of the deferential worker' (p. 92).

The key concept in analysing and comparing plural societies is that of *power*. A crucial cause of instability and conflict in such societies centres round the apportionment of control over resources, and the decision-making process at the parliamentary level. It is for this reason that the rule of proportionality is the most crucial one for plural societies. Blocs of society which are denied power and economic prosperity comparable to that of other blocs will try to institute social change (as in the rise of Indonesian nationalism) which will alter this disequilibrium. Where constitutional rules make proportionality extremely difficult, tension and conflict (as in Guyana and Trinidad) are the likely outcome. The Netherlands provides a clear example of a country in which a satisfactory equilibrium between several blocs can be permanently maintained.

In De Kadt's terminology, conflict in the Netherlands is manifest in so far as the blocs of society have institutionalized the separatism of groups having different interests. This institutional separatism applies too to class conflicts in the secular sphere, in that conservatives and socialists each form separate blocs. In Britain the difference of interest between employers and employed is very real, but recognition of the difference of interest is not overt. The proletariat does not have any kind of bloc consciousness, not does it have any religious conviction or interest. In this kind of socicty power conflicts are *latent*.

Britain possesses one kind of overt conflict which the Netherlands does not—strongly expressed and widely prevalent public hostility to coloured immigrants, translated in practice into widespread discrimination. We have argued that a good deal of the variance in the amount of prejudice observed in Britain can be accounted for by values derived from the style of colonial rule. An important facet of this rule has been the involvement of the proletariat in colonial ideologies.

This idea was developed by Marx in a letter to Engels dated 7 October 1858: 'The British working class is actually becoming more and more bourgeois, so that this most bourgeois of all nations is apparently aiming ultimately at the possession of a bourgeois aristocracy and a bourgeois proletariat as well as a bourgeoisie. Of course this is to a certain extent justifiable for a nation which is exploiting the whole world.'[16] Marx's notion of English workers as bourgeois to the extent that they were involved

[16] Cited by Lenin in *The Split in the Working Class* (Lenin, 1934).

in colonial ideology was taken up by Engels, who wrote to Kautsky on 12 September 1882: 'You ask me what the English workers think of colonial policy? Exactly the same as they think about politics in general, the same as what the bourgeois think. There is no working-class party here, there are only Conservatives and Liberal-Radicals, and the workers merrily devour with them the fruits of the world market.'

Engels extended this analysis in the preface to the second edition of his *Condition of the Working Class in England* published in 1892. He distinguished between 'causes' and 'effects' in studying working-class behaviour. Causes he distinguished as: '(1) Exploitation of the whole world by this country. (2) Its monopolist position in the world market. (3) Its colonial monopoly.' Effects he saw as: '(1) A section of the British proletariat becomes bourgeois. (2) A section of the proletariat permits itself to be led by people who are bought by the bourgeoisie, or at least are in their pay.'[17]

Engels, like Marx, retained the hope that in Britain (as in other countries) the workers would shrug off this shroud of bourgeois values. Lenin took up this view in *The Workers and the Colonies*:

> The English bourgeois, for example, obtains larger revenues from the tens and hundreds of millions of the population of India and of her other colonies than from the English workers. In these conditions, a certain material and economic basis is created for infecting the proletariat of this or that country with colonial chauvinism. Of course, this can only be a passing phenomenon; nevertheless, we must clearly recognize the evil and understand its causes in order to be able to rally the proletariat of all countries for the fight against such opportunism (Lenin, 1934).

What Lenin described—the corruption of the working classes with the values of colonialism—was not 'a passing phenomenon'. The Marxian revolution of the proletariat has not come about; instead the workers have become more rather than less infected with this social chauvinism. Present day working-class racialism in Britain is a clear manifestation of the extent to which workers

[17] Cf. McCreal and Corrigan (1970): 'In Britain not only did certain sections of the labour aristocracy benefit, more than other large sections of the working class, from the "super profits" from colonial domination, but large sections of the British proletariat were mystified by the ideology of "race" and remain so today to a point where they actively collaborate in the oppression of the weakest sections of their own class, including black workers and thus collaborate in their own exploitation.'

are still infected with 'social chauvinism'. Lenin recognized that this corruption of the labour movement by bourgeois ideology might be a more permanent phenomenon than he had originally hoped. Writing in 1916 his tone was angrier, and more desperate:

The opportunists [social chauvinists] are working together with the imperial bourgeois precisely in the direction of creating an imperialist Europe on the backs of Asia and Africa; objectively, the *opportunists* are a section of the petty bourgeoisie and certain strata of the working class which have been bribed out of imperialist super profits and converted into watchdogs of capitalism, into corruptors of the labour movement. . . . It is a *fact* that *certain* groups of workers have already gone over to opportunism and to the imperialist bourgeois (Lenin, 1934, p. 143).[18]

The argument here is that in Britain it is not merely 'certain groups' of workers who have accepted the ideology of bourgeois chauvinism, but the large majority of workers. Hall (1969) has commented on the link between Lenin and some modern theorists of society whose view is close to my own—that the instruments of communication, education, and socialization being in the hands of the ruling classes, ensures the permanent subjection of the proletariat:

Marcuse's book, *One Dimensional Man*, first published in 1964, is surely destined to become one of the critical works of the 20th century, as important in its age as Lenin's *Imperialism* was. . . . Here emerges a vital link, though Marcuse does not stress it, with McLuhan: so complete is the apparatus of the mass media, that the citizens become *willing* slaves, as totally unaware of their condition as if they were hypnotized or drugged. In this state of 'happy consciousness' as Marcuse calls it, a 1984 style tyranny can be maintained without the apparatus of tyranny.[19]

Racialism in Britain (which is especially prevalent among the working classes) is the product, the heir, of the values of imperialism with which their consciousness has been saturated. Through migration since 1945 the exploited colonial peoples—the blacks—are now active competitors with the working classes for jobs and

[18] Cf. Rex (1970, p. 106) on 'the metropolitan citizen's perception of the colonial immigrant . . . in relation to the metropolitan stratification structure'.

[19] As Hall suggests, there are interesting points of comparison too between Marcuse and the social criticisms of Orwell, Lawrence, and Leavis. There are, too, strong parallels with the work of Raymond Williams which we cited above.

houses. Their racialism is likely to be exacerbated for two reasons: their one high status—being white—is threatened as blacks seek to establish that colour shall be irrelevant in the job and housing market;[20] secondly, racialism (like social chauvinism) is functional for the ruling classes in that it diverts attention from the real nature of exploitation and deprivation in society. It is an extremely useful ritual by which a scapegoat may be attacked and denigrated as being responsible for society's ills. St. Clair Drake (1955) has described very succinctly this kind of situation in central Africa in which the 'real' or 'latent' conflicts over land, labour mobility, and political power are hidden, and the 'manifest' conflicts are inter-ethnic ones; conflicts which disguise the real power bases in society. Racialism may perform for the British ruling class precisely the same function that social chauvinism performed in Lenin's analysis of class relations at the turn of the century. It both 'integrates' the proletariat with bourgeois ideology, and serves to institutionalize a kind of manifest conflict while effectively disguising the true nature of power and *inequality*. The consistent appeal of conservatism to the working class on such chauvinist and racialist grounds has been documented by McKenzie and Silver (1968), who point out that without working-class support no Conservative government would ever have been elected in the twentieth century. 'The Unionist government', a pamphlet of 1904 told the workers, 'wants to keep these creatures out of Great Britain. They don't want to see the honest Britisher turned out by these scourings of European slums. They brought in a Bill to check this evil flow of aliens. But Radicals said, No! we don't want to stop the foreign criminal and diseased outcast from coming into this country.'[21]

Later, in 1924 in a pamphlet entitled *The Alien Shall not Steal your Job* the Tory party boasted: 'Under the Unionist Government of 1923 the Aliens Order is strictly enforced, but the Socialist party voted in the House of Commons on 28 February 1923, against maintaining a strict control over alien immigration. Is the Socialist plan to let aliens in, and so hit our people? The Unionist Party plan is to keep aliens out. It helps the British worker.'[22] McKenzie and Silver conclude, '. . . it seems fair to assume that,

[20] For an elaboration of this view see Runciman and Bagley (1969) and Bagley (1970a).

[21] Quoted by Mackenzie and Silver (1968, p. 60).

[22] Quoted in ibid., p. 65.

in so far as they were exposed to a direct statement of the Conservative case by way of the written word, it would have been in large part through the popular literature examined in this chapter' (p. 72). This literature, as the authors show, is riddled with social chauvinism, sentiments offered too in a 1951 Conservative election manifesto: 'Socialists sneered and still sneer at what they call "Imperialism" and think it no discredit that in their term of office countries have left the empire for the first time since the eighteenth century.'[23] Given that the working classes are imbued with the ideology of chauvinism and social superiority, it is not surprising that the Labour Government of 1968 should, through the processes of democracy, pass an immigration act which denied British nationality to coloured people in East Africa. Now it is not merely the Unionist plan to keep out this 'evil flow of aliens'. It is the Labour Party's also.

I have argued that it has been extremely useful for British capitalism to have a proletariat imbued with colonialist values, and using up what surplus revolutionary energy they have by black-baiting.[24] The Netherlands is a capitalist society, and it has also been a major colonial power. But the Dutch working class, on the evidence we have examined, cannot be said to be overly racialist. I suggest that this is because of three inter-acting causes. The first, and most fundamental, has been the place of religion, and religious ideology in Dutch life. Concern to defend one's religion—its values and its ritual—have cut across the traditional boundaries of class. Now, as Max Weber pointed out, classes based on economic interest are often of paramount importance for social organization and conflict; but status groups can cut across class lines. The practice of 'Christian colonialism' has been paternalistic, but in the main kindly, and far more enlightened than British colonialism.

The Dutch scheme, while having no place for democracy, did allow cultural autonomy which, as argued in Chapter 2, was one of the ironies accounting for the Dutch undoing in Indonesia. This respect for cultural autonomy was largely derived from the experience of the tolerance of religious autonomy in the Netherlands. The Netherlands is a plural society, in which conflict of interest

[23] Quoted in ibid., p. 68.

[24] On the high prevalence of racialism in the British working class see Bagley (1970b and 1970e). See too Miller (1968). For references to the practice of 'Paki-bashing' see *Race Today* (May 1970).

is both manifest and institutionalized in the bloc system. There is no need to devise social system mechanisms for integration (such as socialization of the whole population in imperialist values). Social system integration is already based within each bloc on clear ideological interest. What all these ideologies hold in common are Christian notions of ethical behaviour and social responsibility. The revolutionary energies of the Dutch proletariat are absorbed in the rituals of inter-bloc relations. Conflict is grossly overt, and grossly institutionalized. Social system mechanisms, such as the institutionalization of racialism are unnecessary. At the same time racialism would run strongly counter to the formal ideologies of the bloc which are based on: (i) a brotherly affection for one's ideological peers, and (ii) the maintenance of social distance and formal equality in relation to other blocs. In this kind of social system, racialism is both unnecessary and irrelevant. I conclude, therefore, that racialism in Britain may be a social system mechanism which has served to draw the working classes into a culturally integrated value system. In the Netherlands separate blocs of society are culturally integrated by religious values. Racialism is unnecessary as a means of accommodating or channelling conflict, and is also incompatible with the strongly held religious convictions on which both conflict and integration in Dutch society are based. Social conflict and social integration theories of society are not logically antithetical. Societies, conceived as social systems in the Parsonian sense, may be in conflict with one another *within* the geographical boundaries of a country (e.g. the Netherlands). In some countries, such as England, social system integration is maintained by the control of socialization, education, and communication systems over an exploited proletariat. In this way conflict is kept latent by means of social integration controlled by the ruling class.

## THE RELEVANCE OF THE NETHERLANDS MODEL

Lijphart (1968) without mentioning newly emergent societies whose pluralism is the result of colonial rule, proposes two important amendments to pluralist theory. These are: (i) overarching co-operation at the elite level can be a substitute for crosscutting affiliations at the mass level; and (ii) When different groups in society have widely divergent interests and values, self-containment and mutual isolation can be more conducive to stable democracy than a high incidence of overlapping affiliations. Lijphart argues further, 'If one accepts the conclusion that in a divided society stable democracy can be achieved by the combination of mutual isolation of the antagonistic segments of the population and overarching elite co-operation, it follows that *proportional representation and a multiparty system can be salutary to democracy because they strengthen the possibilities of accommodation*' (p. 203, italics in original). These conclusions would suggest that plural societies such as Guyana and Trinidad can best ensure social peace by emphasizing the right to a separate cultural existence of ethnic groups in society, and institutionalizing relationships between them by means of elite and diplomatic negotiations, in terms of equality. Lijphart is anxious to stress that his conclusion 'is not an argument in favour of *apartheid*' (p. 202). Apartheid is a system of pluralism based on gross inequality of power. In order to be stable, and just, plural societies must embody an equal distribution of power between blocs. The relationship, in Aristotle's term, must be one of net equality.

It is possible that within this framework of separatism a policy of co-operation on important issues can be worked out (e.g. on external relations), for there to be a relative harmony and friendliness in everyday interaction. Crowley (1956) writing about Trinidad has recorded how 'creole culture' provides a meeting point for different ethnic groups, while the desirable segments of each cultural bloc are retained intact. 'A Chinese Anglican,' Crowley says, 'finds nothing inconsistent in visiting a Hindu pandit or African obeahman for a love charm to lure a Presbyterian Portuguese girl to his bed and board.' Crowley was writing in the mid 1950s.[25] Since then Trinidad has become independent, and the development of nationalism has probably de-emphasized cultural differences. This (as Oxaal, 1969, points out) has been the specific policy of Dr. Williams's People's National Movement. At the same time, the development of a proletarian consciousness (a kind of nationalism) in one section of the proletariat only (i.e. in Africans) seems to have contributed to the interethnic conflict which originated in Guyana.

[25] Cf. Klass's study (1961) on the cultural persistence of East Indians in Trinidad. Cf. also Bacchus (1969) on the role of education in social change in pluralism in Guyana; and Speckman (1965) on education and the persistence of East Indians in Surinam.

Sociologists[26] have an important task in mapping the degree to which groups in society (i) have a degree of cultural identity to the extent that they form coherent blocs; and (ii) the degree of power inequality between different blocs of society. It is open to them too, to propose constitutional and fiscal means by which this power inequality can be reduced.

## CONCLUSIONS

I began this chapter by pointing to the importance of cultural factors, especially those derived from the style of colonial policy, which could account for much of the difference in racial prejudice in Britain and the Netherlands. Dutch colonial policy has involved the tolerance of different cultural and ethnic groups to a much greater degree than was practised in Britain. Tolerance of diversity has been a feature of Dutch society, which institutionalized harmonious relationships between very diverse ideological groups.

The social system mechanisms of Dutch pluralism, I have argued, could well be imitated by ethnically plural societies in various parts of the world. Britain is not a plural society, except in so far as immigrant minorities, such as Pakistanis, form coherent and discrete cultural groups. The evidence however suggests that both conformity and desire to be assimilated in British society (e.g. by West Indians) and conformity and desire for integration—cultural co-existence and mutual tolerance—(e.g. by Pakistanis) are rejected by the majority of the British population. In the Netherlands by contrast, conforming behaviour is rewarded by acceptance (either through assimilation, or cultural co-existence). The result in Britain is the alienation of British Indians, Pakistanis, and West Indians.

Rejection for an individual whose cultural loyalty is to the mother country, and who does not have an organized or coherent national group or identity to fall back on, may be particularly disastrous. Such rejection, over time, may lead to the development of group consciousness and militant activity as blacks try to wrest some power from the white ruling class. To the extent that blacks become alienated from the institutions of white society, and construct their own institutions transmitting education and cultural values, they will begin to form a separate bloc of society,

[26] I include anthropologists in this term. There is no case for plural separatism here!

and race relations in Britain must be appraised appropriately. In terms of our analysis of class relations in Britain, it is the blacks who form the true proletariat. The white working classes have traded their revolutionary consciousness for racialism and thirty pounds a week. Britain's prosperity is the result of the exploitation of the colonial blacks.[27] These blacks possess the potential for revolutionary activity of a classic, Marxian kind to the extent that their alienation leads them to develop autonomous institutions of education, socialization, communications, and cultural organization.

[27] This exploitation continues on an international basis through the use of tariffs to prevent the processing of raw materials (bauxite, cocoa beans, cane sugar) in the countries in which they are produced. The cost of the prosperity of English chocolate manufacturers such as Rowntree and Cadbury is the relative impoverishment of Ghana. Ghana could process her own cocoa beans and export chocolate to the world were it not for European tariffs making such manufacture uneconomic. Cf. Hayter (1971) on 'aid as imperialism'.

CHAPTER 10

# THE LESSONS FOR BRITAIN

The proportion of coloured immigrants in the Netherlands is similar to the proportion in Britain. The Netherlands is a much more crowded country than Britain, and in comparison with this country has an acute housing shortage. Immigrants to the Netherlands arrived, moreover, in much heavier concentrations than immigrants to the U.K. Despite these facts it appears that the Dutch express markedly less prejudice than their English counterparts, and practise markedly less racial discrimination. Social policy on behalf of immigrants has, moreover, been markedly more generous and systematic than social policy in Britain. Such policy was carried through by a country with somewhat less national wealth per head than Britain. Ironically, by 1972 gross national product per head in the Netherlands had overtaken that of Britain; but for the years to which the analysis refers, Britain's G.N.P. was definitely greater than that of the Netherlands.

The kind of comparative examination of social policy which we have carried out can be useful because it can show how the social services of a particular country can be improved. Britain's major example to the world in this respect is its national health service. But in other fields—provision for children of families in poverty for example—a comparative analysis can show that Britain's services are markedly inferior to the services of a country such as Germany (Bagley, 1970h). The point of making such comparisons is that one can show how the social services of one's country can be improved. On the pessimistic side, it must be said that recommendations by social scientists for changes in government policy seem to have markedly little effect on that policy. The failure of governments to take note of our recommendations concerning poverty in large families (Abel-Smith and Bagley, 1970) is a case in point. The only chance of changing policy at the statute level seems to be with reforms which are politically non-controversial, and cost nothing. Recommendations—and especially expensive recommendations—in the field of race relations are extremely unlikely to have any influence on government policy. But even the moderate proposals for reform in the fields of housing policy put forward by Rex and Moore (1967) and by Cullingworth (1969) have not been implemented.

The situation may well be akin to the progress of public health policy in the nineteenth century. Knowledge and policy recommendations about the spread of disease and its prevention were not lacking; action only came after extensive outbreaks of cholera in major cities. The major difference in this analogy is that by the time any major policy decisions concerning race relations are seriously contemplated, the situation in Britain may be beyond repair in the sense that acute bitterness between ethnic groups cannot easily be alleviated. The descendants of cholera victims do not harbour bitterness; but the bitterness which results from the experience of racial discrimination does not disappear in a generation. Racial prejudice and discrimination are, in a sense, disease processes. But unlike bodily diseases, though we can diagnose cause, we cannot affect any cure. Racism—the malignant neoplasm of British society—may well have too firm a hold, not merely in the bowels but in the brain of this country. The only legislation in the race relations field this country has seen in recent years has been largely negative legislation—the institutionalization of discrimination by some sections of the 1968 Race Relations Act; the denial of citizenship to British citizens on account of their colour in the 1968 Immigration Act; and the whole racist paraphernalia of the 1971 Immigration Act.

A 1971 national opinion poll in Britain on the subject of the Common Market indicated that the Netherlands was the country held in the highest esteem by Englishmen, and that the Dutch (unlike the French and the Germans) were seen in very positive terms. This kindred feeling of the English for the Dutch, which is certainly reciprocated, is traditional, and the two countries have much in common.

Yet their important differences in social structure have been shown by the discussion in the previous chapter. The Dutch are a religious nation, and a great many social institutions are arranged on a religious basis. The same cannot be said of Britain. Although there is an established church, its influence on everyday life, and on political and social attitudes is minimal. The ethic of Christianity should counsel tolerance in the field of race relations, and we would expect that a nation instrinsically committed (as opposed to extrinsic commitment, as defined by Allport [1966]) to religious values would by and large be tolerant and accepting of minorities. It does appear to be true that in the Netherlands intrinsic commitment to religion appears to be associated with tolerance, and that such intrinsic commitment is greater in the Netherlands than in Britain (Bagley, 1971c).

As stressed in the previous chapter, the class divisions which usually operate in industrial societies are to a large extent blurred by the division of Dutch society into plural blocs. Class divisions and class exploitation exist of course, but the necessity for institutionalized racialism as a means of integrating the proletariat with the ideology of 'social chauvinism' does not exist in the Netherlands. The revolutionary energies of the Dutch proletariat are absorbed in the rituals of inter-bloc relations. Conflict is grossly overt, and grossly institutionalized. Social system mechanisms, such as the institutionalization of racialism are unnecessary.

What this analysis implies is that there are important structural and ideological reasons why the Netherlands is a tolerant country. These structural and ideological factors do not exist in Britain. How, then, are we to bring about changes in British society which enable race relations in Britain to be brought up to the Dutch standard?

First of all, it must be said that I do not propose any emulation of the pillarization of Dutch society into religious blocs (although it would seem no bad thing for an Irish society which contains a substantial minority of Protestants). Historical and structural factors have predisposed the Dutch to tolerance in matters of colour; but this tolerance often does not extend, as we have seen, to the treatment of people who are manifestly foreign to, and unacquainted with, Dutch linguistic and cultural norms. This at times extreme zenophobia or chauvinism, which has resulted in very harsh treatment of groups such as Moroccans, again appears to arise from the way the rules governing inter-bloc behaviour have evolved to deal with the peaceful and stable interaction of ideologically diverse groups. Though I have attempted to describe the structural factors underlying Dutch society, I am unable to say *why* religion has been so important to the Dutch nation in the first place; nor can I see any way in which religious ideology (in Allport's intrinsic sense) can become important in an essentially non-Christian nation like Britain.

The underlying sociological schema should be made clear. My position, like that of Rex and Moore in their study of *Race, Community, and Conflict* in Birmingham, is principally a Weberian one. In the final analysis there are only two possible factors which underlie the structural conditions and the norms which inform action. These are *class* and *status*. Though I have in the preceding chapter stressed a Marxist–Leninist analysis of race relations in Britain, there is no doubt that in some situations race relations cannot be seen entirely in terms of their relationships to economic classes. There are important situations—and the Netherlands has been one of them—in which social relations are related to extra-economic factors, in which groups, such as religious groups, have status and meaning over and above class and economic groups.[1]

Since I have described British society in terms of class relationships, social change of the type I recommend—the movement for the achievement of justice in the race relations sphere—must come about through the class struggle, and in particular through non-violent revolutionary pressure of blacks and whites acting in left-wing concord. The personal model which I commend to my readers in this revolutionary struggle is the Catholic Marxist, Archbishop Helder Camara, whom I quoted at the beginning of this book.

## POLICY PROPOSALS

There are two areas in which British policy in race relations can be brought up to the standard of the Netherlands. The first is in the treatment of the East African Asians; the second is in social policy with regard to the reception and care of immigrant workers. It has been symptomatic of the difference between Dutch and English race relations that the Dutch accepted responsibility for a colonial group who remained loyal to the motherland, even after the usefulness of the colony was past. The transportation of Indians to Africa, and their socialization as loyal followers of the British was an extremely useful facet of colonial exploitation. But when the East African Indians were no longer economically or

[1] In this way Weber's theory logically contains Marx's theory of class relationships. See Weber (1948), pp. 192–4 on 'Economic Conditions and Effects of Status Stratification'.

politically useful, they were abandoned, even to the point of denial of British citizenship. If East African Asians were admitted to Britain on the same scale that Indonesians were admitted to the Netherlands, this might mean the addition of a considerable number of coloured immigrants in the space of about five years. Now it may not be expedient for Britain to allow the entry of these people, but it is certainly a moral duty.

The first policy proposal is, accordingly, that the Immigration Act of 1968 which makes a distinction between British citizens on grounds of colour should be repealed. Exceptional efforts should be made for the reception of these refugee Britons in their mother country.

Any change in a country's value system which such policy change involves, requires at least the acquiescence of its leaders. As in the Netherlands, charismatic figures, such as the Queen, might provide active encouragement in the initial reception of these displaced Britons. It would be an excellent example if, for instance, Buckingham Palace (and Lambeth Palace too) could be given over for temporary accommodation. The special social services needed —if they were to be on a Dutch scale—would of course cost money: a provisional estimate would be about £50 million per annum for the next ten years. This is a small amount for a rich nation, though it is considerably more than anything that has been spent on race relations in this country so far.

An important issue to be decided is whether the policy undertaken on behalf of the immigrant Asians shall be one of integration (toleration of the cultural integrity of the group) or assimilation (absorption of the group into the parent society). The Dutch policy with regard to immigrants from Indonesia was one of assimilation. This meant that the immigrants were dispersed throughout the country according to the availability of jobs and houses. The adjustments necessary on behalf of the immigrants sometimes created strains, but over all, and in the perspective of time, the process has been successful.

The danger of initiating a policy of assimilation in the British context is that the values of acceptance of immigrants which would be initiated by official policy would not be taken to heart by the British public. This public, as shown in previous chapters, is largely racialist. The dispersal of immigrants in an assimilationist policy might well result in a situation such as that described by *The Times* on 13 April 1970:

> A Sikh schoolteacher has been forced to leave his council flat in a non-immigrant area of Gravesend after a sustained campaign of intimidation. His wife and children have been stoned, obscenities have been written on the wall of the flats and on his car, and he has been abused by groups of young men. The family have moved to live among Indians where they feel more secure.[2]

It is common practice in London for Asian immigrants to be attacked and beaten[3] and there is little doubt that Asians dispersed to various parts of the country and isolated from the support of kin and friends, would be particularly liable to persecution. A further factor which makes dispersion questionable as an act of policy is the fact that East African Asians, although politically in a position very similar to the Indonesian refugees, do form coherent religious minorities. The Indonesian immigrants, in contrast, were largely Christian, and were therefore absorbed in Dutch denominational social networks. Since England is not at the grass roots a Christian country, there are no networks which immigrants could be absorbed into. West Indians, many of whom were attached to churches in the West Indies, have either fallen away from church life in Britain, or have established their own churches.

The alternative to assimilation, that of integration, is well exemplified in the Dutch treatment of West Indians and migrant workers from Southern Europe and North Africa. The Dutch, both in their colonial and their domestic policy have always paid great attention to the cultural integrity of peoples, such as Moslems in Indonesia or in Surinam, or in the Netherlands. The integration policies for immigrants, as we saw earlier, have been generously endowed and efficiently carried through. We feel that the community relations policy towards West Indians, Asians, and other immigrants should be of a piece: that this policy should be one of integration.

A model of how integration can work in practice has been offered by the Jewish community. Krausz's study of the Jewish community in North London (1969) revealed that in several parts of Edgware, some 40 per cent of the population was Jewish. These Jews are largely endogamous, and give active or tacit support to local synagogues. The evidence suggests that Jews in Britain are tolerated and respected. There is no reason why this pattern should

[2] But see the more optimistic account of the situation in Manchester by Ward et al. (1971).

[3] *Race Today* (May 1970), pp. i-viii.

not be emulated by communities of Pakistani, Indian, and West Indian origin in Britain. Ecologically this would imply 'local dispersal'—some streets would have a majority of residents belonging to the ethnic group concerned, but at an enumeration district[4] level the ethnic group would never be in a majority. Such a policy would also require that the kind of housing commanded by ethnic minorities was of similar quality to that commanded by the population as a whole. My study of a London borough[5] suggested that the kind of local dispersal which the integration policy would imply had already been achieved in practice. However, immigrants have been excluded from middle-class housing, and from council housing. They occupy, perforce, housing of poor quality. Their command over housing resources is a direct result of racial discrimination in housing.

If social justice is to prevail, immigrants must be given the opportunity to compete for housing on equal terms with the rest of the population. In particular an equitable allocation of council housing would be an excellent means of local dispersal. Yet there is evidence that coloured immigrants are severely disadvantaged in this sphere. The Cullingworth Report (1969) on *Council Housing Purposes, Procedures and Priorities* commented:

> . . . a majority of West Indians who live in the underprivileged areas of our cities are not there by choice and could afford better housing if only they could get it. They often pay more rent than their white neighbours for accommodation with poorer amenities. Many West Indians are the archetype of the council house tenant; skilled artisans whose wives are prepared to go out to work to add to the family resources. If the present obstacles are removed it seems likely that they will follow the Irish into acceptance in the public sector. That others would willingly buy homes on credit is shown by the extent of home ownership among West Indians which is far higher than in the English working class. All these people need to be helped to get out of the areas in which they are so often involuntarily segregated. It does not follow that they would choose to be dispersed in isolation from one another; nor is there anything to be gained in isolating them from one another. If families or friends wish to stay together it should be possible to

[4] An enumeration district is the smallest area on which ecological analyses can usually be based, and consists of about 200 households—the average area which one census enumerator can cover.

[5] 'Coloured Neighbours', *New Society* (7 August 1969), pp. 213–4; see too, 'Those Not Rehoused', *New Society* (21 May 1970), pp. 873–4; John Rex's paper, 'The Formation of Ghettoes in Britain's Cities', given to the Institute of Race Relations annual conference, September 1968; and the P.E.P. Report (1967).

offer them rehousing in the same neighbourhood on an estate. There is equally no need for planners to reproduce the large groupings that have grown up by accident or necessity in the inner city (p. 134).

The Cullingworth Committee continues, 'Dispersal is a laudable aim of policy, but this policy needs pursuing with full respect for the wishes of the people concerned. Dispersal of immigrant concentrations should be regarded as a desirable consequence, but not the overriding purpose, of housing individual immigrant families on council estates. The criterion of full, informed, individual choice comes first' (p. 136). I would strongly endorse this view.

How can immigrants be given access to council housing on equal terms with the native population? The ways in which this might be done form the second policy proposal: Immigrants of all kinds—white and coloured, and internal British migrants, should be treated alike in the consideration of the allocation of council housing; there should be no differential waiting period for consideration, as is operated in some English boroughs. The policy of local dispersal should be publicized, and immigrants encouraged to seek council housing.

The evidence reviewed suggests that the Netherlands has made exceptional efforts in providing a firm basis for the integration of immigrants of all kinds. As immigrants become accustomed to Dutch mores and lifestyles, an atmosphere of tolerance and acceptance will mean an increasing degree of assimilation. Dutch policy in this matter, which has been explicitly stated, is that the immigrant makes a better citizen if he has a strong self-identity, is proud of being a Surinamer, or a Spaniard, or a Turk. Such a person is much more likely to make a good worker and a good citizen than one who is alienated, depressed, and bewildered by poor housing, lack of knowledge of his host society, and the experience of discrimination in housing and employment.

If Britain enters the Common Market; if the provisions in the 1971 Immigration Act for treating Commonwealth immigrants like other immigrants are enforced; and if the recommendation of the Survey of Race Relations that, 'admission to this country is in future to be applied equally to aliens and Commonwealth citizens' (Rose [1969], p. 748), are accepted, then the Dutch policy of providing initial services for the orientation and integration of immigrants should be especially relevant to the British situation. If, for example, the kinds of services provided by De Poort in The Hague were emulated in a comparable urban area, these would require that all new immigrants unaccompanied by their families be offered free accommodation, at least for their first year in England. During this time they would be subjected to intensive orientation and language courses, and counselling. If they wished to bring their families to Britain, community relations social workers would seek housing for them (which should, in the absence of discrimination be a much simpler task than in the Netherlands, since Britain's housing problem is less acute). A social worker would visit the immigrant's family in their own country, and counsel them in their role of migrants and, if necessary, arrange for a loan for their fare.

At present the Community Relations Commission in Britain supports eighty local community relations councils with an annual budget of £395,000. This sum employs about sixty community relations officers.[6] The remainder of this sum goes on administrative costs of the head office in London, and on national publicity and education work. However, the costs of running an office for a community relations officer to work from are supposed to be met by the local authority. But there is no statutory obligation upon the local authority to meet these costs.

> As a result the officer, supported only by a paper organization, is left to make race relations work without even the resources necessary to run an office. The task in a borough like Brent with a population of a quarter of a million and a high concentration of coloured immigrants, or in Birmingham with a population of a million is clearly impossible.... Although the Commission is manifestly unable to deal with the situation, the government gives tacit approval of its incompetence by continuing to withhold finance, and by refusing to redirect its policy.[7]

It is clear that community relations in Britain require a great deal more finance, and support of all kinds from the central government. If the excellent Dutch policy is to be emulated with any success a massive increase in finance will be required.

I propose that there should be one community relations officer for every 1,000 immigrants (both white and coloured) of less than ten years' standing.[8] In addition, grants should be made towards

[6] See 'Is Money Enough?', *Race Today* (January 1970), pp. 25–6, and 'Lord Windlesham: Man at the Home Office Helm', *Race Today* (May 1971), pp. 167–8.

[7] 'Is Money Enough?', op. cit.

[8] The stated ideal in Dutch community relations is one community worker to 500 immigrant workers. The ratio is at present 1:800, and an expansion of these services is therefore planned (Ebbeling, 1971).

the capital costs of providing free residential accommodation for newly arrived immigrants. Additional social workers would be needed to staff these residential centres, on the basis of one social worker per fifty residents. These social workers would be specially trained, and have educative as well as social work functions.

I am proposing the expansion of community relations services which would cost up to £50,000,000 in annual expenditure, including interest payment on loans for capital costs. If this proposal seems extraordinary, or revolutionary, it should be borne in mind that I am merely urging that expenditure on community relations in Britain should be brought up to the Dutch level. One should not forget, either, that the Netherlands has a much more acute housing problem.

The 'situation testing' (see Chapter 9) in the Netherlands, carried out as parallel to the situation testing of the English P.E.P. Report, suggested that discrimination in employment is much less prevalent in the Netherlands than in Britain. The ending of such discrimination is of vital importance for race relations in Britain. If substantial numbers of highly qualified and articulate young people are denied jobs commensurate with their qualifications because they are coloured, we cannot expect them to accept such a fate passively. They will have every motivation, and every right, to engage in radical political activity of a revolutionary kind. There is the danger that community relations activities and the educational system will produce articulate individuals, well-versed in the formal values of British society, who nevertheless may be rejected by the white power structure. From such alienation grow the grass roots of revolt.[9]

I propose that the Race Relations Act of 1968 as it relates to discrimination in employment should be strengthened: the Race Relations Board should have the power to subpoena witnesses, and should publish proceedings of conciliation committees, including the names of all parties. The Board too should initiate its own research programme of situation testing, and testing of the kind undertaken by Jowell and Prescott-Clarke (1970) to test the adequacy of the law in this respect.

My proposals will apply equally to the Britons in East Africa who are at present denied entry to their mother country because of their colour. This is blatant racial discrimination and, as urged in my first proposal, must be ended. Because such immigration

[9] Cf. Bagley (1970a) for an elaboration of this point.

will involve large numbers of people coming to Britain relatively quickly, a number of special services and activities will be necessary. First of all, the moral and spiritual leaders of the country must declare publicly the morality and rightness of this policy, and the moral duty of citizens to support it in every possible way. It would be excellent if palaces, vicarages, manses, and presbyteries could be used for temporary accommodation for these immigrants. It is difficult at this stage to forecast how large a number would come to Britain; if numbers were as large as those from Indonesia we could expect, making allowances for population size, as many as 200,000 in the space of a few years.

I propose that a special Ministry of Integration should be established to direct and co-ordinate the reception of these immigrants. In the first stages of immigration special accommodation centres should be set up. Local authorities should monitor all available vacant housing, both private and public, and a quota of 5 per cent of all council housing falling vacant (both new and old) should be allocated for these immigrants. A similar quota of employment vacancies should be made. In carrying out this policy, special attention should be paid to the principal of local dispersal, so that the immigrants should not be isolated from friends and kin. For immigrants without funds, interest-free loans should be given for clothing and furniture, and low interest loans for house purchase. The estimated cost of these services will amount to £50,000,000 a year. This is less, in marginal terms, than the Dutch spent on services for immigrants from Indonesia. I would expect the programme of services for these British Asians to be financed annually for ten years.

All these policies, as the Dutch have acknowledged, cost money. Where is it to come from? An expenditure as great, in proportional terms, as that made by the Netherlands would be easier for Britain to make, since its marginal effect would be less than that of the Dutch expenditure. Since the need for providing integration services for immigrants arises very largely because of Britain's colonial enterprises (which have been a source of immense wealth) it is justifiable to class this expenditure under the general rubric of developmental aid.

The Pearson Commission recommended that the developed countries should spend 1 per cent of the gross national product on aid. The Labour Government, in its 1964 election manifesto promised to increase the share of Britain's G.N.P. devoted to this purpose. In 1964 official aid amounted to 0·53 per cent of G.N.P.; in 1970 the proportion stood at only 0·39 per cent.[10] The difference, in cash terms, between 0·39 per cent of G.N.P. and 1 per cent is a little over £200,000,000. Half of this sum would amply cover the cost of providing services for all kinds of immigrants, including British Asians. I suggest that any government could meet the cost of these services by meeting the fulfilments of the '1 per cent on aid' quota, which several European countries have met without difficulty.[11]

I suggest that the cost of the services recommended should be met by reserving between one-quarter and half of 1 per cent of the gross national income for this purpose. This would amount to an annual budget on community relations (including payment of interest on loans for capital expenditure) of approximately £100,000,000.

## THE FUTURE OF RACE RELATIONS IN BRITAIN

What's going to happen to race relations in Britain? I hope that some or all of the recommendations I have made will be accepted at the governmental level, though previous experience of trying to change social policy at this level leaves me somewhat pessimistic. I think that one can be fairly certain that unless something radical is done race relations in Britain will deteriorate. The principle reason for this is the alienation of immigrants—and especially of second generation black people in Britain. Conformity, as stressed in the previous chapter, is being rewarded not by justice (as in the Netherlands) but by rejection. This must inevitably lead to a struggle by black people for political and social power. The struggle may take some of the forms which the struggle by black people has taken in the United States.

[10] *Sunday Times* (24 May 1970). The projected amount of aid will reach 0·47 per cent of the gross national product by 1974 (*Guardian*, 25 May 1970). The present Conservative government is committed to increase aid to a level of 0·7 per cent of G.N.P. by 1975. In 1970–1 the allocation of overseas aid was in fact *underspent* by £60 millions! (*Guardian*, 23 May 1971). The total amount of official aid given by Britain in 1970–1 was £188·9 millions, or 0·37 per cent of G.N.P. (H.M.S.O., 1971).

[11] The £100,000,000 annual expenditure proposed is but a fraction of Britain's annual expenditure on armaments. It is, ironically, one-tenth of the £1,000 millions by which share prices increased when the Conservatives won the 1970 election; see '£1,000 m. joy day as shares leap', *Evening Standard* (London, 19 June 1970). The defence budget will account for £2,300,000,000 by 1974 (*Guardian*, 29 October 1970).

If justice is not forthcoming, I would endorse such a struggle, and urge that it should take, as the late Martin Luther King urged, non-violent forms. If violence does emerge, it will hardly be the fault of black people. Mr. Powell has predicted that in fifteen years black and white will be fighting.[12] I suggest that this prediction is on the part of some people not their fear, but their hope. If violence does emerge the major responsibility will be that of Mr. Powell and his followers. These followers, I have argued (Bagley, 1971b), are by and large racialist, and constitute a majority of the British population.

Paradoxically at a certain level, race relations are excellent. A great deal of interracial mixing is going on, between a small minority of the white population, and black immigrants. Nearly 20 per cent of fertile marriages involving a partner from the West Indies, Africa, India, or Pakistan involve a white partner (Bagley, 1971d). The children, and the grandchildren, of such marriages are in Mr. Powell's terminology immigrants, and are one reason why, according to Powell, the number of immigrants in Britain is increasing! The greatest amount of interracial mixing goes on in areas such as Notting Hill, London; Moss Side, Manchester; and Handsworth, Birmingham. These are areas occupied by people, both black and white, who have been excluded from the major strata of society. They form a special underclass, a 'housing class' in Rex's term (1971). They are the true proletariat. If there is hope, it lies here, in a group of people who have rejected the racist values of British society on the basis of either personal ideology (like the new left) or of group experience.

12 'White fighting black in 15 years—Powell', *Guardian* (3 May 1971).

## APPENDIX

# THE STRUCTURE AND CORRELATES OF PREJUDICE AND SOCIAL ATTITUDES IN THE NETHERLANDS SAMPLE

In addition to attitude data, I have also collected data on religious affiliation and behaviour for the Dutch sample. I hypothesized that prejudiced individuals would tend to be deviant from the major religious institutions of society: that although they might declare formal allegiance to a particular church, their involvement in the activity of that church would be low. In addition to this hypothesis I was interested in finding out whether prejudice showed any variation according to age, sex, and occupational groupings, and to what extent the items of prejudice measured would correlate with items in the Wilson-Patterson scale of conservative values.

I have investigated these aspects of prejudice by means of the methods of principal components analysis. In terms of the hypothesis concerning religious behaviour and values, one would expect a factor to emerge which identified individuals who are prejudiced, declare a religious affiliation but are infrequent church attenders, do not hold office in their church, and infrequently give to their church. The subjects to which this analysis was applied are the 279 individuals in the quota sample referred to in Chapter 7.

The variables included in this analysis are as follows:

1. Young Professional;
2. Professional (AB);
3. Clerical and Supervisory (C1);
4. Skilled Manual (C2);
5. Semi and unskilled manual (DE);
6. Age;

7. to 50. The following items from the Dutch version of the Wilson-Patterson C-scale: death penalty; evolution theory; strip-tease shows; sabbath observance; beatniks; patriotism; modern art; self-sacrifice; working wives; birth control; military drill; co-education; divine law; socialism; white superiority; cousin marriage; moral training; suicide;

abortion; overseas empire; student pranks; licensing laws; electronic music; chastity; royalty; women judges; mini-skirts; teenage drivers; apartheid; nudist camps; church authority; disarmament; censorship; white lies; mixed race marriage; strict rules; beat music; strait-jackets; casual living; divorce; inborn conscience; Surinamese immigration; Bible truth; pyjama parties;

51. The total score on the 50-item scale of conservative values;
52. Sex of subject;
53. Occupational class expressed as a linear variable;
54. Coloureds inferior;
55. Discriminatory regulations for entry of coloured;
56. Lack of sympathy for coloured people in difficult conditions;
57. Derogatory statements about coloured people;
58. Sack the coloured worker;
59. Refuse to let council house to coloured;
60. Promote the white worker;
61. Subject has church affiliation;
62. Subject R.C.;
63. Subject Dutch Reformed;
64. Subject Re-Reformed;
65. Subject Humanist;
66. Church attendance (twice a week through to almost never);
67. Contributing to church funds[1] (regular/sometimes/almost never);
68. Subject holds some office in a church organization;
69. Subject has a church affiliation, but attends less than once a month;
70. Prejudice score (total score on items 54–58 and 60; minimum score 0, maximum 6);
71. Subject rejects marriage of a child or brother or sister to a Surinamer on religious grounds (i.e. would not approve of such a relative marrying a coloured man if he was of a different religion but would accept such a marriage if Surinamer were of same religion);
72. Subject rejects marriage of child or brother or sister to a Surinamer on grounds other than religion (i.e. would have no objection of marriage of relative to man of different religion, but would object to marriage of relative to a coloured man).

[1] The wording of this item is taken from the questionnaire used by Gadourek (1961) in his study of Sassenheim.

THE ANALYSIS

I have, first of all, examined the product moment correlations between the six-item prejudice scale and a number of demographic items (Table A:1). This analysis shows that age and occupation are significantly related to prejudice, but sex is not. Roman Catholic church membership is significantly associated with prejudice, while Re-Reformed Church membership, being Humanist, attending church regularly, and giving to church regularly are all inversely related to prejudice. Being a church member but infrequently attending church has a marked and highly significant correlation (·43) with prejudice. This initial analysis suggests that older, working-class individuals, Roman Catholics, and those having a religious affiliation but not involved with the life of their church may be prejudiced. Table A:2 shows the degree to which Re-Reformed are conformist in their religious behaviour. Catholics, despite the sanction of mortal sin, frequently do not attend Mass on Holy Days of Obligation. The further analysis of the data has been by means of principal components analysis, which establishes the underlying structure of the data. One can examine, for example, whether Roman Catholic church membership, being older and working class, and not attending church regularly, are associated with the same sub-group of individuals, or refer to different groups of individuals. For this analysis I have used the principal components programme written by Hendrickson and White (1964).[2] The routine prescribed extracted the first twelve principal components (the eigenvectors of the matrix), and rotated them to a promax solution. The factors thus extracted were systematically reduced to three, then two factors. These 'higher order factors' indicate the major structuring of the data. The rationale underlying principal components analysis is to reduce a large body of inter-correlated variables to a smaller number of factors. The correlation of any individual item with any factor can then be demonstrated.

The first six of the twelve first-order rotated factors are presented in Tables A:3 to A:8. Factor loadings of below 0·30 have been left out of these tables since the predictive value of such loadings is low. We have, however, in every case given the loadings on the Conservatism score and on the Prejudice score, since it is of interest to see whether each factor has any appreciable loading on these two items.

The first factor (Table A:3) appears to be an 'Age versus Youth' factor. It represents the views of older people, who tend to be skilled workers or middle class, and Re-Reformed church members who are

[2] I am grateful to Owen White for statistical advice in using this programme. The analysis was carried out on the FA5 Programme of the I.B.M. 7090 computer of Imperial College, London.

*Table* A:1. *Correlations between Prejudice and Demographic Variables in a Dutch Survey of Attitudes to Surinamers*

| | *Age* | *Sex (Female)* | *Class (High to Low)* | *Roman Catholic* |
|---|---|---|---|---|
| Correlation of Six-item Prejudice scale | ·25 | ·09 | ·22 | ·21 |
| | *Dutch Reformed* | *Re-Reformed* | *Humanist* | *Frequency of Church Attendance* |
| Correlation of Prejudice scale | ·08 | —·13 | —·12 | —·15 |
| | *Regularly giving to Church Funds* | *Having a Function in Church* | *Church member but Infrequently Attends* | |
| Correlation of Prejudice scale | —·11 | —·05 | ·43 | |

278 d.f. Correlations of ·12 and beyond are significant at the 5 per cent level.

*Table* A:2. *Correlations between Religious Denominations and Religious Behaviour in a Dutch Sample*

| | *Rejecting Inter-Faith Marriage* | *Frequency of attending Church* | *Frequency of giving to Church Funds* | *Having a Church Function* | *Affiliated to a Church, but not a Regular Attender* |
|---|---|---|---|---|---|
| Roman Catholic | ·04 | ·15 | ·12 | —·03 | ·31 |
| Dutch Reformed | —·05 | ·07 | ·19 | ·01 | ·19 |
| Re-Reformed | ·22 | ·48 | ·32 | ·21 | —·12 |

278 d.f. Correlations of ·12 and beyond are significant at the 5 per cent level.

generally conservative, and especially reject a number of institutions associated with youthful freedom and indulgence. The young professionals, by contrast, are in favour of such institutions. The loading of the Prejudice score is near zero.

*Table* A:3. *Factor I: Age versus Youth*

| *Conservative Scale Items* | *Loading* |
|---|---|
| Electronic music | ·62 |
| Pyjama parties | ·61 |
| Teenage drivers | ·58 |
| Beat music | ·50 |
| Modern art | ·40 |
| Provos | ·38 |
| Mini-skirts | ·36 |
| Conservatism score | ·44 |
| *Prejudice Items* | |
| Prejudice score | —·04 |
| *Demographic Variables* | |
| Age | ·81 |
| Young professional | —·75 |
| Professional | ·43 |
| Skilled worker | ·38 |
| Class (high to low) | ·31 |
| Re-Reformed church member | ·30 |
| *Proportion of Variance* | 14·5% |

Factor II (Table A:4) I have termed 'Protestant-Conformist'. Both Dutch Reformed and Re-Reformed Church members have appreciable loadings on this factor; they attend church regularly, donate regularly to their church, and are conservative, especially on a number of religious items.

The third of the first-order factors (Table A:5) is clearly a 'Racialist' one. It has high loadings on C-scale items which define racialism, but it does not have a high loading on the conservatism scale as a whole. There is a very high loading (·98) on the Prejudice score, and on the six items making up this scale, as well as on refusal to let a council house to a Surinamer, and objection to interracial marriage on other than religious grounds. The high loadings on this factor indicate the internal reliability of the prejudice scale. These findings are in accord with those of Bagley (1970g) from a factor-analytical validation of this scale with a British population. Of particular interest is the loading of being affiliated to a church, but rarely attending it. This finding is in line with the hypothesis that prejudice might be the province of those unintegrated with the life of their church.

*Table* A:4. *Factor II: Protestant-Conformist*

| *Conservative Scale Items* | *Loading* |
|---|---|
| Divine law | —·74 |
| Bible truth | —·68 |
| Sabbath observance | —·63 |
| Chastity | —·56 |
| Church authority | —·55 |
| Self-denial | —·44 |
| Conservatism score | —·33 |
| *Prejudice Items* | |
| Prejudice score | —·01 |
| *Demographic Variables* | |
| Donating to church regularly | —·73 |
| Attending church regularly | —·70 |
| No church affiliation | —·59 |
| Clerical worker | —·37 |
| Re-Reformed church member | —·34 |
| Dutch Reformed church member | —·31 |
| Professional | —·39 |
| *Proportion of Variance* | 7·8% |

*Table* A:5. *Factor III: Racialist*

| *Conservative Scale Items* | *Loading* |
|---|---|
| Surinamese immigration | ·56 |
| Interracial marriage | ·47 |
| White superiority | ·39 |
| Apartheid | ·30 |
| Conservatism score | ·09 |
| *Prejudice Items* | |
| Prejudice score | ·98 |
| Sack coloured* | ·81 |
| Promote white* | ·72 |
| No sympathy for coloured* | ·70 |
| Coloureds inferior* | ·67 |
| Refuse to let to coloured | ·66 |

| | |
|---|---|
| Discriminatory regulations for Surinamese entry* | ·53 |
| Hostile statements about coloured* | ·51 |
| Reject interracial marriage on grounds other than religion | ·41 |
| *Demographic Variables* | |
| Church affiliation, but rarely attends church | ·31 |
| *Proportion of Variance* | 5·3% |

*Table A:6. Factor IV: Class Values*

| *Conservative Scale Items* | *Loading* |
|---|---|
| Co-education | —·60 |
| Evolution theory | —·46 |
| Moral training | ·42 |
| Self-denial | ·31 |
| Conservatism score | —·03 |
| *Prejudice Items* | |
| Coloureds inferior | —·53 |
| Prejudice score | ·08 |
| *Demographic Variables* | |
| Professional | ·84 |
| Skilled worker | —·58 |
| *Proportion of Variance* | 4·6% |

The fourth factor (Table A:6) I have termed 'Class Values', since its highest loadings are on two occupational groupings, professional (·84) and skilled worker (—·58). The professionals are liberal on co-education and evolution theory, and conservative on moral training and self-denial. This factor also loads strongly (—·53) on considering Surinamers to be inferior. Now, this does not mean that professionals tend to think that coloureds are inferior, but that there is a small but significant sub-group who consider Surinamers inferior. This point can be illustrated by the correlation of this item (0·0574) in the original correlation matrix with being professional. This correlation is, of course, negligible. What the technique of principal components analysis has

* Indicates items making up the P scale.

*Table A:7. Factor V : Female-Puritanical*

| *Conservative Scale Items* | *Loading* |
|---|---|
| Striptease shows | —·70 |
| Nudist camps | —·58 |
| Divorce | —·39 |
| Legalized abortion | —·38 |
| Women judges | —·38 |
| Pyjama parties | —·36 |
| Conservatism score | —·25 |
| *Prejudice Items* | |
| Prejudice score | ·03 |
| *Demographic Variables* | |
| Sex (female) | —·70 |
| *Proportion of Variance* | 3·1% |

*Table A:8. Factor VI : Imperialist*

| *Conservative Scale Items* | *Loading* |
|---|---|
| Overseas empire | —·74 |
| Patriotism | —·54 |
| Socialism | —·51 |
| Military drill | —·45 |
| Disarmament | —·42 |
| Royalty | —·42 |
| Censorship | —·40 |
| Apartheid | —·33 |
| Strict rules | —·31 |
| Death penalty | —·31 |
| Conservatism score | —·36 |
| *Prejudice Items* | |
| Prejudice score | ·01 |
| *Demographic variables* | |
| Nil significant | |
| *Proportion of variance* | |

done is to extract from the total matrix a sub-group of correlations which together form a significant factor. This finding means that when professional workers are racialist (which, as shown in Chapter 8, is only rarely) they express this in terms of considering Surinamers inferior to them. On the other items measuring prejudice they are, however, neutral or liberal.

Factor V (Table A:7) has high loadings on sexual items, and on female sex, and I have termed it 'Female-Puritanical'. It has, rather surprisingly, no loading on any religious affiliation. Factor VI (Table A:8) I have termed 'Imperialist', since its proponents favour overseas empire, patriotism, military drill, censorship, strict rules, and the death

*Table* A:9. *Second-Order Factor A: Racialist-Church Defaulters*

| *Conservative Scale Items* | *Loading* |
|---|---|
| Death penalty | ·51 |
| Interracial marriage | ·50 |
| Mini-skirts | ·47 |
| Surinamese immigration | ·44 |
| Disarmament | ·44 |
| Beat music | ·43 |
| Electronic music | ·42 |
| Provos | ·36 |
| Modern art | ·35 |
| Apartheid | ·35 |
| Military drill | ·34 |
| Royalty | ·30 |
| Conservatism score | ·35 |
| *Prejudice Items* | |
| Reject interracial marriage, not on religious grounds | ·60 |
| Hostile statements about coloured | ·53 |
| Discriminatory regulations for Surinamese entry | ·50 |
| Coloureds inferior | ·48 |
| No sympathy for coloured | ·40 |
| Prejudice score | ·53 |
| *Demographic Variables* | |
| Church affiliation, but rarely attends church | ·58 |
| Dutch Reformed church member | ·45 |
| Age | ·39 |
| Professional | ·36 |

penalty, and are opposed to socialism and disarmament. No demographic or prejudice scale items load significantly on this factor.

The rotation of the original factors to produce 'higher order factors'[3] reduces the original twelve components extracted to three, and then to

*Table* A:10. *Second-Order Factor B: Working-Class Conservatives*

| *Conservative Scale Items* | *Loading* |
|---|---|
| Legalized abortion | —·64 |
| Military drill | —·56 |
| Censorship | —·45 |
| Women judges | —·44 |
| Evolution theory | —·42 |
| Working wives | —·41 |
| Socialism | —·40 |
| Teenage drivers | —·39 |
| Empire building | —·37 |
| Inborn conscience | —·37 |
| White superiority | —·35 |
| Church authority | —·34 |
| Divorce | —·33 |
| Strict rules | —·32 |
| Patriotism | —·31 |
| Suicide | —·30 |
| Conservatism score | —·47 |
| *Prejudice Items* | |
| Promote white | —·55 |
| Refuse to let to coloured | —·47 |
| Sack coloured | —·33 |
| Prejudice score | —·22 |
| *Demographic Variables* | |
| Class (high to low) | —·79 |
| Unskilled worker | —·63 |
| Young professional | ·53 |
| Roman Catholic church member | —·46 |
| Re-Reformed church member | ·44 |
| Function in church | ·38 |
| Professional | ·32 |

[3] See Hendrickson and White (1964) for a statistical description of this process. See too Hope (1968), a general exposition of this method.

two. The first of the second-order factors (Table A:9) has been labelled 'Racialist–Church Defaulters' since individuals with high scores on this factor have high loadings on the prejudice scale, and on some of the items contributing to this scale. However, there are no appreciable loadings on the items referring to the promotion and sacking of the coloured worker, or on letting him a council house. Individuals with high scores on this component tend to be professionals, Dutch Reformed church members, and infrequent church attenders.

Factor B (Table A:10), the second of the second-order factors defines working-class conservatism and racialism, and especially the values of unskilled workers. The racialism of these workers takes a different form from that of the professionals in the previous factor—the three significant items are refusal to promote the coloured man; advocating that the coloured man should be sacked in a lay-off; and advocating that the coloured man shouldn't be given a council house.

*Table* A:11. *Second-Order Factor C: Calvinist Values*

| *Conservative Scale Items* | *Loading* |
|---|---|
| Chastity | ·56 |
| Striptease | ·48 |
| Casual living | ·46 |
| Nudist camps | ·45 |
| Church authority | ·42 |
| White lies | ·41 |
| Bible truth | ·35 |
| Sabbath observance | ·34 |
| Divorce | ·32 |
| Pyjama parties | ·31 |
| Birth control | ·30 |
| Conservatism score | ·45 |
| *Prejudice Items* | |
| Rejecting interracial marriage, on religious grounds | ·44 |
| Prejudice score | —·02 |
| *Demographic Variables* | |
| Attending church regularly | ·74 |
| Donating to church regularly | ·68 |
| Re-Reformed church member | ·49 |
| No church affiliation | —·45 |
| Function in church | ·40 |

This interesting finding suggests that middle-class racialists tend to be derogatory and condescending about Surinamese immigrants, while working-class individuals are hostile in areas of employment and housing, areas in which they may feel threatened by the immigration of Surinamers.

Table A:11 shows the loadings on the third of these second-order factors. I have termed this 'Calvinist Values' since it refers to Re-Reformed church members who attend church regularly, give to their church funds regularly, and who take some part in organized church life. Such individuals are conservative on inter-faith (and therefore on interracial marriage), but they are not racialist. Their conservatism on sexual and religious items is very much in accord with the picture of Calvinists which has emerged in previous studies. The loading on 'Apartheid' is low and negative (—·02) suggesting that these individuals are not in sympathy with the apartheid ideology of the extreme Calvinists of South Africa. Again, this finding is in line with the discussion in Chapter 6.

The major structure of the data is represented by the two final, third-order factors (Tables A:12 and A:13). The first of these, 'Working-Class Racialism' has high class loadings, and also loads highly on Roman Catholic church membership, and attending church infrequently. It also has an age loading suggesting that this finding applies to older individuals. This finding about age is important, since it indicates that these deviant Catholics are *not* individuals who are in the vanguard of liturgical reform in the Catholic Church (van der Plas and Suer, 1968), since these reformers are young men and women. These working-class, middle-aged Catholics have rejected their church's teaching on regular attendance at Mass, and the Catholic ideology on abortion. They seem, too, to have rejected Catholic teaching on tolerance in race relations. Since they have rejected the *medium* of this teaching—the teaching of the priest, and the enunciation of formal instructions to the faithful from bishops which are read by the priest from the pulpit—it is not surprising (both from a theological and a sociological point of view) that these individuals have lapsed into base and worldly values.

The second of these third-order factors has been entitled 'Religious Conformity'. Individuals so identified are conservative on a number of religious, moralistic, and sexual items, and they reject inter-faith marriage (and therefore marriage to a Surinamer of a different religion, but will accept marriage to a Surinamer of the same religion). These individuals tend to be older, Re-Reformed church members who attend church regularly, and contribute to church funds regularly. They are unlikely to be skilled workers. The loading of the prejudice score on this factor is near to zero.

*Table* A:12. *Third-Order Factor 1: Working-Class Racialism*

| *Conservative Scale Items* | *Loading* |
|---|---|
| Censorship | ·51 |
| Evolution theory | ·51 |
| Apartheid | ·51 |
| Provos | ·50 |
| Surinamese immigration | ·49 |
| Co-education | ·48 |
| Modern art | ·45 |
| Socialism | ·45 |
| White superiority | ·44 |
| Casual living | —·43 |
| Empire building | ·39 |
| Inborn conscience | —·36 |
| Suicide | ·33 |
| Legalized abortion | ·30 |
| Interracial marriage | ·31 |
| Patriotism | ·31 |
| Conservatism score | ·51 |
| *Prejudice Items* | |
| Reject interracial marriage on grounds other than religion | ·54 |
| Refuse to let to coloured | ·48 |
| Hostile remarks about coloured | ·42 |
| Promote white | ·38 |
| Discriminatory regulations for Surinamese entry | ·38 |
| Sack coloured | ·37 |
| Coloureds inferior | ·34 |
| No sympathy for coloured | ·34 |
| Prejudice score | ·58 |
| *Demographic Variables* | |
| Class | ·72 |
| Skilled worker | ·57 |
| Church affiliation, but rarely attends church | ·56 |
| Young professional | —·53 |
| Roman Catholic church membership | ·46 |
| Unskilled worker | ·39 |
| Attending church regularly | —·37 |
| Re-Reformed church member | —·34 |
| Donating to church regularly | —·32 |
| Age | ·30 |

Table A:13. *Third-Order Factor 2 : Religious Conformity*

| *Conservative Scale Items* | *Loading* |
|---|---|
| Casual living | —·47 |
| Chastity | —·46 |
| Divine law | —·44 |
| Self-denial | —·43 |
| Nudist camps | —·42 |
| Beat music | —·42 |
| Bible truth | —·38 |
| Striptease shows | —·36 |
| Sabbath observance | —·36 |
| Church authority | —·36 |
| Mini-skirts | —·35 |
| Working wives | —·33 |
| Royalty | —·33 |
| Disarmament | —·33 |
| Legalized abortion | -·31 |
| Birth control | —·30 |
| Divorce | —·30 |
| Conservatism score | —·59 |
| *Prejudice Items* | |
| Reject interracial marriage on grounds of religion | —·50 |
| Prejudice score | —·03 |
| *Demographic Variables* | |
| Skilled worker | ·56 |
| Donating to church regularly | —·50 |
| Age | —·42 |
| Attending church regularly | —·38 |
| Re-Reformed church member | —·33 |

### *A Principal Components Analysis of the Schildersbuurt Data*

A further principal components analysis has been carried out on the data eliciting attitudes to Moroccans in the Schildersbuurt sample of fifty working-class individuals.[4] For technical reasons the number of variables was reduced in order that there were less variables than subjects; because of the small numbers involved only the two final

[4] This kind of analysis has not been carried out on the data on attitudes to Italians, since no C-scale or religious data were collected for this sample.

components are presented. These components are extracted from the rotation of the twelve first-order factors accounting for 73 per cent of the variance. Because of the need to reduce the number of variables, only fourteen of the C-scale items have been used. These are variables concerned with religious and racial items, which are of particular interest in the context of the present analysis. The correlations of prejudice with religious and demographic variables are given in Table A:14. The magnitude of these correlations is very similar to the comparable correlations in Table A:1, except that Roman Catholics appear to be less 'racialist', and Dutch Reformed more so.

*Table* A:14. *Correlations between Prejudice and Demographic Variables in a Dutch Survey of Attitudes to Moroccans*

| | *Age* | *Sex (female)* | *Unskilled Worker* | *Roman Catholic* |
|---|---|---|---|---|
| Correlation of Six-item Prejudice scale | ·21 | ·15 | ·06 | ·02 |

| | *Dutch Reformed* | *Re-Reformed* | *Church Attendance* |
|---|---|---|---|
| Correlation of Prejudice scale | —·14 | —·17 | —·16 |

| | *Regularity of giving to Church* | *Church Member but attends Infrequently* |
|---|---|---|
| Correlation of Prejudice scale | —·18 | ·31 |

49 d.f. Correlations of ·26 and beyond are significant at the 5 per cent level.

*Note*: None of these respondents declared themselves to be 'Humanist'. The numbers having a church function were too small to be included in the analysis.

The first of these higher-order factors ('Protestant–Conservative') shown in Table A:15 represents the religious conformity of older Re-Reformed and Dutch Reformed church members. They are conservative on interracial marriage on religious grounds, but would accept marriage with a Moroccan of the same religion. In particular, they are likely to be liberal on the issue of letting a house to a Moroccan. Nevertheless, the six-item P-scale does have a loading of —·19 on this factor, suggesting an undercurrent of hostility to Moroccans. This is compatible with events such as the 'Schildersbuurt incident' described in Chapter 6.

The second of the higher-order factors has been termed 'Racialist' (Table A:16) since it has high loadings on a number of items in this field. Individuals who hold such values tend to be unskilled workers who are Roman Catholics but who rarely attend church, and who also reject the idea of moral training. The loadings on these higher-order factors is very much in line with the principal components analysis of the data on attitudes to Surinamers, which represented a more heterogenous occupational population. The factor structure is dominated by, on the one hand, Protestant or Calvinist conformity, and on the other by a racialist sub-group who also tend to be Catholics unintegrated with the life of their Church. One notable difference between loadings on these higher-order factors and the results from the survey of attitudes towards Surinamers is the loading of —·19 on the prejudice score compared with the loading of —·03 in the earlier sample. This finding almost undoubtedly reflects the higher general prevalence of hostility towards Moroccans in the population surveyed.

*Table* A:15. *Attitudes to Moroccan Immigrants: Higher-Order Factor A, Protestant–Conservative*

| *Conservative Scale Items* | *Loading* |
|---|---|
| Sabbath observance | —·44 |
| Divine law | —·54 |
| Church authority | —·58 |
| Bible truth | —·56 |
| Conservatism score (50-item scale) | —·62 |
| *Prejudice Items* | |
| Reject interracial marriage on religious grounds | —·59 |
| Let to Moroccan | ·32 |
| Prejudice score | —·19 |
| *Demographic Items* | |
| Dutch Reformed church member | —·44 |
| Re-Reformed church member | —·35 |
| Attending church regularly | —·36 |
| Giving to church regularly | —·35 |
| Church affiliation, but not a regular attender | ·47 |
| Age | —·51 |

*Table* A:16. *Attitudes to Moroccans: Higher-Order Factor B, Racialist*

| *Conservative Scale Items* | *Loading* |
|---|---|
| Moral training | ·41 |
| Overseas empire | —·37 |
| Censorship | —·42 |
| Mixed race marriage | —·54 |
| Moroccan immigration | —·37 |
| Conservatism score | —·32 |
| *Prejudice Items* | |
| No sympathy for Moroccans | —·67 |
| Sack the Moroccan | —·47 |
| Promote Dutch worker | —·50 |
| Refuse to let to Moroccan | —·44 |
| Moroccans inferior | —·37 |
| Discriminatory regulations for Moroccan entry | —·31 |
| Opposed to marriage with Moroccan on grounds other than religion | —·30 |
| Prejudice score | —·59 |
| *Demographic Items* | |
| Regular church attender | ·63 |
| Gives regularly to church | ·61 |
| Unskilled worker | —·36 |
| Roman Catholic church member | —·33 |
| Church affiliation, but rarely attends church | —·31 |

## CONCLUSIONS

The investigation of the underlying structure of the data on attitudes to Surinamers in a sample of 279 residents of The Hague and Amsterdam has identified a number of interesting sub-groups of individuals. The components so identified have represented the values of older people, working-class people, women, and Protestants. A significant racialist sub-group has emerged. There is strong evidence for concluding that racialism is the province of a small group of deviants, who are deviant not only from dominant values in the Netherlands (tolerance towards coloured immigrants who conform to Dutch mores), but who are deviant also from the value system and social control networks of the religious denominations to which they nominally belong. This deviance takes two forms. The 'ideal types' are: (*a*) middle-class and middle-aged individuals who have a nominal affiliation to the Dutch Reformed church, but who are unintegrated with the life of their church. Their racialism takes the form of feelings of superiority and contempt for Surinamers; (*b*) working-class Catholics, middle-aged and unintegrated with the life of their church. Their racialism takes the form of hostility to Surinamers in the employment and housing spheres. A third 'ideal type' has emerged representing conformity rather than deviance; Re-Reformed church members, conservative on many issues, highly involved with the life of their church, and liberal in the sphere of race relations.

The same kind of higher-order factor structure has emerged in the analysis of data on attitudes to Moroccans. However, although Catholics in this sample tend to be 'church defaulters' and also to be particularly hostile to Moroccans, prejudice does have some loading on the component identifying religious conformity in Protestants. This reflects the over all higher level of hostility to the recently-arrived Moroccans, in comparison to the generally tolerant regard for Surinamers. In a statistical sense hostility to Moroccans cannot be said to be deviant, although *extreme* hostility appears to be the province of deviants from religious institutions. Such individuals would almost certainly be hostile to Surinamers as well as to Moroccans. The over all expression of hostility to Moroccans in the working-class residents of the Schildersbuurt is, I would argue, part of the social control process which seeks to socialize Moroccans into Dutch modes and standards of public and inter-personal behaviour. The more tolerant attitudes to Italians and to Surinamers almost certainly reflects the fact that these individuals have to a much greater extent learned the rules of such behaviour.

# Bibliography


Abel-Smith, B. and Bagley, C. (1970). 'The problem of establishing equivalent standards of living for families of different composition'. In *Concepts of poverty* (ed. P. Townsend). London, Heinemann.

Adorno, T. and others (1950). *The authoritarian personality*. New York, Harper.

Allport, G. (1958). *The nature of prejudice*. New York, Doubleday Anchor Books.

—— (1966). 'The religious context of prejudice'. *Journal for the Scientific Study of Religion*, vol. 5, pp. 447–57.

Antilles Information Service (1961). *Netherlands Antilles: their geography, history and political, economic and social development*. Curaçao, Government Information Service.

Amersfoort, J. M. M. van (1968). *Surinamers in de Lage Landen: de ontwikkeling en problematiek van de Surinaamse imigratie naar Nederland*. The Hague, State Publishing Office.

—— (1971). *De sociale positie van de Molukkers in Nederland*. The Hague, State Publishing Office.

—— (1972). Personal communication.

Bacchus, M. (1969). 'Education, social change, and cultural pluralism'. *Sociology of Education*, vol. 42, pp. 368–85.

Bagley, C. (1967). 'Anomie, alienation and the evaluation of social structures'. *Kansas Journal of Sociology*, vol. 3, pp. 110–23.

—— (1968a). 'Racial barriers I: Holland Unites'. *New Society*, 2 March, pp. 339–40.

—— (1968b). 'Migration, race and mental health: a review of some recent research'. *Race*, vol. 9, pp. 343–56.

—— (1969a). 'Coloured Neighbours'. *New Society*, 7 August, pp. 213–14.

—— (1969b). 'Alienation and human fulfilment: a case study of South Africa'. *Journal of Human Relations*, vol. 17, pp. 12–25.

—— (1969c). 'Incest behaviour and incest taboo'. *Social Problems*, vol. 4, pp. 505–19.

—— (1969d). 'A survey of problems reported by Indian and Pakistani immigrants in Britain'. *Race*, vol. 11, pp. 65–76.

—— (1969e). 'The social aetiology of schizophrenia in immigrant groups'. *Race Today*, vol. 1, pp. 170–4.

—— (1970a). 'Race relations and theories of status consistency'. *Race*, vol. 11, pp. 267–88.

—— (1970b). *Social structure and prejudice in five English boroughs.* London, Institute of Race Relations.

—— (1970c). 'Racial and religious values in South African Catholics'. Unpublished.

—— (1970d). 'A comparative study of mental illness among immigrant groups'. In *Proceedings of the Anglo-French conference, University of Sussex, 1968* (ed. F. Henriques). The Hague, Mouton.

—— (1970e). 'Racial prejudice and the "conservative" personality: a British sample'. *Political Studies*, vol. 18, pp. 134–41.

—— (1970f). 'On the construction and reliability of a prejudice scale'. *Race*, vol. 12, pp. 371–4.

—— (1970g). 'Those not rehoused'. *New Society*, 21 May, pp. 873–4.

—— (1970h). *The cost of a child: problems in the measurement and relief of poverty.* London, Institute of Psychiatry.

——(1971a). *The social psychology of the child with epilepsy.* London, Routledge.

—— (1971b). *Race relations and the British press: an empirical study.* Mimeo.

—— (1971c). 'Relation of religion and racial prejudice in Europe'. *Scientific Study of Religion*, vol. 9, pp. 219–25.

—— (1972). 'Patterns of intermarriage amongst ethnic groups in England'. *Phylon*, in press.

Banton, M. (1955). *The coloured quarter.* London, Cape.

Baschwitz, K., et al. (1956). *Het gerepatrieerdenvraagstuk in de Nederlandse pers.* Amsterdam, Instituut voor Perswetenschap aan de Universiteit van Amsterdam.

Beijer, G. and Oudegeest, J. J. (1952). *Some aspects of migration problems in the Netherlands.* The Hague, Martinus Nijhoff.

Beijer, G. (1961). *Characteristics of overseas emigrants.* The Hague, Government Publishing Office.

Berghe, P. van den (1967). *Race and racism.* New York, Wiley.

Berkel, H. W. H. van (1964). *Surinamers in Amsterdam.* Amsterdam, Sociale Akademie, Dissertation.

Beyer, A. E. (1965). *Surinaamse arbeiders in Nederland.* Assen, Van Gorcum.

—— (1966). 'Surinamese labourers in the Netherlands'. London. Paper given to R.A.I./I.R.R. conference.

Boer-Laschuyt, T. de (1959). 'Eurasian repatriants in Holland'. *R.E.M.P. Bulletin*, vol. 8, pp. 23–45.

Böhning, W. R. (1972). *The United Kingdom, the European Community and the migration of workers.* London, Oxford University Press for the Institute of Race Relations.

Bovenkerk, F. (1971). 'Ook Turken willen fatsoenlijk woenen'. *Haagse Post*, 7 July, p. 6.

Bovenkerk, F. and Galen, J. van (1971). 'Nederland hoe langer hoe kleuriger'. *Haagse Post Deze Week*, 7–13 April, pp. 44–50.

Bruyn, W. (1965). *Het recht op apartheid: inleiding tot de Nederlandse problematiek.* Arnhem, Derkesen.

Buikhuizen, W. (1971). 'Criminaliteit onder Ambonezen'. *Nederlands Tijdschrift voor Criminologie*, June.

Burney, E. (1967). *Housing on trial.* London, Oxford University Press for the Institute of Race Relations.

Buve, R. (1963). 'Surinaamse slaven en vrije negers in Amsterdam gedurende de achtiende eeuw'. *Bijdragen tot de taal—land—en Volkenkunde*, vol. 119, p. 1.

Caldwell, M. (1968). *The modern world: Indonesia.* London, Oxford University Press.

Camara, H. (1968). *Church and colonialism.* London, Sheed and Ward.

Chaudhury, I. (1950). *The Indonesian struggle.* Lahore, Ferozons.

Colman, A. and Lambley, P. (1970). 'Authoritarianism and race attitudes in South Africa'. *Journal of Social Psychology*, vol. 82, pp. 161–4.

Coolhaas, W. Ph. (1960). *A Critical survey of studies on Dutch colonial history.* The Hague, Nijhoff.

Cressey, P. F. (1935). 'The Anglo-Indians: A disorganized marginal group'. *Social Forces*, vol. 14, pp. 263–8.

Crowley, D. (1956). 'Plural and differential acculturation in Trinidad'. *American Anthropologist*, pp. 817–24.

Cullingworth, J. B. (1969). *Council housing purposes, procedures and priorities.* London, H.M.S.O.

Dahm, B. (1971). *History of Indonesia in the 20th century.* London, Pall Mall.

Daniel, W. (1968). *Racial discrimination in England.* London, Penguin Books.

Deakin, N. (1968). 'The Dutch experiment revisited'. *Institute of Race Relations Newsletter*, March, pp. 121–3.

Defleur, M., and Westie, F. (1958). 'Verbal attitudes and overt acts'. *American Sociological Review*, vol. 23, pp. 667–73.

Despres, L. (1967). *Cultural pluralism and nationalist politics in British Guiana.* Chicago, Rand McNally.

Deugd, H. de (1970). *Chinese immigration in Nederland.* Amsterdam, the author.

Dincer, N. (1962). 'Emigration and immigration in Holland: policy and organization'. The Hague, Institute of Social Studies, dissertation.

Donnison, D. (1967). *The government of housing.* London, Pelican Books.

DRAKE, ST. CLAIR (1957). 'Some observations on interethnic conflict as one type of intergroup conflict'. *Journal of Conflict Resolution*, vol. 1, p. 64.

DURKHEIM, E. (1951). *Suicide*. London, Routledge.

EBBELING, G. (1971). 'Minorities in Holland'. *Race Today*, vol. 3, p. 381.

ELLEMERS, J. E. (1964). 'The determinants of emigration: an analysis of Dutch studies on migration'. *Sociologia Neerlandica*, pp. 41–58.

EMMERIK-LEVELT, H. van and TEULINGS, A. (1970). *De buitenlandse arbeiders in de Nederlandse pers*. University of Leiden.

ELIAS, N. and SCOTSON, J. L. (1965). *The established and the outsiders*. London, Cass.

ERNST, M. (1967). *The comparative international almanac*. New York, Macmillan.

EX, J. (1966). *Adjustment after migration*. The Hague, Nijhoff.

EISENSTADT, S. N. (1952). 'The process of absorption of new immigrants in Israel'. *Human Relations*, vol. 5.

FALLERS, L. A. (1958). *Immigrants and associations*. The Hague, Mouton.

FENDRICK, M. (1957). 'Perceived reference group support: racial attitudes and overt behaviour'. *American Sociological Review*, vol. 32, pp. 960–70.

FISCHER, L. (1959). *The story of Indonesia*. New York, Harker.

FURNIVALL, J. S. (1944). *Netherlands India: a study of plural economy*. London, Cambridge University Press.

—— (1948). *Colonial policy and practice: a comparative study of Burma and Netherlands India*. London, Cambridge University Press.

GADOUREK, I. (1961). *A Dutch community*. Groningen, Wolters.

—— (1969). 'Political radicalism and social change: a macro-sociological analysis of some recent trends as reflected in a sample of 100 communities in the Netherlands'. *Sociolgia Neerlandica*, vol. 5, pp. 38–56.

GADOUREK, I. and others (1961). 'Involvement in cultural system in the Netherlands; its measurement and social correlates'. *Social Forces*, vol. 40, pp. 302–8.

GASTMANN, A. (1968). *The politics of Surinam and the Netherlands Antilles*. Puerto Rico, Institute of Caribbean Studies.

GEERTZ, C. (1963). *Peddlers and princes: social and economic modernisation in two Indonesian towns*. Chicago, University of Chicago Press.

GESCHWENDER, J. (1968). 'Status inconsistency, social isolation and social unrest'. *Social Forces*, vol. 46, pp. 477–83.

GEYER, R. F. (1967). *Buitenlandse arbeidskachten beknopte uitgave. Resultaten van een arderzoek onder Spaanse en Nederlandse werknemer in het Rijnmondgebied*. Rotterdam, Stichting tot Onderzoek van de Arbeidssitatie in het Rijnmondgebied.

GIBBS, J. and MARTIN, W. (1964). *Status integration and suicide.* Oregon, University of Oregon Press.

GOUDSBLOM, Johan (1967). *Dutch society.* New York, Random House.

GWYNN, S. (1966). 'How immigrants go Dutch'. *Institute of Race Relations Newsletter*, January, pp. 19–24.

HALL, P. (1969). 'The new English bible?' *New Society*, 29 February, pp. 288–9.

HANSEN, H. (1971). 'Integratie Ambonezen moet in eigen kring beginnen'. *De Volkskrant*, 3 August, p. 6.

HARTOG, J. de (1969). *The children.* London, Atheneum Press.

HAUG, M. R. (1967). 'Social and cultural pluralism as a concept in social system analysis'. *American Journal of Sociology*, vol. 13, pp. 294–304.

HAYTER, T. (1971). *Aid as imperialism.* London, Penguin Books.

HEEK, F. van (1936). *Chineesche Immigranten in Nederland.* Amsterdam, publisher unknown.

—— (1954). *Het geboorte-nivean der Nederlandse Rooms-Katholieken.* Leiden, Stenfert Kroese.

HEEREN, H. J. (1967). *Transmigratie in Indonesie.* Meppel, Boom.

HENDRICKSON, A. and WHITE, P. (1964). 'Promax: a quick method for rotation to oblique simple structure'. *British Journal of Statistical Psychology*, vol. 17, pp. 65–70.

H.M.S.O. (1971). *British aid statistics: statistics of economic aid to developing countries 1966–1970.* London, H.M.S.O.

HETHERINGTON, T. (1971). 'The Race Relations Board—where now?' *Race Today*, vol. 3, pp. 382–4.

HILL, C. (1967). *How colour prejudiced is Britain?* London, Panther Books.

HOLLAND, Sir M. (1965). *Housing in Greater London.* London, H.M.S.O. Cmnd. 2605.

HOLLANDER, A. den (1967). 'Social description: the problem of reliability and validity'. In Jongmans and Gutkind (eds.) *Anthropologists in the field.* Assen, van Gorcum.

HOEFNAGELS, H. (1961). 'Nederland een sociaal paradijs?' *Sociologische Gids*, vol. 8.

HOETINK, H. (1967). *The two variants in Caribbean race relations.* London, Oxford University Press for the Institute of Race Relations.

HOFSTEDE, B. P. (1964). *Thwarted exodus: post-war overseas migration from the Netherlands.* The Hague, Martinus Nijhoff.

HOFSTEE, E. W. (1952). *Some remarks on selective migration.* The Hague, Martinus Nijhoff.

HOGEBRINK, L. (1970). 'Opposition to government policy on migrant workers in the Netherlands'. *Migration Today*, No. 15, pp. 16–23.

HOOGERWERF, A. (1965). 'Latent socio-political issues in the Netherlands'. *Sociologica Neerlandica*, vol. 2, pp. 161–79.

HOOGVELT, A. (1969). 'Ethnocentrism, authoritarianism, and Powellism'. *Race*, vol. 11, pp. 1–12.

HOPE, K. (1968). *Methods of multivariate analysis*. London, University of London Press.

HUGGETT, F. (1971). *The modern Netherlands*. London, Pall Mall Press.

HUGHES, J. (1968). *The end of Sukarno*. London, Angus and Robertson.

HURWITZ, J. (1955). 'Marginal men of India: an inquiry into the history of the Anglo-Indian'. *Indonesia*, vol. 8, pp. 129–47.

HUXLEY, A. (1939). *After many a summer*. London, Chatto and Windus.

INDONESIA (1969). 'Indonesia's political prisoners'. *Indonesia*. January–February.

ISHWARAN, K. (1959). *Family life in the Netherlands*. The Hague, Van Keulen.

JAHODA, M., DEUTSCH, M. and COOK, S. (1951). *Research methods in social relations: with special reference to prejudice*. New York, Dryden.

JOWELL, R. and PRESCOTT-CLARKE, P. (1970). 'Racial discrimination and white-collar workers in Britain'. *Race*, vol. 11, pp. 397–418.

KADT, E. J. de (1965). 'Conflict and power in society'. *International Social Science Journal*, vol. 17, pp. 454–71.

KAHIN, G. Mc. (1952). *Nationalism and Revolution in Indonesia*. New York, University of Cornell Press.

KENNEDY, R. (1942). *The ageless Indies*. New York, John Day.

KEUR, John Y. and KEUR, Dorothy L. (1955). *The deeply rooted: a study of a Drents community in the Netherlands*. Assen, Van Gorcum.

KHLEIF, B. (1958). 'Research on Dutch policy towards the Amboinese in Holland'. Institute of Social Studies, The Hague, Dissertation.

KLASS, M. (1961). *East Indians in Trinidad: a study of cultural persistence*. New York, Columbia University Press.

KRAAK, J. H. et al. (1957). *De repatriering uit Indonesie een onderzoek naar de integratie van de gerepatrieerden uit Indonesie in de Nederlandse samenleving*. The Hague, Government Publishing House.

KRAUSZ, E. (1969). 'The Edgware survey: occupation and social class'. *Jewish Journal of Sociology*, vol. 11, pp. 75–95.

KROEF, J. M. van der (1954). *Indonesia in the modern world*. Bandung, Masa Baru.

KROEF, J. (1953). 'The Eurasians in Indonesia'. *American Sociological Review*, vol. 18, pp. 484–93.

KRUIJT, C. (1960). *Zelfmoord. Statistich—sociologische verkenningen*. Assen, Van Gorcum.

KRUIJT, J. P. (1959). *Verzuiling*. Zaandijk, Heijuis.

LA PIERE, R. (1934). 'Attitudes vs actions'. *Social Forces*, vol. 13, pp. 230–7.

LENIN, V. (1934). *Lenin on Britain*. London, Lawrence and Wishart.

LIDDLE, R. W. (1970). *Ethnicity, party, and national integration—an Indonesian case study*. New Haven, Yale University Press.

LIER, R. A. J. van (1949). *Samenleving in een grensgebied*. The Hague, Nijhoff.

—— (1955). 'Social and political conditions in Surinam and the Netherlands Antilles: introduction'. In *Developments toward self-government in the Caribbean*. The Hague, van Hoeve.

—— (1950). *The development and nature of society in the West Indies*. Amsterdam, Royal Institute of the Indies.

LIJPHART, A. (1966). *The trauma of decolonization: the Dutch and West New Guinea*. New Haven, Yale University Press.

—— (1968). *The politics of accommodation: pluralism and democracy in the Netherlands*. Berkeley and Los Angeles, University of California Press.

LOHMAN, J. and REITZES, D. (1954). 'Deliberately organized groups and racial behaviour'. *American Sociological Review*, vol. 32, pp. 298–301.

LONGEMANN, J. H. A. (1955). 'The constitutional status of the Netherlands Caribbean territories', in *Developments towards self-government in the Caribbean*, pp. 46–7. The Hague, van Hoeve.

MACKENZIE, R. (1968). *Angels in marble*. London, Heinemann.

MAGUBANE, B. (1969). 'Pluralism and conflict situations in Africa—a new look'. *African Social Research*, vol. 1.

MALEFIJT, A. (1968). *The Javanese in Surinam*. Assen, van Gorcum.

MALZBERG, B. (1967). 'Internal migration and mental disease among the white population of New York State, 1960–1961'. *International Journal of Social Psychiatry*, vol. 13, pp. 184–91.

MARIEN, M. (1971). 'Het Zuidmolukse radicalisme in Nederland: nationalistische of emancipatiebeweging?' *Sociologische Gids*, vol. 18, pp. 62–76.

MCGREAL, J. and CORRIGAN, P. (1970). 'Ideology in *Colour and Citizenship*'. London, Graduate Syndics of the London School of Economics. Mimeo.

MCVEY, R. (1963). *Indonesia*. New Haven, Human Relations Area Files.

MEERLOO, J. A. M. (1961). 'Terreur en paniek'. *Elseviers Weekblad*, vol. 9, 11 November.

MICHOLSON, W. (1970). *Man and his urban environment*. Reading, Mass., Addison-Wesley.

MILLER, H. (1968). 'A study of the effectiveness of a variety of teaching techniques for reducing colour prejudice in a male student sample (aged 15–21)'. Dissertation, London University.

MITCHELL, H. (1963). *Europe in the Caribbean: the policies of Great Britain, France and the Netherlands towards their West Indian territories*. Edinburgh, Constable.

MITRASING, F. (1959). *Tien jaar Suriname*. Leiden, University Press.

MOBERG, David O. (1961). 'Religion and society in the Netherlands and in America'. *American Quarterly*, vol. 13, No. 2, pp. 172–8.

—— 'Social differentiation in the Netherlands'. *Social Forces*, vol. 39, No. 4, pp. 333–7.

Mol, J. (1961). 'Churches and immigrants'. *R.E.M.P. Bulletin*, Supplement No. 5.

—— (1963). 'The functions of marginality'. *International Migration*, vol. 1, 175–7.

—— (1959). 'Theoretical frame of reference for the international patterns of religion and the adjustment of immigrants'. *R.E.M.P. Bulletin*, vol. 7, pp. 21–43.

Motta, R. M. C. (1964). 'Towards a study of alienation amongst some foreign workers in the Netherlands'. The Hague, Institute of Social Studies, Dissertation.

Muaja, A. J. (1958). *The Chinese problem in Indonesia*. Djakarta, New Nusantara.

Murari, T. (1971). 'Bastards of the Raj'. *Guardian*, 20 March.

Netherlands Ministry of Foreign Affairs (1956). *Suriname en de Nederlandse Antillen in de Verenigde Naties*. The Hague, The Ministry.

Netherlands Ministry of Housing and Building (1964). *Housing in the Netherlands*. The Hague, The Ministry.

Netherlands Ministry of Cultural Affairs, Recreation and Social Welfare (1965). *Repatriation*. The Hague, The Ministry.

—— (1968). *Reception and social guidance of migrant workers*. The Hague, The Ministry.

—— (1969). *Ambonezen in Nederland*. The Hague, The Ministry.

—— *Niewsbrief* (periodical). The Hague, The Ministry.

Nettl, P. (1967). *Political mobilization*. London, Faber and Faber.

Nicholls, D. (1971). 'East Indians and Black Power in Trinidad'. *Race*, vol. 12, pp. 443–59.

Nooij, A. J. J. (1969). 'Political radicalism among Dutch farmers'. *Sociologia Ruralis*, vol. 9, pp. 43–61.

Oxaal, I. (1969). 'Race, pluralism and nationalism in the British Caribbean'. *Journal of Biosocial Science*. Supplement 1, pp. 153–62.

—— (1970). 'Plural society theory and race relations in the West Indies: a brief introduction'. Paper given to Race Relations Group of the British Sociological Association, London School of Economics.

Palmier, H. (1962). *Indonesia and the Dutch*. London, Oxford University Press for the Institute of Race Relations.

Parsons, T. (1952). *The social system*. London, Tavistock.

—— (1963). 'On the concept of political power'. *Proceedings of the American Philosophical Society*, vol. 107, pp. 232–62.

Parsons, T. and Shils, E. (1951). *Towards a general theory of action*. Cambridge, Mass., Harvard University Press.

Patterson, S. (1957). *The last trek*. London, Routledge.

—— (1969). *Immigration and race relations in Britain, 1960–1967*. London, Oxford University Press for the Institute of Race Relations.

P.E.P. (1967). *Racial discrimination*. London, Political and Economic Planning.

PEN, Jan (1963). 'The priority of housing'. *Delta*, vol. 6, no. 2, pp. 17–31.

PETERSEN, William (1955). *Planned migration: the social determinants of the Dutch-Canadian movement*. Berkeley, University of California Press.

PETTIGREW, T. (1958). 'Personality and socio-cultural factors in intergroup attitudes: a cross-national comparison'. *Journal of Conflict Resolution*, vol. 2, pp. 29–42.

PINNER, F. (1965). 'Parental overprotection and political distrust'. *Annals of the American Academy of Political and Social Science*, vol. 301, pp. 58–70.

PLAS, van der M. and SUER, H. (1968). *Those Dutch Catholics*. London, Chapman.

POLLS, Amsterdam. Journal of the Netherlands Institute of Public Opinion.

POOLE, L. (1951). *The Caribbean commission*. Colombia, University of Carolina Press.

POPA-RADIX, P. J. A. (1968). 'Reception and social guidance of migrant workers'. *Sociale Zorg*, 31 July.

PRAAG, C. van (1971). 'Het overheidsbeleid in zake allochtone groepen'. In H. Verwey-Jonker. *Allochtonen in Nederland*. The Hague, State Publishing House.

PRESSER, J. (1965). *Downfall: the persecution and extermination of the Dutch Jewish community, 1940–1945*. The Hague, National Institute of War Archives.

QUERIDO, A. (1968). *The development of socio-medical care in the Netherlands*. London, Routledge.

RAYNOR, L. (1968): 'Agency adoptions of non-white children in the United Kingdom'. *Race*, vol. 10, pp. 153–62.

REIJNDERS, C. (1969). *Van Joodsche natien tot Joodse Nederlanders 1600–1942*. University of Utrecht, Dissertation.

REX, J. (1960). 'The plural society in sociological theory'. *British Journal of Sociology*, vol. 10, pp. 114–24.

—— (1970). *Race relations in sociological theory*. London, Weidenfeld and Nicholson.

—— (1971). 'The concept of housing class and the sociology of race relations'. *Race*, vol. 12, pp. 243–301.

REX, J. and MOORE, R. (1967). *Race, community, and conflict*. London, Oxford University Press for the Institute of Race Relations.

RICHARDSON, A. (1961). 'The assimilation of British immigrants in a Western Australian community—a psychological study'. *R.E.M.P. Bulletin*, vol. 9, pp. 1–76.

RICHMOND, A. (1967). *Post-war immigrants in Canada.* Toronto, University of Toronto Press.

ROSE, E. J. B. and ASSOCIATES (1969). *Colour and citizenship.* London, Oxford University Press for the Institute of Race Relations.

RUNCIMAN, W. and BAGLEY, C. (1969). 'Status consistency, relative deprivation and attitudes to immigrants'. *Sociology*, vol. 3, pp. 359–75.

RUSSETT, B. and others (1964). *World handbook of political and social indicators.* New Haven, Yale University Press.

SAMPSON, A. (1970). 'Doing our own thing'. *The Observer*, 12 July, p. 21.

SCHAKELS (Periodical). Uitgave van het kabinet van de Vice-Minister President, The Hague.

SCHARF, A. (1964). *The British press and Jews under Nazi rule.* London, Oxford University Press for the Institute of Race Relations.

SCHRIEKE, B. (1955). *Indonesian sociological studies: selected writings.* The Hague, Bandung.

SIMONS, M. S. M. (1962). 'Italiaanse arbeiders in de Limburgse mijnstreek in Twente'. *Mens en Maatschappij*, vol. 37, pp. 223–46.

SKINNER, G. W. (1963). 'The Chinese minority'. In *Indonesia.* New Haven, Human Relations Area Files, ed. R. McVey.

SMIT, C. (1962). 'De liquidatie van een imperium: Nederland en Indonesie 1945–1962'. Amsterdam, Dissertation.

SMITH, M. G. (1960). 'Social and cultural pluralism'. *Annals of the New York Academy of Sciences*, vol. 83, pp. 763–77.

SMITH, R. T. (1971). 'Race and political conflict in Guyana'. *Race*, vol. 12, pp. 415–28.

*Sociaal den Haag* (1969). 'Eigen trefcentrum voor antillianen in de oort was een broodnodige zaake'. January–February, pp. 13–15.

SOEDERHUIZEN, J. (1964). 'Einige gegevenis omtrent het verblijf van Surinamers in Amsterdam'. Amsterdam, Social Academy, Dissertation.

SPECKMANN, J. D. (1964). 'Pluraliteit in de Surinaamse samenleving'. *Social Congress*, vol. 11, pp. 250–9.

—— (1965). *Marriage and kinship among the Indians of Surinam.* Assen, Van Gorcum.

STAAY, A. van der (1971). 'De buitenlandse werknemers'. In H. Verwey-Jonker (ed.), *Allochtonen in Nederland.*

STICHTING HAAGS . . . (1969). *De Poort—verslag van de verkzaamhed. 1 Juli 1965–1 April 1969.* The Hague, *Stichting Haags Katholiek Jongeren Centrum, Stichting Begleiding Buitenlandse Werknemers, en Stichting voor Antillianen.*

SURIE, H. G. (1971). 'De gerepatrieerden'. In H. Verwey-Jonker (ed.), *Allochtonen in Nederland.*

SUVARNATEMEE, P. (1966). 'Thai people in the Netherlands'. The Hague, Institute of Social Studies, Dissertation.

SWART, A. (1970). 'Rassendiskriminatie en de Nederlandse strafivet.' *Delikt. Delink.*, vol. 1, pp. 65–81.

TAFT, R. (1961). 'The assimilation of the Dutch in Australia'. *Human Relations*, vol. 14, p. 265.

TARTER, D. (1969). 'Toward prediction of attitude-action discrepancy'. *Social Forces*, vol. 47, pp. 398–405.

TAYLOR, A. M. (1960). *Indonesian independence and the United Nations.* Ithaca, Cornell University Press.

THOLENAAR VAN RAALTE, J. (1965). 'Migratie en integratie van Surinamers in Nederland'. Amsterdam, Dissertation.

——(1965). 'Surinamers in the Netherlands'. *Het Algemeen Handelsblad*, 19 March.

THOMPSON, E. B. (1967). 'Surinam: multiracial paradise at the crossroads'. *Ebony* (Feb.), pp. 112–120.

THURLING, J. (1972). 'The case of Dutch Catholicism: a contribution to the theory of the pluralistic Society'. *Sociologia Neerlandica*, pp. 118–36.

VANDENBOSCH, A. (1944). *The Dutch East Indies.* Berkeley and Los Angeles, University of California Press.

VELDEN, A. van der (1968). 'The situation of migrant workers (Italians and Spaniards) in the Ijmond region'. Paper given to the Seminar on Children of Migrant Workers: Problems and Policies, at the International Children's Centre, Paris, December.

VELLINGA, M. and WOLTERS, B. (1971). 'De Chinezen'. In H. Verwey-Jonker (ed.), *Allochtonen in Nederland.*

VERWEY-JONKER, H. (ed.) (1971). *Allochtonen in Nederland.* The Hague, State Publishing House.

VEUR, van der P. W. (1960). 'Eurasian Dilemma in Indonesia'. *Journal of Asian Studies*, vol. 20, pp. 45–60.

—— (1969). *Education and social change in colonial Indonesia.* Ohio, Center for International Studies.

WAGENFELD, H. (1971). 'Reply to Boekhuizen'. *Nederlands Tijdschrift voor Criminologie*, September.

WEBER, M. (1948). *From Max Weber: essays in sociology* (eds. H. Gerth and C. Wright Mills). London, Routledge.

WEHL, D. (1948). *The birth of Indonesia.* London, Allen and Unwin.

WEIMA, J. (1964). 'Authoritarianism, anti-Catholicism, and the integration of religious values'. *Social Compass*, vol. 11, pp. 13–25.

—— (1965). 'Authoritarianism, religious conservatism and sociocentric attitudes in Roman Catholic groups'. *Human Relations*, vol. 18, pp. 231–9.

WELLS, A. (1970). 'Towards a non-pathological view of judgemental attitudes'. *Race*, vol. 12, pp. 219–28.

WERTHEIM, W. F. (1956). *Indonesian society in transition.* The Hague, van Hoeve.

WILDER, J. S. (1967). 'Indonesian women in The Hague: colonial immigrants in the Netherlands'. New York University, Dissertation.

WILLIAMS, R. (1961): *The long revolution*. London, Chatto and Windus.

WILSON, A. (1971). *The Observer atlas of world affairs*. London, Philip.

WILSON, G. (1970). 'Is there a general factor in social attitudes? Evidence from a factor analysis of the conservatism scale'. *British Journal of Social and Clinical Psychology*, vol. 9, pp. 264–9.

WILSON, G. and PATTERSON, I. (1968). 'A new measure of conservatism'. *British Journal of Social and Clinical Psychology*, vol. 7, pp. 264–9.

WITTERMANS, T. (1955). 'Social organization of Ambonese refugees in Holland'. London University, Dissertation.

—— (June 1955). 'Functional aspects of "Pela" among Ambonese refugees'. *Indonesie*, vol. 8, June, pp. 214–30.

—— (1956). 'Het begrip communicatie basis bij de analyse van communicatieprocessen'. *Mens en Maatschappij*, vol. 30, November, pp. 372–89.

WITTERMANS, T. and GIST, N. P. (1962). 'The Ambonese nationalist movement in the Netherlands: a study in status deprivation'. *Social Forces*, vol. 40, pp. 309–17.

WORKS, E. (1969). 'Types of racial discrimination'. *Phylon*, vol. 30, pp. 223–33.

YANES, de, M. F. (1962). 'Housing: the west and the rest of the Netherlands'. The Hague, Institute of Social Studies, Dissertation.

ZIELHUIS, L. and GIRDHART, R. (1971). *Migratie uit Suriname*. The Hague, Afdeling Wetenschappelijk onder zoek en Planning.

ZINKIN, T. (1964). 'Orchids in the land of tulips'. *The Spectator*, 3 April, p. 438.

# INDEX